REMEMBERING SEVEN PROPHETS

REMEMBERING SEVEN PROPHETS

MEMORIES OF FRANCIS M. GIBBONS
AS TOLD TO DANIEL BAY GIBBONS

Sixteen Stones Press

HOLLADAY, UTAH

Copyright © 2015 by Daniel Bay Gibbons

All rights reserved. No part of this publication may be reproduced, distributed or transmitted in any form or by any means, including photocopying, recording, or other electronic or mechanical methods, without the prior written permission of the publisher, except in the case of brief quotations embodied in critical reviews and certain other noncommercial uses permitted by copyright law.

Book layout, typography, and cover design ©2015 by Julie G. Gibbons. Photo credits: all cover photographs from the private collection of Francis M. Gibbons, used by permission. Sixteen Stones Press logo design by Marina Telezar.

Sixteen Stones Press
Publisher website: www.sixteenstonespress.com

Remembering Seven Prophets
by Daniel Bay Gibbons

Paperback ISBN 978-1-942640-08-0
eBook ISBN 978-1-942640-09-7

In Memory of

Helen Bay Gibbons

November 4, 1921
to
August 2, 2015

TABLE OF CONTENTS

INTRODUCTION 1
   "A Plutarch to the Presidents of the Church" 1
   "A Scribe to the Prophets" 2
   "I am their witness" 3

FRANCIS M. GIBBONS—PREPARED TO SERVE 5
   "An interview with the Prophet" 5
   "The man you are looking for" 5
   "The time is now" 7
   "Frank can't afford not to do it" 8
   "My world was upended" 10
   "A unique preparation" 11
   "I was enthralled" 11
   "Instinctively drawn to Harold B. Lee" 14
   "Go get the boy up" 18
   "Sit in the leading councils" 19
   "To make a great life" 20
   "Go see Bjork Cederlof" 22
   "This is your house" 23
   "Brother Joseph Anderson" 24
   "He walked toward me" 25
   "Raised up by the Lord" 27

JOSEPH FIELDING SMITH 29
   Joseph Fielding Smith Chronology 30
   "A contemporary of fifteen Prophets" 37
   "The long shadow of history" 38
   "A trunk which had belonged to Hyrum" 40
   "A most distinguished name" 42
   "Watching the stone cutters" 43
   "The shadow of persecution" 44

"Very little money" 46
"We got a scolding from the Prophet" 48
"A defender of the doctrine" 49
"They crossed the Atlantic" 50
"The most prolific writer" 52
"A widower at age thirty-one" 53
"I guess we'll have to sell the cow" 55
"His father's private secretary" 57
"A new family home on Douglas Street" 58
"A lesson on the Word of Wisdom" 59
"The evils of profanity" 60
"Let's go and watch the football game" 61
"A widower for the second time" 62
"Their unusual courtship" 63
"Fun-loving and full of life" 65
"Awakened by the sound of jackboots" 66
"Bowed down with grief" 67
"Physically vigorous and active" 69
"As excited as a schoolboy" 70
"First impressions of the Prophet" 72
"Constantly praying within himself" 74
"One of the kindest men" 75
"A delicious sense of humor" 77
"Coax President Smith to sing" 78
"President Smith is here!" 79
"Who is that woman in your office?" 80
"The handshake of a man in his prime" 81
"He never ate meat" 82
"A deep love for the temple" 83
"Next day he was back at his desk" 85
"A widower for the third time" 86
"A quorum of Apostles on foreign soil" 87
"God be with you, 'til we meet again" 88
"Compensation for a lifetime" 89
"He died peacefully" 90

HAROLD B. LEE ... 93

- Harold B. Lee Chronology ... 95
- "The humbleness of his upbringing" ... 101
- "Harold, stay away from that building" ... 102
- "A reputation as a brilliant young man" ... 103
- "An aura of light" ... 105
- "Elder Talmage kindly pulled him aside" ... 106
- "He visited Fern Tanner and Joan Jensen" ... 108
- "His most distinguishing characteristic" ... 110
- "He had a very vivid dream" ... 112
- "A model to help the poor" ... 114
- "His Patriarch was living in poverty" ... 115
- "To put the quorums to work" ... 116
- "A clear impression" ... 117
- "The dean of the younger men" ... 118
- "When you're winning, don't gloat" ... 120
- "A young ballplayer with his coach" ... 122
- "The most Christlike man" ... 123
- "A description of the Savior" ... 124
- "Good job, boy!" ... 126
- "A general feeling" ... 129
- "Possessed with an evil spirit" ... 130
- "A first-rate intellect" ... 131
- "He blessed her even as Hannah of old" ... 132
- "This young man could fill any position" ... 135
- "With a view to what the man may become" ... 137
- "The most important moment of his life" ... 138
- "A master at priesthood leadership and delegation" . 139
- "His daughter appeared" ... 141
- "Serve His people" ... 142
- "A free interchange of ideas" ... 145
- "Where would the Savior appear?" ... 146
- "A very gentle and thoughtful letter" ... 148
- "A song about President Lee" ... 149
- "Preach optimism, not pessimism" ... 150

"Spirits from beyond the veil" 151
"They understood" 152
"Experiences too sacred to discuss" 153
"He twice felt hands upon his head" 154
"He didn't look once at the colors" 155
"I know who your husband will be" 156
"The man we can least afford to lose" 159
"The two Prophets stood upon Mars Hill" 161
"We have come to the land of miracles" 163
"The entire church was a single family" 166
"He saw three men sitting at a table" 167
"Let every man learn and act" 169
"An unseen presence in the circle" 170
"The architect" 171
"The man to lead God's people" 172
"Foxes have holes and birds have nests" 174
"One final conversation" 175
"No righteous man dies before his time" 177

SPENCER W. KIMBALL 179

Spencer W. Kimball Chronology 181
"A man of many qualities" 189
"To name him 'Roberts'" 190
"The epitome of perfection" 191
"A son of Arizona" 192
"A truly touching scene" 193
"Reminiscing about Uncle Golden" 194
"An identity problem" 195
"You sound like a Woolley" 197
"I have fallen among cutthroats" 198
"A sweet and mild whisper" 199
"A whole corps of doctors" 200
"Spencer, you are not to die!" 201
"A special blessing" 202
"A modern-day Job" 203
"A special covenant with the Lord" 205

"The most stubborn man" 206
"Deep compassion" 209
"A pretty frightening thing to face" 210
"He moved forward speedily" 211
"The President framed in my doorway" 212
"A truly unique leadership style" 214
"Humble yet supremely confident" 216
"Round-the-clock working habits" 217
"A Prophet in perpetual motion" 218
"He abhorred vacations" 220
"A pencil in his hand" 222
"I don't want to be saved" 223
"Never stand still" 224
"To die in the harness" 225
"A keen sense of humor" 227
"Are you willing to share?" 228
"You didn't kill this, did you?" 229
"Would you gentlemen like a cocktail?" 230
"Do not fail to give me a ticket" 231
"His delicious sense of humor" 233
"To go to the front of the line" 234
"With all the love of which I am capable" 235
"How is Henry?" 236
"Remember, I love you" 238
"A visionary, not an administrator" 239
"Plowing new ground" 241
"The inspiration of dreams" 242
"Kaleidoscopic sermons" 243
"Unprepared sermons" 244
"The day of the Lamanite" 245
"The Apostle to the Lamanites" 247
"Baptizing illegal aliens" 248
"To raise up strong leaders" 249
"He motioned to Brother Martins" 250
"A map of Africa came into his mind" 253
"blacks and the priesthood" 254

"A wakeful night"... 255
"The native Brazilian missionaries"........................ 256
"A manifestation of the will of God"....................... 257
"A spiritual personage in the room" 258
"alone in the Upper Room" 260
"He had a good, warm feeling" 261
"Unanimity among the Brethren"............................ 262
"The prayerful struggle in the temple".................. 263
"I have never seen a more historic day".................. 265

EZRA TAFT BENSON 267

Ezra Taft Benson Chronology 269
"A portrait of President Benson" 275
"His birth was a great miracle" 278
"Two Prophets walked out of the same farmland"..... 279
"He became a man at age twelve"............................ 280
"Bunkmates on either side of him died" 281
"A beautiful girl in a sports car"............................. 283
"Our Benson" 285
"The young couple"... 287
"A striking contrast" 288
"An exemplary Latter-day Saint family" 289
"The Scoutmaster shaved his head"........................ 290
"The cabin itself was a sacred place"...................... 291
"Cities leveled by intense bombing"........................ 293
"you ought to accept" 294
"Joseph in Pharaoh's Kingdom"............................... 295
"To open doors for the Church" 296
"He cultivated a sense of family" 299
"He learned to think on his feet" 300
"He occasionally told a good story" 301
"We'll see if your spiritual antenna is up" 303
"Two future Church Presidents" 306
"The prophetic mantle".. 308
"No empty chairs"... 309
"What's best for the Kingdom?" 311

"I look upon you as a true friend" 312
"Poise and self-control" 313
"No weapon that is formed against thee" 314

HOWARD W. HUNTER 315

Howard W. Hunter Chronology 317
"A home of books" 323
"We don't ragtime music" 325
"Church leaders who were lawyers" 327
"His call to the Apostleship" 328
"Think" 331
"Sweet, hopeful, and uncomplaining" 332
"A loving husband" 333
"His wisdom and vision were vindicated" 334
"He was uniformly kind to everyone" 335
"Junior member of the Twelve" 336
"How Prophets are raised up" 338
"Three stake presidents in agreement" 340
"A sweet and kind a spirit about him" 341
"Very cordial and quite passive" 343
"He took great delight in children" 344
"Unity among the highest leaders" 345
"A man wholly without guile" 346
"The Church is a friend to Islam" 348
"Absolute faith in the Priesthood" 349
"The timetable of the Lord" 351
"LeGrand will return!" 352

GORDON B. HINCKLEY 355

Gordon B. Hinckley Chronology 357
"Son and grandson of stake presidents" 361
"Known among all nations" 363
"The example of Robert Louis Stevenson" 366
"A patriarchal blessing" 367
"Close association with two Apostles" 368
"We will give you 15 minutes" 369

"Someday I'm going to run this place"......................371
"He was the workhorse"..373
"President Lee saw what was ahead"......................375
"The land of miracles" 376
"Conciliation and negotiation" 378
"We want to compose this matter" 380
"I want to see how you do it" 381
"Influence in the highest councils"........................382
"He used the Talmage Room as his office"...............384
"His articulate supremacy"......................................387
"Impelled by President Hinckley's talk" 388
"a grueling deposition" 389
"A recurring phenomenon" 390
"A highly developed sense of humor" 391
"The decision to sell their home"............................392
"A place unique in Church history"........................394
"You brethren go forward" 396
"I'm just about at the end of the road" 398
"The two octogenarians went running"...................400
"Poise and adroitness"...401
"The dominant administrator" 403
"A counselor *in* the First Presidency" 405
"Providential timing"...407
"I wished that Moroni had a howitzer" 409
"A miracle of the first magnitude" 410
"The checked everything but my I.Q." 412
"Not afraid to move forward"...................................413
"No shrinking violet"..414
"Within the bounds of his authority" 415
"A mark of his greatness" 416
"He was walking a very tight rope"..........................417
"The situation had never existed before" 418
"The office of Archbishop".......................................420
"Broad delegations of authority" 424
"President Hinckley bore a heavy burden" 426
"One of our greatest Presidents" 427

THOMAS S. MONSON 429
    Thomas S. Monson Chronology 431
    "I have a new bishop for *you!*" 435
    "Long on caring and short on statistics" 436
    "Have courage, my boy, to say yes" 437
    "He saw Tom Monson sitting on the end seat" 438
    "A special young man" 440
    "Love and admiration for President Clark" 441
    "A consummate team player" 442
    "Called to the attention of President McKay" 443
    "He did say 'the Twelve,' didn't he?" 444
    "To tell her about the calling" 445
    "Some far-reaching event" 446
    "The youngest Apostle" 447
    "A happy warrior" 448
    "A striking profile" 449
    "Cordiality and friendliness" 450
    "My mentor" 451
    "A very skilled administrator" 453
    "He recognizes, encourages and builds up" 454
    "They often showed deference" 456
    "The most aggressive member of the Twelve" 457
    "A sweeping change" 458
    "Making the gospel clear to the masses" 459
    "He prayed during the entire journey" 460
    "A future temple in East Germany" 461
    "He had a vivid dream" 463
About the Author 464
Index 465

INTRODUCTION

This book is a collection of the personal reminiscences of Francis M. Gibbons about the last seven Presidents of the Church. Now in his ninety-fifth year, Francis M. Gibbons is the oldest living General Authority or former General Authority of the Church, and perhaps the greatest student on the lives of the Prophets of this dispensation. From 1970 through 1991 he served, first, as the secretary to the First Presidency, and second, as a member of the First and Second Quorums of Seventy. During that time he served personally with Presidents Joseph Fielding Smith, Harold B. Lee, Spencer W. Kimball, Ezra Taft Benson, Howard W. Hunter, Gordon B. Hinckley and Thomas S. Monson.

As a son of Francis M. Gibbons, I have been deeply interested in his unique life and perspective on the Presidents of the Church. This book is the fruit of approximately one hundred hours of interviews I conducted with Dad during the years 2001 to 2011, and then since July of 2011 following my return from presiding over the Russia Novosibirsk Mission of the Church.

Dad has two unique qualifications to speak and write about the Prophets: he is the Church's most prolific biographer of the Prophets, and he labored for sixteen years as their scribe and secretary.

"A Plutarch to the Presidents of the Church"

First, over the past forty-five years, Francis M. Gibbons has become "a Plutarch to the Presidents of the Church." This unusual phrase has reference to Plutarch, the ancient Greek writer, who became the most famous biographer in history, the "Father of Biography." Many years ago Dad shared with my mother his special aspiration to become "a Plutarch to the Presidents of the Church, and through their lives to write the history of the Church." If any man or woman deserves the title "Plutarch to the Presidents of the Church," it is my father, Francis M. Gibbons. Over the past four decades he has become by far the most prolific writer of biographies of the Presidents of the Church, writing a full-length biography of every Prophet from Joseph Smith to Gordon B. Hinckley. Dad's biographies of the Prophets have been very popular, selling many hundreds of thousands of copies. Thirteen of his presidential biographies have been included in Brigham Young University's list of "Sixty Significant Mormon Biographies." He has truly become "a Plutarch to the Presidents of the Church."

"A Scribe to the Prophets"

Second, Francis M. Gibbons has been a personal witness and observer of the character of the last seven Presidents of the Church: Presidents Joseph Fielding Smith, Harold B. Lee, Spencer W. Kimball, Ezra Taft Benson, Howard W. Hunter, Gordon B. Hinckley, and Thomas S. Monson. He knew these men personally. He worked with them. While serving from 1970 to 1986 as the secretary to the First Presidency and later as a member of the Seventy, Dad associated with them on a daily basis. He was a "Scribe to the Prophets," as were William Clayton, Wilford Woodruff, Joseph F. Smith, William F. Gibbs, Joseph Anderson, and others before him.

"I am their witness"

When Dad was sustained as a General Authority in April of 1986, after many years serving as the faithful scribe for the Presidents of the Church, he said:

> The Church is led by prophets, seers, and revelators. I am their witness. I testify that they are honorable, upright, dedicated men of integrity, committed to teaching the principles of the gospel, who strive with all of their might to prepare a people ready for the return of the head of the Church, Jesus Christ, at His second coming.

This work, *Remembering Seven Prophets*, shares many unique stories, anecdotes, insights, and testimonies about the last seven Presidents of the Church, which are nowhere else available.

I offer this work for the enlightenment and inspiration of the reader and as a tribute to the memory of the seven Presidents of the Church featured in these pages. I also love and honor these great men, and add my witness to that of my father that they were and are Prophets of God!

Daniel Bay Gibbons
August 5, 2015
Holladay, Utah

Francis M. Gibbons—Prepared to Serve

By Daniel Bay Gibbons

"An interview with the Prophet"

It is a clear and crisp spring morning in April of 1970. A forty-eight year old lawyer in a business suit pauses on the sidewalk in front of 47 East South Temple in Salt Lake City. Straightening his tie, he looks up at the Church Administration Building with its twenty-four Ionic columns forming a colonnade around the structure. The lawyer glances at his watch. He has an eight o'clock a.m. appointment inside the building with three men. It will be an interview with the Prophets, ninety-three year old Joseph Fielding Smith, who three days earlier was sustained as the tenth President of The Church of Jesus Christ of Latter-day Saints. Also in the meeting will be President Smith's counselors, President Harold B. Lee and President N. Eldon Tanner. The lawyer has left word with his legal secretary that he will return to the law office by mid-morning. As he climbs the eighteen granite steps and passes the ornamental bronze torches flanking the front doorway, he does not yet know that he will not be returning to his law office today—or ever.

"The man you are looking for"

In April of 1970, things were going well in the world of my father, Francis M. Gibbons. He was just turning forty-nine, was a partner in one of the finest law firms in the state, with an extensive clientele and a busy trial calendar.

Over the years he had been exceedingly frugal with his money and had been able to pay off the mortgage on his modest home in 1964. He now commanded a good income, and even had great prospects of becoming a wealthy man within a few years time. In the Church, Dad was in the early months of his service as a Bishop in the Yalecrest Ward, having been called on the very day of President David O. McKay's death in January. He was happily married, with four children, two daughters and two sons promised in his patriarchal blessing. Now, this orderly world of Francis M. Gibbons was about to be turned upside down.

During the General Conference sessions of April 1970, Dad attended in the Tabernacle, using his new bishop's pass. At the Solemn Assembly on Monday, April 6, President Joseph Fielding Smith was sustained as the tenth president of the church with Harold B. Lee and N. Eldon Tanner as his counselors. Also sustained were Elder Boyd K. Packer as a member of the Quorum of the Twelve, and Elders Joseph Anderson, David B. Haight, and William H. Bennett as Assistants to the Twelve. Joseph Anderson, as it turns out, was a member of the Dad's ward. Dad recalled the events of that evening:

Late that evening, my wife Helen and I took a box of candy over to Joseph Anderson, who was a member of the ward, to congratulate him. During our visit, which was of about an hour's duration, he mentioned the difficulty the Brethren had been having to find someone to understudy him and ultimately take his place as secretary to the First Presidency, a position he had occupied for almost fifty years. As he discussed his duties (attendance at the meetings of the First Presidency and the Quorum of Twelve and following through on administrative matters for them) the Spirit witnessed to me that this was a work for which I had been subconsciously preparing myself all of my life. I said nothing at the time, but later when I was alone with Helen I mentioned the feeling to her. As so often is the case with us, she had received the same impression. In fact, she said that so strong was the feeling with her that she almost told Brother Anderson, "Frank Gibbons is the man you are looking for."

Dad spent a largely sleepless night as he pondered the impression he had received while in the home of Joseph Anderson and praying fervently for direction. The next morning, Tuesday, he phoned Joseph Anderson at 7:00 a.m. and asked if he could come in to see him later that day. Joseph Anderson later told Dad that after hanging up the telephone, Joseph Anderson turned to his wife, Norma, and said, "Frank Gibbons is going to offer his services to the Brethren." Norma answered, "Surely Frank wouldn't give up his legal practice to do that." Joseph's only answer was, "Well, we shall see."

"The time is now"

On Tuesday morning Dad visited with Joseph Anderson in his office in the Church Administration Building at 47 East South Temple. Dad recalled that:

> I went in at 10:00 a.m. and told him of my impression and told him further that if the Lord and the Brethren wanted me, I was available to assist where possible. He asked, "Would you accept a job at a thousand dollars a month?" I answered affirmatively. What I didn't tell him was that I would have been willing to work for nothing for the privilege of working closely each day with the prophets. I felt that now is the

time for me to decide whether to make a great life or a lot of money.

On Wednesday Brother Anderson called Dad and asked whether he could come in to meet with the First Presidency early the next morning. Dad recalled:

> At the time, Joseph Anderson asked whether I had had a change of heart. When I answered no, he said, "Frank, I want you to know that I'm very proud of you," a comment, which, alone, is almost compensation enough for leaving an honored and loved profession and the rewards, it has given to me.

After hanging up the phone with Joseph, Dad told his legal secretary that he would be gone for the rest of the day. He got in his car and drove across the valley to Copperton, where he parked his car facing the Salt Lake Valley and spent the afternoon in meditation and prayer. Dad said that as he drove back across the valley, the Spirit whispered to him, "The time is now."

"Frank can't afford not to do it"

Shortly before 8:00 on Thursday morning, April 9, 1970, Dad returned to the Church Administration Building where he was greeted by Joseph Anderson and then ushered immediately into the beautiful, wood-paneled Council Room of the First Presidency located on the first floor. There he was introduced to the members of the First Presidency, President Joseph Fielding Smith and his counselors, Presidents Harold B. Lee and N. Eldon Tanner. Dad recalled what followed:

> I met with the First Presidency and Brother Anderson that morning at 8:00 a.m. My impression was

that I was there to be interviewed. It soon became apparent the Brethren had already made a decision when President Tanner commented, "The only question I have is how you can afford it." To this President Lee responded, "Frank has come to the point in his life where he knows he can't afford not to do it." Nothing was said about the nature or scope of my duties, about my compensation, or about my title, if, indeed, I am to have one.

It was a matter of great interest to me that the Brethren had almost been prepared to make a decision about calling someone else before conference. Several men had been under active consideration. However, President Lee had said to the other members of the, "Let's wait until after conference to make the decision." In connection with this, President Tanner observed to President Lee, "You have the inspiration with you sometimes, don't you?"

Other things said at the time and mentioned later by Joseph confirmed my earlier impression that this is a work to which I have been called by the Lord and for which I have been subconsciously preparing for a long time.

Following the rather brief discussion about my call, the First Presidency moved quickly into the business before them, which consisted of about 30 items. President Lee took the lead in most matters, with President Tanner actively entering the discussion in most instances and leading out in some. President Smith's role was a passive one for the most part, although he interjected comments on two or three occasions. When he did so they were meaningful and to the point and indicated a good grasp of the subject matter under discussion

I was asked to join the Brethren at the meeting with the Twelve in the temple, which commenced at 10:00 a.m. and concluded at 2:00 p.m. Before this meeting started, I was taken around the circle and introduced to each of the Twelve.

At this meeting I took in short hand the blessings given to Elder Boyd K. Packer and Brothers Anderson, Haight, and Bennett, as well as their responses and acceptances of the charge given to them. It was amazing how readily my shorthand skill came back to me after such a long period of relative disuse. It is a most curious thing to me that this skill is an essential one to enable me to hold the position, yet it is a minor part of my duties.

"My world was upended"

Dad recently commented on his long preparation to serve in the unique role of secretary to the First Presidency and of the speedy unfolding of events surrounding his call in 1970:

Within the period of a week, my world was upended. There can be little doubt that a spiritual impression I had in the Assembly Hall in the spring of 1946 during a talk by Elder Albert E. Bowen prepared me for this change. It is doubtful I could so easily have turned my back on a lucrative and promising profession had not the thought been planted long ago that the time would come when I would be confronted with the decision whether to make a lot of money or to make a great life. I was, therefore, preconditioned to walking away from my law practice without a backward glance. And this I proceeded to do.

"A unique preparation"

There is a remarkable spiritual aspect to the unique preparation and training of Francis M. Gibbons for his service as secretary to the First Presidency, which he often reflected upon. Dad recently told me, "I have been reflecting upon my early life and have frankly been amazed how God has mercifully blessed me with revelatory insights at every major turn in the road of my life and led me to service to the First Presidency."

I will describe the amazing chain of spiritual experiences that provided an obscure boy with the unique skills and training he needed to one day serve the Prophets, and directed his life's trajectory from rural Arizona to the office of the First Presidency.

"I was enthralled"

Dad grew up in the rural town of St. Johns, Arizona, the youngest child of Andrew Smith Gibbons and Adeline Christensen. His father was a State Superior Court Judge with jurisdiction over the vast Apache County, which included most of northeast Arizona. Judge Gibbons served on the bench until 1930, presiding over a varied trial calendar, hearing both civil and criminal matters. Because the Superior Court was a court of record under the Arizona Constitution, the court employed a full-time court reporter, Ward Heap, who took down a verbatim transcript of all court proceedings.

Dad and his older brother and sisters often visited their father in his courtroom. At the time, Dad would have been less than nine years old. The courtroom and judge's chambers were located on the second story of the courthouse, which was one of the largest buildings in St. Johns. Dad especially loved being in his father's chambers, which were located immediately adjacent to the judge's bench in the courtroom. Dad has commented on his fascination with a rotating bookcase in his father's law library, and with what Dad called "the peculiar odor that permeated all of the St. Johns courthouse, which was an admixture of stale tobacco smoke, chewing tobacco, and chemicals that were used to clean and sweep the floors." The courtroom itself was a large, impressive room with richly carved wood paneling, a raised bench for the judge, and special built-in desks or enclosures for witnesses, the jury, the clerk, and the court reporter. Dad's family has enjoyed telling of the occasion when Dad's sister, Ruth, hid herself under the bench, and her father, Judge Gibbons, did not discover her presence until after he had commenced his court session and he felt Ruth tickling his leg.

As for Dad, in visiting his father's courtroom he was most impressed with the transcription work of Ward Heap, the court reporter. This, of course, was before the days of mechanical or electronic recording devices, and court reporters made verbatim transcripts using only a pen, ink, and their skill at shorthand. Dad recalled:

> I was enthralled with the work of the court reporter, Ward Heap. He had an ink well that was affixed to a ring that he put on his left index finger, and then he used a dip pen and would dip into the ink well and write very fast. I was fascinated by that and that was the thing that motivated me to study shorthand so as to become a court reporter.

So impressed was eight- or nine-year old Dad with the work of his father's court reporter, that he began to aspire to someday be a court reporter himself. This ambition reached fruition a few years later when, at age seventeen, Dad qualified to become a certified court reporter. This occurred while the family was living in Phoenix, Arizona. After working during the summer to save his money, Dad enrolled in the fall of 1938 at the Arizona School of Commerce, where he studied shorthand under Kitty Dixon, who had been one of the original pupils of John Robert Gregg, who developed the Gregg shorthand system. In addition to taking a course in shorthand, Dad also took courses in typing, bookkeeping, filing systems, business procedures, and finally an advanced course in shorthand.

Though he qualified as a court reporter in 1938, Dad soon abandoned his ambition to work in the judicial system, and instead turned his attention to business, and later to a full-time mission, service in the U.S. Navy, and then his education at the University of Utah and Stanford University. However, he never lost the ability to write rapidly in shorthand. Indeed, Dad continued to make good use of his shorthand skills throughout his life. For example, during at least two years of his schooling at Stanford University, Dad made all of his diary entries in shorthand.

After serving a full-time mission in the Southern States Mission, Dad was inducted into the Navy during World War II. Because of his ability to take shorthand and to type, he was given an officer's rank upon leaving boot camp, and soon found his way onto the staff of Commodore Brittain, where he had frequent need to use his shorthand. Later Dad took class notes in shorthand in his University and Law School classes and kept sporadic diary entries in shorthand for many years, including daily entries for the years 1946 through 1948.

My mother, Helen Bay Gibbons, was also very skilled in shorthand, and so during the years that we children were growing up, through the 1950s and 1960s, they would often communicate with each other in shorthand when they didn't want us to know the subject of the communication. Thus, during these years it was not uncommon for shorthand messages to appear on the refrigerator or on the desk written between Dad and Mom in shorthand.

Because recording devices are not used in the meetings of the First Presidency, and especially in the Upper Room of the Temple, the ability to take shorthand rapidly and accurately is one of the least, but at the same time one of the most essential, qualifications for a secretary to the First Presidency. Thus, Dad's early desires to study shorthand and qualify as a certified court reporter are surely providential and crucial in his long preparation to serve with the Brethren.

"Instinctively drawn to Harold B. Lee"

Many years following the death of President Harold B. Lee's death, Dad recalled:

> Aside from my own father, there is no man who has had a more profound influence on my life than President Harold B. Lee. Nor, with that same exception, is there any man whom I love and respect more or whose approval I want more than his. These feelings seem to trace to a spiritual relationship I cannot explain or define. I remember as if it were yesterday the first time I saw and heard President Lee. It was at a stake conference in Phoenix, Arizona, in about 1939 or 1940,

before Elder Lee had been called to the Twelve. He was there representing the Welfare Committee with Elder John A. Widtsoe, who was the visiting authority. I cannot remember what he said in his talk, but I shall never forget his appearance and demeanor nor the profound effect he had upon me. He carried a prophetic influence about him. It was characterized by a sense of energy and urgency, which seemed to permeate his being. I found the expressions on his face and the air and stance of his person as compelling and provocative as anything he said. I felt instinctively drawn to Harold B. Lee then, and although I did not speak to him or shake hands with him, I remember standing quite close to him when Bishop John H. Udall introduced himself to the visitor, and how impressed and thrilled I was to be that close to one whom I instinctively recognized as a great man. I had no inkling at that time that I would one day work closely with him in the office of the First Presidency.

It was not long after Brother Lee's visit to Phoenix on the occasion I have mentioned that he was called as a member of the Twelve—April 1941. I was then twenty years old, and it was a few months before my father had died. It is difficult to explain, but at that time, I felt a special kinship to President Lee, almost as if we were destined to be associated in some special way in the future. I also felt that some day he would be the President of the Church.

Another portentous event occurred in 1949 while Dad was studying law at Stanford University in Palo Alto, California. Dad and Mom had been unable to have children after nearly four years of marriage, which was a source of great sorrow and concern to the young couple. Each of them had been promised both sons and daughters in their patriarchal blessings. Though Dad and Mom had consulted with the best doctors in the Bay area and prayed fervently for the Lord to fulfill the promised blessings, yet they were still unable to conceive. Dad also had great concern about his schooling and his life's future course.

In this context, Dad and Mom were invited on the evening of March 2, 1949, to meet with a large group of LDS students at the home of their friends and fellow Stanford students, Ernie and Maurine Wilkins. Maurine was the daughter of Elder Harold B. Lee of the Quorum of Twelve, and Elder Lee was visiting at the Wilkins home in Palo Alto at the time.

Dad recorded in his diary that "prior to going into the meeting I prayed that I might be given intelligence as to how to make a success of my effort to gain my education." That evening, Elder Lee visited at length with the enthralled students crammed into the little living room of the Wilkins' apartment. Among other things, he spoke about the office and function of the Holy Ghost and its differentiation from the light of Christ. He also recounted the experience of giving a special priesthood blessing to a brilliant medical student, who had approached Elder Lee prior to an important exam, and of the literal fulfillment of that blessing. Dad was moved powerfully to be in the close presence of one of the Apostles and took careful notes of everything that was taught during the evening. Later that night, Dad confided his deep impressions in his diary, commenting on "Brother Lee's penetrating grasp, not only of the principles of the Gospel, but of events of current interest."[1] Then Dad made the following significant notation in his diary:

> I have had the impression tonight that I shall yet be more closely associated with Brother Lee in a way I do not now realize—Time will tell whether these impressions are well grounded.[2]

After this evening, Dad had no further contact with Elder Lee for a period of more than twenty-one years, until the fateful day in April of 1970 when he began his service with the First Presidency. Of course, Dad was "closely associated" with President Harold B. Lee for the last three years of the President's life, thus literally fulfilling the unique impression he had received as a young student.

Mom had impressions of her own following the evening with Elder Lee, for the next day, while Dad was at school, she paid an unannounced visit to the Wilkins' home where she asked Elder Lee to give her a special blessing. He agreed, and laid his hands on her head on the spot, promising her, among other things, that she would conceive and become a mother. This blessing was literally fulfilled within a few months, when Helen conceived their first daughter and ultimately bore four children, two girls and two boys, in fulfillment of the promises in Dad's and Mom's patriarchal blessings.

Though he had no further contact with Elder Lee, Dad continued to feel himself strongly drawn toward this magnetic and spiritual giant. In October of 1965, Dad was deeply impressed by Elder Lee's masterful conference sermon, in which he urged every member to obtain a testimony for himself, warning that "the time would come

---

[1] FMG Diary, Wednesday, March 2, 1949.
[2] FMG Diary, Wednesday, March 2, 1949.

when we will not be able to live on borrowed light." Afterward Dad recorded this significant statement: "When Elder Lee spoke on Sunday, I was impressed again with his great spiritual strength. It would be a wonderful experience to be able to work closely with this great prophet."[3] Finally, Dad had a most portentous dream on May 3, 1966. He recorded: "Last night I had one of the rare dreams which I was able to remember afterward. I was in conversation with Elder Harold B. Lee of the Quorum of Twelve."[4]

"Go get the boy up"

One of the most crucial experiences of Dad's preparation occurred shortly after the death of his father, Judge Andrew Smith Gibbons, in December of 1940. His father, then age sixty, was struck by a car as he was walking across a street in downtown Phoenix, Arizona, and died shortly thereafter. At the time, Dad was almost wholly inactive in the church, as were most other members of his family. Dad recalled:

Not long after we had buried Father, Mother came to my bedroom early one Sunday morning in a high state of excitement. She said she had been awakened by my Father who appeared in her bedroom and who said to her in a clear, distinct voice, "Go get the boy up and get him off to Priesthood meeting." This incident has had a positive influence in my church and Priesthood activity over the years. As time passes, the reality of this event looms larger in the mind of my Mother.

---

[3] FMG Diary, Monday, October 4, 1965.
[4] Diary, Tuesday, May 3, 1966

"Sit in the leading councils"

Dad served as a missionary in the Southern States Mission from 1942 until 1944, assigned for most of that time in the mission office in Atlanta, Georgia, where he concluded his mission serving as the mission secretary under President Heber Meeks. On February 22, 1944, Dad was honorably released by President Meeks in Atlanta, and he departed that day to drive to Salt Lake City with two fellow missionaries, also released that day, including Elder Jack Anderson, who later achieved fame as a columnist in Washington, D.C. Before leaving Atlanta, Dad took his leave from President Meeks. He recorded in his missionary diary:

> Old missionary ties were severed today. . . . Bid farewell to President and Mother Meeks, both of whom had tears in their eyes. Prior to my departure was given some timely advice by President Meeks. He promised me that if I proved faithful, the time would come when I would sit in the leading councils of the church.[5]

As a mature man, Dad has commented that this prophecy, uttered to a twenty-two year old man by his mission president, is significant both for what it says and what it does not say. It says, of course, that Dad, if faithful, would one day "sit" in the leading councils of the Church. It does not say, however, that Dad would be a "member" of those councils. In retrospect, this prophecy has been fulfilled to a remarkable degree. For sixteen years Dad "sat" in all of the leading councils of the Church, including the presidency meetings of the First Presidency, the temple meetings of the Council of the First Presidency and the Twelve, the weekly meetings of the First Presidency and the

---

[5] FMG Diary, Tuesday, February 22, 1944

Presiding Bishopric, the annual meeting of the Council on the Disposition of the Tithes, the regular meetings of all General Authorities, and other meetings of the leaders of the Church at the highest level.

"To make a great life"

Shortly after Dad's discharge from the Navy in 1946, another significant event occurred which ultimately prepared him for and pointed him toward his ultimate service to the leading Brethren of the Church. At the time, Dad was twenty-five years old and married, but had had no University training and was uncertain as to his future career plans. He had given some thought to the possibility of studying law, like his father, but no definite plans had as yet crystallized. Thus, these questions about his future life's work dominated Dad's thoughts and prayers in the early weeks of his discharge from the Navy.

In this searching and prayerful state of mind, Dad and Helen read in the newspaper in the spring of 1946 that Elder Albert E. Bowen would be speaking at a stake conference session in the Assembly Hall on Temple Square the next Sunday. Elder Bowen was then a member of the Quorum of the Twelve, who had distinguished himself as a practicing lawyer before his call. Dad felt a strong desire to attend to hear Elder Bowen in the hopes that something would be said which would provide him with guidance. In attending this meeting, Dad recorded that, "I had the vague feeling that Elder Bowen could shed some light on the seemingly dark future which lay ahead of me. . . . I began to pray inwardly that the Lord would reveal something to me. . . ."[6] Helen agreed to attend the meeting with Dad,

---

[6] FMG Autobiography, Volume II, page 29-30.

although Dad did not divulge to her his reasons for wanting to attend. Dad recorded what then occurred at the meeting:

> At the Assembly Hall, we took our seats on the south side, beneath the balcony, and near the front. Throughout the meeting, I repeated the silent prayers I had begun to offer earlier in the morning. During Elder Bowen's talk, he paused in the midst of it, and, turning his head to the right, which was in our direction, he uttered this sentence: "There often comes in a man's life a time when he must decide whether to make a lot of money or a to make a great life." As he said this, I received a powerful witness of the spirit, accompanied by the burning sensation in the breast. What made the incident even more significant to me at the time was the fact that this statement seemed to have little relevance to the subject he was developing in his talk.[7]

As the meeting ended and Dad and Mom filed out of the Assembly Hall, Dad was "electrified" by a comment which Mom made to him: "Frank, I can't escape the idea that at one point in his talk today, Elder Bowen was speaking directly to you and to no one else."[8]

> For the next twenty-five years, Dad thought often of this profound experience, and believed that the day would come when he would be faced with the choice presented by Elder Bowen—whether "to make a lot of money or a to make a great life."

---

[7] FMG Autobiography, Volume II, page 30.
[8] FMB Autobiography, Volume II, page 30; see also, Record Book, page 94

"Go see Bjork Cederlof"

A further step along the way was a remarkable impression Dad received after he had passed the Utah Bar exam and was trying, without success, to begin his law practice. In 1967 he wrote:

> At the time I passed the Utah State Bar in the fall of 1951, I was unknown to the legal profession in Salt Lake. Neither did I have an entrée through powerful or influential relatives or friends. In these circumstances, I had to aggressively seek a connection with a firm. I did this by listing all of the top rated firms from Martindale-Hubbell, a law directory, and by systematically contacting them about employment. I spent several weeks doing this, but got no results. Finally, I decided to open my own office and strike out alone. I then commenced a canvass of the office buildings for space and discovered this was as hard to find as employment. I investigated many different possibilities, but found nothing suitable. In the meantime I continued to pray for guidance. While I experienced periods of discouragement and disappointment, I felt deep down that events would work out satisfactorily for me. Subsequent developments proved this faith and confidence to be well founded.
>
> One December day I was continuing my search for office space. As I walked east across State Street near Fourth South to look at some space owned by Attorney Edward Clyde, my mind for some reason turned to my friend, Bjork Cederlof, who, I knew, worked for a Coal Company which officed in the Newhouse Building. As I thought of Bjork, it occurred to me that he might be able to put me in touch with the owners of that

building, who, I hoped, might in turn be able to rent me an office. Following through on this impression, I contacted Bjork later in the day. To my surprise, I found that the man who controlled the company Bjork worked for also owned the Newhouse Building. Bjork gladly introduced me to this gentleman (Clyde Thompson) and through him, I was later able to rent two small rooms on the seventh floor. At the time Mr. Thompson rented this space to me, he said that the firm which represented him officed in the same building on the sixth floor and, as he understood it, needed some assistance. Without my asking him to do it, Mr. Thompson went to this firm and told them about me. Because of this introduction, I was able to work out an arrangement with this firm (Senior and Senior) under which I worked on a part-time basis for them. Later, I went on a salary basis working for them full time. As it turned out, this firm enjoyed a national reputation in the field of natural resources law and public lands. I could not have made a better connection, professionally, than this one. It all came about because I heard and heeded the whisperings of the still, small voice. God be thanked for it.[9]

"This is your house"

Early in his law practice with Senior and Senior, Dad was asked to probate the estate of the Dupaix family. The executor, Ray Dupaix, kept suggesting to Dad that he ought to buy the old family home that had belonged to his parents, which was located at 1784 Yale Avenue on Salt Lake's east bench. Dad put Ray off, but ultimately agreed to

---

[9] Record Book, pages 88-90

look at the house. When Dad and Mom drove up and saw the house in 1954, they both had the impression, "This is your house!" Though they had little money, they were able to make a down payment and purchased this home, which they lived in for the next quarter of a century and raised their four children there.

As it turns out, had my parents never purchased this particular house, Dad never would have met the man who was most instrumental in bringing him into the office of the First Presidency.

"Brother Joseph Anderson"

The home that Dad and Helen purchased in 1954 was located on Salt Lake City's east bench in the Yalecrest Ward of the Bonneville Stake. One of the members of the Yalecrest Ward was Brother Joseph Anderson, who had served as the secretary to the First Presidency since 1922. Joseph had served on the Bonneville Stake High Council for many years. In January of 1964 Dad was serving as the stake mission president and noted in his diary that:

> Brother Joseph Anderson, Secretary to the First Presidency of the Church, and member of the Bonneville Stake High Council, spoke to our missionaries this morning. He has occupied his present position for almost 42 years, having started in it in 1922. He reviewed for us some of the highlights of the Church's achievements during recent years. . . . He bore a strong testimony of the divinity of the work and affirmed that the Brethren are Prophets of God.[10]

---

[10] FMG Diary, Sunday, January 19, 1964.

Within a few months, Dad would also be called to the high council, where he would serve with Brother Anderson. At the time, this high council also included Brothers Russell M. Nelson and Joseph B. Wirthlin, both of whom would later be called as members of the Quorum of Twelve. In 1969, Dad was sustained as the stake executive secretary in a stake conference meeting and noted in his diary: "After the meeting I was set apart to the work by President Russell M. Nelson, assisted by his counselors, Albert R. Bowen and Joseph B. Wirthlin."[11]

In the coming years Dad had frequent contact with Brother Anderson. For example, in January of 1965 they had a long discussion about Brother Joseph's work with the First Presidency. Dad wrote in his Diary that Joseph had "reported all of the General Conferences since 1922 when he became secretary to President Grant."[12]

"He walked toward me"

President David O. McKay died on January 18, 1970. This, incidentally, was the same day on which Dad was sustained and ordained as the bishop of the Yalecrest Ward, having been called by his stake president, Russell M. Nelson. Between President McKay's death and Dad's call to serve with the Brethren in April of 1970, one final signpost pointing him toward his ultimate service appeared in Dad's life. On the night of Monday, March 23, 1970, Dad had a very vivid and sacred dream, in which he was present in a meeting presided over by President McKay, with others of the Brethren present, where the Brethren were discussing the affairs of the Church. Dad then recorded, "When he noticed me, President McKay, not knowing my name, asked

---

[11] Diary, Sunday, May 25, 1969
[12] FMG Diary, Sunday, January 3, 1965.

someone sitting near him about my identity, and learning it, he walked toward me and extended his hand." Dad greeted President McKay in tears, and the Prophet then conferred a special priesthood blessing upon Dad." Dad did not hear the words of the blessing, as he awoke from this dream with a start. He recorded that "the dream carries strange implications."[13] Within seventeen days of receiving this dream, Dad would find himself in the Upper Room of the Salt Lake Temple, acting as the secretary to the First Presidency.

One of the most moving aspects of Dad's dream is a parallel dream which Dad's predecessor, Joseph Anderson, had at about the same time. Several months after Dad's call, Elder Anderson came to see Dad for tithing settlement, Dad serving as the bishop of Elder Anderson's ward at the time. Dad later told me:

> When Joseph Anderson came in for tithing settlement that day, he told me that not long before he was called as an assistant to the Twelve, he had a vivid dream of President McKay, who was young and vigorous, who showed great love and concern for Joseph and who indicated that Joseph should be called to a high position in the Church. He said that he got the impression that the Church leaders who pass to the other side have influence on the choices made of earthly leaders on the same principle of delegation that exists here now. On this basis, he concluded that President McKay was instrumental in his call.

---

[13] FMG Diary, Monday, March 23, 1970.

"Raised up by the Lord"

There was no doubt in Dad's mind that the unique series of events that preceded his call as secretary to the First Presidency were directed by heaven. Mom once observed to the family that it seemed as if the Lord had prepared Dad his whole life for his future service, bringing him from the obscurity of St. Johns to a state of readiness near the center of the Church. Elder Joseph Anderson once told Dad that he knew Dad had been "raised up by the Lord to serve as secretary to the First Presidency."

JOSEPH FIELDING SMITH

Tenth President of The Church of Jesus Christ
of Latter-day Saints

January 1970 – July 1972

Joseph Fielding Smith Chronology

July 19, 1876
Joseph Fielding Smith is born in Salt Lake City to Joseph F. Smith and Julina Lambson Smith.

January 1879
The U.S. Supreme Court issues its decision in *Reynolds v. United States*, which upheld the constitutionality of the Morrill Anti-Bigamy Act of 1862, which had criminalized the Latter-day Saint practice of plural marriage. Joseph Fielding Smith's family is dramatically affected by efforts to arrest and prosecute his father, President Joseph F. Smith.

April 26, 1898
Joseph Fielding Smith is married to his first wife, Louie Shurtliff, in the Salt Lake Temple.

May 13, 1899
Joseph Fielding Smith departs for his mission to England with his older brother, Joseph Richards Smith.

March 30, 1908
Joseph Fielding Smith's first wife, Louie Shurtliff Smith, passes away.

November 2, 1908
Joseph Fielding Smith is married to his second wife, Ethel Reynolds, in the Salt Lake Temple.

April 7, 1910
In a surprise announcement, Joseph Fielding Smith is sustained as a member of the Quorum of the Twelve Apostles. After his call to the Apostleship, he continued to serve as the confidential secretary for his father, Church President Joseph F. Smith.

November 19, 1918
Elder Joseph Fielding Smith's father, President Joseph F. Smith., passes away. One of his last services to his father was to record his vision of the dead, which now appears as section 138 of the Doctrine and Covenants.

1921
Elder Joseph Fielding Smith is appointed as Church Historian.

1922
Elder Joseph Fielding Smith publishes his book, *Essentials in Church History*. He would eventually write more than twenty books.

1925
Elder Joseph Fielding Smith builds a new family home on Douglas Street in Salt Lake City.

August 26, 1937
Elder Joseph Fielding Smith's second wife, Ethel Reynolds Smith, passes away.

April 12, 1938
Elder Joseph Fielding Smith marries his third wife, Jessie Evans, in the Salt Lake Temple

April 21, 1939
Elder Joseph Fielding Smith leaves Salt Lake City for extended tour of European Missions. He would not return home until November of 1939.

July 4, 1939
Elder Joseph Fielding Smith is awakened in Florence, Italy, by the movement of Mussolini's fascist troops.

August 23, 1939
Elder Joseph Fielding Smith oversees the evacuation of all missionaries serving in Germany prior to the outbreak of World War II.

September 3, 1939
Elder Joseph Fielding Smith goes to Copenhagen, Denmark, where he oversees the evacuation of all missionaries serving in Europe.

November 1939
Elder Joseph Fielding Smith returns home after being in Europe for seven months.

March 4, 1942
Elder Joseph Fielding Smith's son Lewis is drafted.

1944
Elder Joseph Fielding Smith delivers two series of radio lectures entitled "The Signs of the Times" and "The Restoration of All Things."

December 29, 1944
Joseph Fielding Smith's son Lewis is killed in action in North Africa.

June 1945
Elder Joseph Fielding Smith is called as President of the Salt Lake Temple.

August 8, 1950
Elder Joseph Fielding Smith is sustained as Acting President of the Quorum of the Twelve Apostles following the death of Elder George F. Richards.

April 9, 1951
President Joseph Fielding Smith is sustained as President of the Quorum of the Twelve Apostles following the death of President George Albert Smith.

September 1958
President Joseph Fielding Smith travels to England and Western Europe for the dedication of the London Temple and special training in the Swiss Temple.

November 1958
President Joseph Fielding Smith travels to the South Pacific for missionary and member meetings.

October 1960
President Joseph Fielding Smith leaves for an extended tour of South America, where he holds meetings in Brazil, Uruguay, Argentina, Chile, Peru, Ecuador, and Guatemala.

November 1963
President Joseph Fielding Smith travels to Australia for missionary and member meetings.

October 29, 1965
President Joseph Fielding Smith is called as additional counselor in the First Presidency.

Summer of 1966
President Joseph Fielding Smith accompanies President David O. McKay for an inspection of Church history sites in Missouri.

January 18, 1970
President David O. McKay passes away.

January 23, 1970
President Joseph Fielding Smith is ordained and set apart as the tenth President of the Church.

August 3, 1971
President Joseph Fielding Smith's third wife, Jessie Evans Smith, passes away.

August 26, 1971
President Joseph Fielding Smith arrives in Manchester, England, for the Church's first Area Conference. The night before the Conference, Joseph Fielding Smith presides at a special Council of the First Presidency and the Quorum of the Twelve, the first such meeting held on foreign soil since 1840.

July 2, 1972

President Joseph Fielding Smith dies peacefully in the home of his daughter, Amelia Smith McConkie, seventeen days before his ninety-sixth birthday.

"A Contemporary of Fifteen Prophets"

President Joseph Fielding Smith might have touched the lives of more Church leaders than any other President of the Church. The grandnephew of the Prophet Joseph Smith, he was a contemporary of the succeeding fifteen Prophets of this dispensation. He was born July 19, 1876, during the lifetime of President Brigham Young. He lived during the lifetime of each of the Presidents of the Church who preceded him except for the Prophet Joseph Smith. As a boy and a young man, he was personally acquainted with Presidents John Taylor, Wilford Woodruff, and Lorenzo Snow. He served in the Quorum of the Twelve during the administrations of his father, President Joseph F. Smith, and then under Presidents Heber J. Grant, George Albert Smith, and David O. McKay. By the time he was ordained as the tenth President of the Church on January 23, 1970, he had personally witnessed nearly a century of Church history. He was also a contemporary of the six Church Presidents who succeeded him after his death (as of November of 2014), having served in the First Presidency or the Quorum of the Twelve with Presidents Harold B. Lee, Spencer W. Kimball, Ezra Taft Benson, Howard W. Hunter, Gordon B. Hinckley, and Thomas S. Monson.

Thus, President Smith represents a sort of welding link, connecting all Church Presidents, past and present.

"The Long Shadow of History"

The long shadow of history hung over Joseph Fielding Smith from the moment of his birth. He had the most unique upbringing of any of the Prophets I had the privilege of working under. He was born, of course, into the most distinguished family in the Church. From his birth, he was surrounded by many who were intimately acquainted with the earliest period of Church history. His father, President Joseph F. Smith, was the son of Hyrum Smith and the nephew of Joseph Smith and had boyhood memories of living in Missouri and in Nauvoo.

President Smith was also very close to his great-aunt Thompson, Mercy Fielding Thompson, who was a plural wife of his grandfather, Hyrum Smith, and was personally acquainted with Joseph and Emma Smith. She was able to share with her grandnephew firsthand impressions of the personalities and perspectives of first-generation Latter-day Saints. He was also personally acquainted with Church Presidents John Taylor, Wilford Woodruff, and Lorenzo Snow, and many of the older Apostles who had been contemporaries of his great-uncle Joseph Smith, Jr., and his grandfather Hyrum Smith. These associations gave President Smith a special and unusually vivid sense of history.

The sense of history that Joseph Fielding Smith acquired through these relationships was sharpened by the natural inclinations of his mother, Julina Lambson Smith. She was a remarkably intelligent and perceptive woman. Before her marriage to Joseph F. Smith, she had been an employee in the Church Historian's Office. There she acquired a keen interest in Church history and doctrine, which I'm sure she passed on to her son, resulting in his lifelong passion for history.

"A Trunk Which Had Belonged to Hyrum"

President Joseph Fielding Smith had inherited a very old trunk, which had belonged to Hyrum Smith, and an old safe, which had belonged to his father, President Joseph F. Smith. These had been stored, unopened, for decades in President Smith's home on Douglas Street and later in his apartment in the Eagle Gate in downtown Salt Lake City.

After he became the President of the Church in 1970, President Smith gave the safe to the Church. I was with the Prophet when it was opened and inventoried. As we went through the items, President Smith provided fascinating information about the contents and about his family and personal history.

There were so many things of special historic significance inside this old safe that it was almost overwhelming. It was a special experience to be in the presence of the aged Prophet when these things were brought forth. It gave me a sense of President Smith's deep personal connection to the past. Inside the safe there was a veritable treasure trove of documents, journals, letters, and artifacts of great historical significance to the Smith family and the Church. Among the items in the safe were an old family Bible almost four hundred years old, numerous journals and other documents dating back to the earliest days of the Church, memorabilia from Kirtland and Nauvoo, artifacts related to the martyrdom of Joseph and Hyrum in the Carthage Jail, and many, many other fascinating things.

Upon his death, President Joseph Fielding Smith also bequeathed to the Church the old trunk in his possession. Shortly after the Prophet's death, I accompanied President

Smith's sons Joseph and Douglas, President Gordon B. Hinckley, and several others to inspect this old trunk. It had belonged to his grandfather, Hyrum Smith, and was brought across the plains in a covered wagon by his grandmother, Mary Fielding Smith, and his father, Joseph F. Smith. The trunk bore a nameplate with the inscription, "Hirum Smith, Hancock County, Illinois." In it were several items of clothing that had belonged to Hyrum Smith, including his Nauvoo Legion uniform, some personal belongings of Joseph F. Smith, and some miscellaneous old newspapers and other documents. The trunk had not been opened in some time, and it was necessary to get the help of a locksmith before the trunk could be opened.

These experiences seeing and handling these Smith family artifacts, preserved for nearly a century and a half by President Joseph F. Smith and his son, President Joseph Fielding Smith, represent some of the most interesting and inspiring hours I have ever spent in my life.

"A MOST DISTINGUISHED NAME"

Joseph Fielding Smith was a child of great promise and he was given a most distinguished name.

His father, President Joseph F. Smith, had six wives and nearly fifty children. I understand that Joseph Fielding Smith's mother, Julina Lambson, had been promised that her first son would bear his father's full name, Joseph Fielding Smith, even though he had an older brother who was several years older. Like his father, Joseph Fielding Smith was named after the Prophet Joseph Smith. He was also named after his grandmother, Mary Fielding Smith, an early English convert who married Hyrum Smith in Kirtland in 1837. So the name was full of significance, both for the Church and for the young Joseph Fielding Smith personally.

It is interesting that during his early life, he always identified himself as Joseph F. Smith, Jr., but following the death of his father, the Prophet, he began to refer to himself as Joseph Fielding Smith.

"WATCHING THE STONE CUTTERS"

When I first began working with President Smith in 1970, it was almost an everyday occurrence to hear the Prophet speak of matters occurring in the 1880's or 1890's like it was yesterday. He was born in 1876, and so his memory stretched many years before the completion of the Salt Lake Temple. One day I had a sweet conversation with the Prophet as we walked from the Church Administration Building to the temple. He told me about his boyhood and how he would go each summer to Little Cottonwood Canyon with his father, President Joseph F. Smith, to stay in a little rustic cabin the family had there. While in the canyon, he and his father would hike over to watch the quarrymen hew the massive blocks of granite to be transported to Temple Square. He also said that his boyhood home was on 100 North Street, close to Temple Square, and he reminisced with me about how he would often run over to watch the stone cutters at work on the temple. He said that it was fascinating to watch them shape the great stones that were raised in place on the walls and towers. He also mentioned attending the dedication of the Salt Lake Temple in 1893, when he was sixteen years old, and seeing the venerable aged Prophet, President Wilford Woodruff, in his immaculate white suit as he dedicated the sacred building.

"The Shadow of Persecution"

I was privileged to have several conversations with President Joseph Fielding Smith about his boyhood. He remembered his childhood in the 1870's and 1880's with great fondness, despite the difficult circumstances under which his family lived. President Smith grew up under a kind of shadow, which was the heavy anti-Mormon persecution then waged by the federal government against the Church. So his boyhood was happy within the home, but often difficult and traumatic outside. The trauma came from the countless times his father had to leave home to avoid arrest because of his practicing plural marriage. In the late 1870's, when the Prophet was only a toddler, the U.S. Supreme Court issued its opinion, *Reynolds v. United States*, upholding the constitutionality of the Morrill Anti-Bigamy Act. This ruling was a serious blow to the Church and to Joseph F. Smith and many other Latter-day Saints who were then practicing plural marriage. It essentially made criminals of an entire generation of Mormons, and aggressive federal enforcement followed under the Edmunds-Tucker Act. Many Church leaders were imprisoned or forced into hiding and exile in the aftermath of the *Reynolds* case. President Joseph Fielding Smith's father was no exception, and he took President Smith's mother and his younger sister and left for Hawaii, where he lived for about three years. So for a time during his adolescence, President Joseph Fielding Smith was deprived of the companionship of his father as he evaded arrest.

During his father's long absence, President Smith continued to live with his brothers and sisters and his father's other wives in the only family home on 100 North in

Salt Lake City. Young Joseph always called his father's other wives "aunties." There was a great deal of affection in that large, unusual family. So Joseph Fielding Smith really lived a life of simple happiness. I'm sure this happiness came principally from being part of an unusually close-knit and unified family consisting of his parents, the "aunties," and many brothers and sisters. Most of the siblings, of course, were half brothers and sisters, but I understand from members of the family that none of the children were ever regarded as a "half-brother" or a "half-sister," and in fact they were offended if anyone ever referred to them as such. In the Smith family, they were all brothers and sisters, without regard to which mother gave them birth.

The shadow of persecution that hung over the family never really lifted until Joseph Fielding Smith was in his mid teens. Even after his father's return from Hawaii, he was unable to openly visit or support his wives and children. This sad state of affairs continued until 1891, when Joseph F. Smith and other Church leaders received a federal pardon from U.S. President Benjamin Harrison.

"Very Little Money"

While rich in family heritage, President Joseph Fielding Smith's family was poor in the wealth of the world. President Joseph F. Smith lived very frugally. There was much love, but very little money. He had few opportunities to accumulate money during his lifetime. Almost from his boyhood he was engaged full time in missionary work and Church leadership service.

All members of the family worked to provide means to live. President Joseph Fielding Smith's mother was a midwife, who delivered babies as a way to supplement their income. She became exceptionally skilled at her work as a midwife. It is reported that she delivered nearly a thousand babies in her career without ever having a mother or an infant die in childbirth. Young Joseph Fielding Smith contributed to the family income by becoming his mother's chauffeur, driving her to visit her patients in the family carriage. He had a favorite horse named Meg, and whenever needed, he would hitch Meg up to the carriage. At all hours of the day or night, and in all weather, Joseph made himself available to drive his mother to her work. He also earned money by working in the warehouse at the old ZCMI store carrying heavy boxes and moving goods from one place to another, tasks that resulted in a permanent injury to his shoulder.

There was very little money in the family to provide for an education for the young man. He did attend two years at the old LDS College, after which he began working as his father's secretary, taking dictation, writing letters, and conducting research. It is interesting to contemplate this special relationship of father and son, the President of the

Church working side by side with his secretary, who would, in his high old age, also become the President of the Church.

"We Got a Scolding from the Prophet"

President Smith often recalled an experience he had as a boy when he was scolded by the Prophet. When the Tabernacle Choir sang at the World's Fair in Chicago in the early 1890's, Joseph Fielding Smith was invited to attend and traveled on the train with a group that included President Wilford Woodruff. President Smith would have been about sixteen years old at the time. During the long train trip, he spent much of his time visiting with a son and daughter of President Woodruff, and they became good friends. The three teenagers explored the train and had a grand time together. One day the trio procured a watermelon and took it to the rear of the train, where they sat on the open platform laughing, talking, eating watermelon, and spitting seeds over the low railing onto the tracks behind. Word of this behavior apparently found its way to President Woodruff, and when the teenagers returned to the Prophet's private car, he gave them a good talking to. President Smith said, "We got a scolding from the Prophet!"

"A DEFENDER OF THE DOCTRINE"

Not long before his call to serve as a missionary, when he was about twenty years old, President Joseph Fielding Smith was given a patriarchal blessing by his uncle, John Smith, who was the oldest son of Hyrum Smith. The blessing was remarkable. It essentially laid out the young man's entire life before him.

There were two very significant promises in the blessing. He was told that he would "sit in counsel" with his brethren and "preside among the people." He was also promised that he would "live to a good old age." President Smith ultimately lived to age 95. The only Presidents who surpassed him in age were President David O. McKay, who lived to age 96, and President Gordon B. Hinckley, who lived to age 97.

President Smith's oldest son, Joseph Fielding Smith, Jr., told me that his father had received a second patriarchal blessing after he had been a member of the Twelve for about three years. In it he was promised that he would become preeminent as an expounder of the gospel and as a defender of the doctrine taught by the Prophet Joseph Smith.

"They Crossed the Atlantic"

As an additional means of supporting the family, Joseph's mother, Julina, often took boarders into the large family home on 100 North Street in Salt Lake City. One such boarder was a young woman named Louie Shurtliff, who was a student at the University of Utah, from Ogden, Utah. President Smith fell in love with this girl and began to court her, and the two were married in the Salt Lake Temple in 1898. About a year later, Joseph Fielding Smith was called to serve a mission for the Church in Great Britain. It was quite common in those days to call married men into the mission field. The wives of these missionaries were left to fend for themselves at home, with the help of their families. During President Smith's mission to England, his wife moved back home to Ogden to live with her parents.

President Smith traveled to his field of labor in England with his older brother, Joseph Richards Smith. They crossed the Atlantic in a sailing ship. It is interesting to contemplate that a Prophet who served in the years after men landed on the moon spent his boyhood and young manhood in a world of horses and buggies and sailing ships!

Arriving in Liverpool, young Joseph was assigned by his mission president to serve in Nottingham, England. In Nottingham Joseph first experienced the great derision and hostility then shown towards Mormons in England. A few days after his arrival, while leaving the missionaries' rented room, Joseph and his companion were surrounded by a gang of rowdy English boys who taunted the Elders and sang a parody of a Church hymn, "Chase me girls to Salt

Lake City, where the Mormons have no pity." Elder Smith was also shocked at the gross immorality he witnessed, including public drunkenness and immoral acts committed openly in public parks. He said that he saw more wickedness in his first two weeks in England than in his entire life at home.

In England the proselyting activities consisted almost exclusively of door-to-door and street contacting. He did not see much success. After several months, Elder Smith was transferred to Derby, where he served as a senior companion to a man in his thirties. The work in Derby was as unsuccessful as it had been in Nottingham. After a time in Derby, Elder Smith and his companion were transferred back to Nottingham, where his junior companion was called as the conference president. Elder Smith was now the junior companion. This was a shock, but Elder Smith humbly accepted the junior role. He served as a junior companion the rest of his mission! I'm sure that this experience schooled him in the way of the priesthood. It also prefigured his life of service in the Church. He spent almost his entire life in a junior role. It was only in his high old age that he finally had a chance to preside.

The work in England was very unfruitful during the time of President Smith's service there. Despite all his diligent labors, he did not baptize a single convert during his entire mission.

During his mission he immersed himself deeply in the study of the scriptures and Church history. He reported that even his senior companion, the conference president, deferred to the younger Elder Smith in doctrinal and scriptural matters. He also had the gift of healing, and many people who came to him for blessings were healed of sicknesses.

"THE MOST PROLIFIC WRITER"

After returning home from his mission, Elder Joseph Fielding Smith was hired as a clerk in the Church Historian's Office. Thus began an association with the Historian's Office that lasted his entire life. Ultimately he served as an assistant historian and then for many decades as the Church historian. When he commenced his service, he worked under Anthon H. Lund, the Church historian, whose assistants were Orson F. Whitney, B. H. Roberts, and Andrew Jenson. All of these men were skilled researchers and writers and became role models for young Joseph Fielding Smith, who soon established himself as a writer. His first published work was entitled *Asael Smith of Topsfield,* which explored the Smith family heritage in New England. This was followed by *Blood Atonement and the Origin of Plural Marriage,* and *Origin of the Reorganized Church and the Question of Succession.* Eventually Joseph Fielding Smith published more than twenty books. He is the most prolific writer of any of the modern Prophets.

In 1921, after his call to the Apostleship, he became the Church Historian, leading the office in which he had worked for twenty years, since his return home from his mission to England. In 1922, his book *Essentials in Church History* was published, which became one of the most popular works of history ever published in the Church, going through dozens of editions and being translated into many foreign languages.

"A WIDOWER AT AGE THIRTY-ONE"

Joseph Fielding Smith and his wife Louie built a small home in Salt Lake City and became the parents of two daughters. Their names were Josephine and Julina. Joseph was soon called to the Salt Lake Stake high council and as a member of the Young Men's General Board.

Then, his life was shattered when his wife Louie passed away suddenly in early 1908 from pregnancy-related complications. Joseph was suddenly a widower at age thirty-one, with two little daughters.

Into this family tragedy stepped Joseph's kindly and loving father, President Joseph F. Smith, then President of the Church. The Prophet invited his son to move into the Beehive House, then the official residence of the President of the Church, where the motherless daughters would have care while their father pursued his work in the Church Historian's Office.

Within a few months after the death of Joseph's young wife, his father tactfully, but clearly, suggested that he ought to remarry, and for the sake of the little orphaned girls, remarry soon.

Working in the Church Historian's Office was a young woman, Georgina Ethel Reynolds, who was the daughter of Elder George Reynolds, a former assistant secretary to the First Presidency, and then a member of the First Council of Seventy. Elder Reynolds had been the plaintiff in a court case against the United States government challenging the constitutionality of the Federal anti-Mormon legislation. The case *Reynolds v. United States* had made Ethel's father famous among Latter-day Saints. Joseph began to court Ethel discreetly. They were married in the Salt Lake Temple on November 2, 1908. Ethel became a loving mother to little Josephine and Julina, and life returned more or less to normal for President Smith and his young family.

"I GUESS WE'LL HAVE TO SELL THE COW"

In 1910 Joseph Fielding Smith's life was again turned upside down. While sitting in General Conference, with no advance notice whatsoever, he heard his name presented as a member of the Quorum of the Twelve Apostles. He was only thirty-three years old. In many ways, this event altered his life far more than the death of his wife two years earlier. Things would never be the same for the young man and his family.

His comment to his wife after his surprising new call was, "Well, I guess we'll have to sell the cow!"

He approached the calling humbly and prayerfully, despite immediate opposition. Shortly after he was sustained, the anti-Mormon newspaper, *The Salt Lake Tribune*, published a vicious editorial entitled, "The Church of the Smiths," which criticized the calling of the Prophet's young son to the Apostleship. The Tribune pointed out that seven of the Church's twenty-seven General Authorities were members of the Smith family. It accused the Prophet of "Smith-i-sizing the Mormon Church," then went on to paint the Church and its President and his family in words of mockery and disdain.

As a member of the Quorum of the Twelve, Joseph Fielding Smith traveled almost every week, often under difficult circumstances. He went by railway and by horse and carriage, even reaching remote Mormon communities in the American west on horseback. He invariably stayed with local Church leaders rather than in hotels.

In his early years of apostolic service, he developed a pattern for speaking which would remain with him throughout his life. He tried to preach pure doctrine from the scriptures. He developed a reputation for speaking boldly and directly about many subjects. Though his sermons could be quite stern, away from the pulpit he was filled with good humor and kindness. He also liked to have fun, and during conference visits he would often participate in athletic competitions with the young men in outlying communities.

"His Father's Private Secretary"

After his call to serve as an Apostle, Joseph Fielding Smith continued serving as his father's private secretary. His father, President Joseph F. Smith, of course, was then the President of the Church. He continued in this special assignment from 1910 until the Prophet's death in 1918. It was a blessing to his father to have a son serving by his side. Young Joseph Fielding Smith was undoubtedly a great help and comfort to the rapidly aging Joseph F. Smith. Father and son often traveled together. One of the last trips they took together occurred in 1914, when the pair traveled in a private railway car throughout the Southern States and the American Midwest. In Independence, Missouri, the Prophet dedicated a new chapel, and father and son called on their cousin, Joseph Smith, III, the son of the founding Prophet, who was then president of the Reorganized Church.

In his capacity as personal secretary to the Prophet, Joseph Fielding Smith met daily with his father and conferred with him on the most sensitive matters involving Church administration. A few days before his father's death on November 19, 1918, he recorded Joseph F. Smith's vision of the redemption of the dead, which is now known as Section 138 of the Doctrine and Covenants.

It is touching to think of these two, working side by side during these years. The venerable Prophet, Joseph F. Smith, who had personally known the Prophet Joseph Smith, and the young Apostle, Joseph Fielding Smith, who would live to preside over the Church in the age of space travel.

"A NEW FAMILY HOME ON DOUGLAS STREET"

Following his call to the Apostleship, Joseph and his second wife, Ethel, lived in a small house in Salt Lake City, but soon purchased a large lot on Salt Lake's east bench. There in 1925, they built a new family home on Douglas Street to accommodate their growing family of ten children. There were, of course, Josephine and Julina, the two daughters of Joseph's deceased first wife, Louie. Then by the time the family moved into their new house, his second wife Ethel had given birth to eight additional children: Emily, Naomi, Lois, Joseph, Amelia, Lewis, Reynolds, and Douglas.

The new house on Douglas Street had ample bedrooms for all of the children and also space outdoors for the children to play. Since Joseph was an active father who loved sports, the new home had a large lawn, a tennis court, horseshoe pits, and other athletic equipment for the children (and their father) to enjoy. Two years after moving into the new home, an eleventh and final child was born: Milton (whose nickname was "Mitt").

President Joseph Fielding Smith was always very loving and kind toward his eleven children. He never saw one of his children or grandchildren but that he gave them a kiss.

I had the blessing of being personally acquainted with four of the sons of President Joseph Fielding Smith: Joseph Fielding Smith, Jr., Lewis Smith, Reynolds Smith, and Douglas Smith. His relationship with each of these sons reveals much about his character.

"A Lesson on the Word of Wisdom"

When I was younger, I often played golf with President Smith's son, Reynolds Smith, whom we always called "Reyn." Reyn once told me that when he was a student at Roosevelt Junior High School, he had a friend who brought a package of cigarettes to school one day and persuaded Reyn to "try just one puff." When school ended the boys went to an out-of-the-way cul-de-sac near the Junior High, where they thought no one would be watching. They each took a cigarette, lit it with a match, and began to smoke. Reyn told me that at that precise moment a car drove up the cul-de-sac. It was President Smith! Reyn said that he rolled down the car window and said, "Reynolds," a name he used only rarely. "I want to talk to you tonight when you get home!" He then drove away. Reyn fretted over his transgression the rest of the day and finally had the courage to return home for dinner. Not a word was spoken during the meal, but afterwards President Smith invited his son into his study for "a lesson on the Word of Wisdom." Afterwards, President Smith exacted a promise from Reyn that he would never again smoke a cigarette as long as he lived, a promise which Reyn kept.

"THE EVILS OF PROFANITY"

President Smith fully supported his sons in all of their athletic endeavors. When in the city, he always went to watch athletic events in which his sons were competing, and he did not allow his Church duties to interfere. Douglas Smith, President Smith's youngest son, was a fellow member of the Bonneville Stake, and served as my counselor in the stake presidency during the time that his father presided over the Church. Douglas played football for East High School, which was not far from the Smith home. He told me that his father always came to watch him play football when the Apostle was in town. On one occasion, Doug was injured early in the game. At halftime, the players went into the locker room, carrying Doug with them. President Smith was watching in the stands and made his way to the locker room to check on his son's condition. Doug was lying on the floor of the locker room when his father entered, just in time to hear the football coach, Mickey Oswald, deliver an impassioned halftime exhortation to the players. Doug said that Coach Oswald was angry, and was using "boatswain master's language" laced with mild profanity. Hearing the rough language, President Smith delivered an impromptu sermon on the evils of profanity and the merits of circumspect speech. Meanwhile, Doug pretended to be unconscious on the floor to avoid the embarrassment of facing his teammates and his coach.

"LET'S GO AND WATCH THE FOOTBALL GAME"

Of all of President Joseph Fielding Smith's sons, Mitt Smith was perhaps the most athletically gifted. Mitt played quarterback on the University of Utah football team. President Smith would attend every home game possible, always arriving early and sitting on the east side of Ute (later Rice-Eccles) Stadium on the University of Utah campus. He was an avid fan and knew all the ins and outs of the game and was not above standing on his feet with the other partisan fans to yell his protest of a bad call.

President Marion G. Romney, who for decades served with President Smith as a member of the Quorum of the Twelve, told me this illuminating story: One General Conference, the University of Utah was playing a football game at Ute Stadium during the Saturday evening priesthood session of Conference. Before the session, President Smith came up to President Romney on the stand in the Tabernacle, leaned over and whispered to him, "Marion, let's go up and watch the football game." President Romney told me that he declined, because he had his young son George with him in the Tabernacle, and did not want to set a bad example for him. President Romney told me that after the opening song and prayer, and when the Tabernacle lights were dimmed for the first speaker, Joseph Fielding Smith slipped quietly out of the Tabernacle to go alone to Ute Stadium to see his son play football.

There are doubtless those who would criticize him for leaving General Conference to watch a football game, but I tend to think President Smith had his priorities absolutely right in this case. President Smith was always a father first.

"A WIDOWER FOR THE SECOND TIME"

Joseph Fielding Smith's second wife, Ethel, was a woman of intelligence and substance and served on the Relief Society General Board for many years. Because Louie's daughters were older, they took responsibility around the home when Ethel traveled on Relief Society business, or when she accompanied her Apostle husband on his ecclesiastical duties. One such trip took Joseph and Ethel on an extended tour of the Central States Mission, including visits to Church history sites in Missouri and Illinois. Joseph and Ethel also took vacation trips with their eleven children.

Beginning in the 1930's, Ethel Smith began to suffer from a debilitating illness and despite all the best medical care available, many priesthood blessings, and the fervent prayers of her family and the Saints, she passed away in 1937. Thus, the Prophet was a widower for the second time, at age sixty-two.

"Their Unusual Courtship"

Several of the younger children still lived at home at the time of the death of their mother, Ethel Reynolds Smith, which placed a great burden on the sixty-two-year-old Apostle.

As in the case of the death of his first wife, Louie Shurtliff Smith, Joseph felt that it would be unwise to delay remarriage, and he began courting Jessie Evans, a well-known contralto who sang with the Mormon Tabernacle Choir. My dear friend, David W. Evans, served in the bishopric of the Garden Park Ward, where President Smith lived at the time of Ethel's death. He told me that when Sister Smith died, he stopped by the home to offer assistance. At first, President Smith declined any help, but then he thought and said, "Oh, there is one thing you might do. Will you ask Jessie Evans to sing a number at the funeral?" David Evans told me jokingly that he has since taken credit for having brought President Smith and Jessie Evans Smith together.

Jessie Evans, who was a quarter of a century younger than Joseph, had never married and worked as the Salt Lake County Recorder. Having decided to court Jessie Evans, Joseph proceeded with caution and tact. Their unusual courtship was a charming interlude, which revealed much about their personalities. Joseph first needed to create an excuse to speak with Jessie Evans, and so one day he called her from the Church Historian's Office. She answered the phone in the Salt Lake County Clerk's Office. He told her that he was prepared to help her to fill gaps in the records of the County with information from the Historian's Office. This led to a series of meetings, which

Jessie unromantically referred to as "interviews." Eventually the couple went on various social outings together, some of which included Joseph's eleven children. They were sealed in the Salt Lake Temple by Church President Heber J. Grant on April 12, 1938.

Jessie Evans Smith had been the sole support of her widowed mother for many years, and Mother Evans moved into President Smith's house on Douglas Street after Jessie's marriage to President Smith. In addition to providing her a home, this allowed Mother Evans to care for the younger Smith boys when President Smith and Jessie Evans Smith traveled together on Church assignments.

"Fun-Loving and Full of Life"

Jessie Evans Smith, the Prophet's third wife, was always known as "Aunt Jessie" to the family and close associates. Aunt Jessie was a *bona fide* character. She was fun loving and full of life and jokes. She was not averse to telling a ribald joke if the urge struck her—and it struck quite often. Example: "The fruit which brought about the expulsion from the Garden of Eden was not the apple in the tree but the pear ('pair') in the grass." She was a first-rate singer and performed with the Tabernacle Choir for almost fifty years. She enjoyed the limelight immensely and never lost an opportunity to bask in it. President Smith's private secretary, Arthur Haycock, remarked that Jessie Evans Smith seemed determined to "gather the rosebuds while she may."

"Awakened by the Sound of Jackboots"

In 1939 President and Sister Smith left Salt Lake City to tour missions in Great Britain and Europe. They visited all the missions in Great Britain, Scandinavia, and Europe. As the tour progressed, the news of impending war grew increasingly ominous. While in Florence, Italy, on July 4, they were awakened by the sound of jackboots as Mussolini's fascist brownshirts marched directly beneath their hotel window. They then traveled to Germany and were in the country on August 23 when Germany signed a non-aggression pact with the Soviet Union. War was imminent between Germany on the one side and Great Britain and France on the other. The First Presidency responded by ordering the evacuation of all missionaries from Germany. President Smith went to Copenhagen, Denmark, where he oversaw the removal of all missionaries to safety. President and Sister Smith finally returned to the United States in November, after seven months abroad.

"Bowed Down with Grief"

One of the Prophet's greatest trials and sorrows was the death of his son, Lewis Smith, who was killed in action during World War II.

After the Japanese attacked Pearl Harbor in December of 1941, it became apparent that President Smith's sons might be called up for military duty, as several were eligible to be drafted. The President's son, Lewis, was the first and became a pilot. Douglas and Reynolds soon followed, joining the Army and Navy respectively.

In January of 1944, the family received the shocking word that Lewis had been killed while flying his plane in North Africa. He had flown to India on military business, returned via Palestine, where he had spent Christmas in Bethlehem, and then, as his plane flew over North Africa, it inexplicably exploded in mid-air. He was buried with military honors in Nigeria, the body later being transported and reburied in Salt Lake City. President Smith took great comfort in knowing that his son was a faithful Latter-day Saint to the end.

I was personally acquainted with Lewis, who was stationed near Mobile, Alabama, during his training as a pilot. He was a fine-looking, spiritual, and quiet young man who was called upon often to speak to the Saints. He had a powerful way of preaching and surely would have developed into one of the Lord's great leaders, had he lived. Shortly after I met him, he was deployed to North Africa.

One of the Prophet's sons-in-law, Hoyt Brewster, told me later that if any father could be said to have a favorite son, Lewis was the favorite of Joseph Fielding Smith. Hoyt told me that he had never seen the Prophet so bowed down with grief as he was upon learning of his son's untimely death during the war.

"Physically Vigorous and Active"

In 1950 President Smith became Acting President of the Quorum of the Twelve, and then President in 1951. One of his major labors in this period was the direction of the missionary work. As he approached his eightieth birthday, he was as physically vigorous and active as a man half his age. He made numerous international trips for the Church, touring the Orient, Europe, England, and the United States.

At home, President and Sister Smith sold the old family home on Douglas Street and moved into the Eagle Gate Apartments, less than a block from his office in the Church Administration Building.

"As Excited as a Schoolboy"

President Joseph Fielding Smith was always very enthusiastic about flying. Though he was born a generation before the Wright brothers' first powered flight in 1903, he was always interested in the latest advancements in airplanes, jets, and spacecraft. Though he never obtained a pilot's license, he frequently asked for the privilege of sitting in the cockpit of grounded aircraft. He always found air travel exhilarating. He was made an honorary brigadier general in the Utah Air National Guard and became acquainted with several pilots, who often took him on flights in military jet aircraft.

I was with him during a trans-Atlantic air trip to England and back in 1971. Though he was then about ninety-five years old, he was as excited as a schoolboy to be flying in a magnificent jet across an ocean.

President Howard W. Hunter told me this charming story about President Smith's love for flying: In contrast to the President's love of airplanes and flying, President J. Reuben Clark hated flying. President Clark, who served in the First Presidency for nearly thirty years, was adamant against flying and would do anything he could to take alternate transportation. One day President Smith played a good-natured joke on President Clark. President Smith invited President Clark to the airport to inspect a new airplane. Standing on the tarmac, admiring the wings and fuselage, President Clark asked, "What does it look like inside, a boxcar?" To that point in his life, President Clark had never flown in an airplane. President Smith invited President Clark inside to satisfy his curiosity. President Clark was then induced to occupy one of the seats, and just for the experience, to buckle up. When he was securely belted in, President Smith gave a prearranged signal, whereupon the flight crew fired the engines up, and the plane took off with its unwilling passenger.

"First Impressions of the Prophet"

I first met President Joseph Fielding Smith in April of 1970 when I was called as the secretary to the First Presidency. I still remember my first impressions of the Prophet. He was the first Church President whose father had also served in that position. At nearly ninety-four years of age, he was also the oldest man in the history of the Church to become its President.

President Smith carried a spirit of peace and contentment about him. He was never hurried and did everything with calmness and deliberation. He was of average height, with white hair, a slightly bent posture, and a somewhat shuffling gait. But his handshake was very strong, his memory was clear, and his mentality vibrant and active.

Even in his nineties, he was in remarkably good physical condition. He was quite robust and in excellent health, although, like virtually all persons of his age, he had minor episodes of forgetfulness and occasionally repeated himself, especially when he was tired. He needed a helping hand from time to time, but he came to the office every day. He walked to various meetings in the Church Administration Building and in the temple under his own power. For his age, his strength physically and mentally was a miracle.

It was a great matter of interest to me and even of inspiration to me to discover that his tendency to repeat himself never occurred either when he prayed or when he ordained or set anyone apart. It was truly remarkable, that on those special occasions, the President was magnified in such a powerful way. This was especially true when he ordained Elder Boyd K. Packer as an Apostle in April of 1970. President Smith did not repeat himself once during the lengthy ordination blessing.

In contrast to President Smith, his two counselors, President Harold B. Lee and President N. Eldon Tanner, were relatively young and physically vigorous men in their early seventies. Because of the confidence he had in his counselors, President Smith made broad delegations of administrative authority to them. They handled a myriad of details, freeing the President to provide a steady, guiding presence. President Smith attended all the meetings of the Brethren and was kept apprised about all aspects of the work, retaining the ultimate authority, with the attendant power to revoke his delegations at any time he elected.

"CONSTANTLY PRAYING WITHIN HIMSELF"

After observing President Joseph Fielding Smith for nearly two years, I frequently had the impression that he was constantly praying within himself. There was something about his demeanor that spoke of a man of faith. He was a man of prayer, as were his father Joseph F. Smith and grandfather Hyrum Smith before him, as well as his great-uncle, the Prophet Joseph Smith. All of these great men solved every problem of life through profound and fervent prayer.

"One of the Kindest Men"

President Joseph Fielding Smith was one of the kindest men I have ever known. This was interesting, because in his public ministry he always portrayed an image of sternness, of aloof rigidity, of taciturnity. Because of his apparent solemn, unsmiling demeanor at the pulpit, President Smith projected a serious, unbending, mirthless image to the Church. He had a reputation in the Church for being rather austere in his preaching and in his prolific doctrinal writing. When he conducted a meeting, everything was on the dot; the meeting started on the minute, and there was no question but that Joseph Fielding Smith was in charge. But this image of a cold, stern leader with little patience for the sinner was so at variance with his everyday personality. Behind the scenes, he was a very loving, compassionate man with a wry sense of humor. He never greeted one of his grown sons but that he embraced him and kissed him on the cheek. He was kind. He was humble. He had a sweet, warm, and forgiving nature.

The First Presidency is the ultimate council of resort in the Church, and during President Smith's presidency I sat with him on countless occasions when he considered appeals from disciplinary councils held throughout the Church. There were many tough cases and many sordid cases. I remember him commenting several times, "Why don't people behave themselves!" And yet, after watching him deal with difficult cases of sin or transgression, I was amazed at how merciful and forgiving he was in almost every instance. He showed great compassion and leniency as he decided these appeals. I felt that if I were ever to be judged by a Church tribunal, I would want Joseph Fielding Smith to be its presiding officer!

"A DELICIOUS SENSE OF HUMOR"

There was a delightful, playful side to President Smith. He often exhibited a very keen, exuberant, delicious sense of humor, with an almost puckish quality to it. He was completely without guile or pretension.

Once when meeting with a recently released mission president, the man expressed concern about his ability to complete his report within the allotted time. President Smith responded, "Well, I suppose we can give you an extra minute."

On another occasion, President Smith set apart several brethren to serve in one of the temples. One of them, who was there with his wife, mentioned to the President that he had married them fifty-one years earlier. Cupping his hand and speaking in an aside to the wife, he said, "Can you ever forgive me?"

I was once walking with President Smith and his second counselor, President N. Eldon Tanner. President Tanner observed to the Prophet. "You certainly move along in a spry manner, President." To this President Smith responded, "I should—I've had plenty of practice."

"Coax President Smith to sing"

President Smith had a sweet relationship with his wife, Jessie. She always had a joke or an anecdote to share. On her kitchen wall hung a placard that announced: "The views of the head of this house do not necessarily represent the views of the management."

When she and the President went in the car, she would always drive. During the years I knew them, they drove a white American Motors Hornet. On one occasion as they were driving away from a chapel where President Smith had spoken, he rolled down his window on the passenger side of the car and called out to a crowd of Saints who had gathered at the curb to wave goodbye. "Watch out," he called in mock alarm. "Woman driver!"

Aunt Jessie had a lovely singing voice and for many years had soloed with the Tabernacle Choir. After their marriage, she would often coax President Smith to sing a duet with her during meetings where they spoke. He invariably referred to these performances as "Do its."

"President Smith is here!"

President Smith was fond of taking drives with his family in his white Hornet. A special memory in our family is the occasion when the Prophet and Aunt Jessie stopped at our Yale Avenue home while out for an evening drive. My youngest son, Daniel, then about thirteen or fourteen years of age, came running to my study calling, "Dad! Dad! President Smith is here! President Smith is here!" In disbelief, I went outside to find the Hornet parked in our driveway with President and Sister Smith seated inside. After a visit during which all the family members were introduced to the Smiths, they drove on.

"Who is that woman in your office?"

President Smith's office, which was in the northeast corner of the main floor of the Administration Building, was visible from the Smith's apartment. With a small telescope, Jessie could see into her husband's office when the blinds weren't drawn. Once she gazed through the telescope to see a sculptured bust of the President's grandmother, which stood on a pedestal in his office. She promptly called on the telephone, demanding to know, "Who is that woman in your office?"

"THE HANDSHAKE OF A MAN IN HIS PRIME"

President Joseph Fielding Smith was a lifelong athlete. Even in his nineties he had the firm handshake of a man in his prime. His physical strength was a result of a lifetime of athletic endeavors. One day I walked with him from the Church Administration Building to the Salt Lake Temple. As we walked, he told me that he played handball for many years at the old Deseret Gym. There was a group of four men, the President and three friends, who played weekly. Then, the President told me, when he was in his seventies, he had a life-changing conversation with a medical doctor. President Smith had been playing handball with his usual foursome and was sitting on a bench in the locker room at the Deseret Gym, sweating and puffing from a hard game. A doctor friend walked by and said "Joseph, you're too old to be playing that hard. If you don't stop, you will drop dead on the handball court one day." In response, President Smith asked whether he was recommending that he completely give up the game. The doctor answered, "Yes!" President Smith said to me, "That was the last game of handball that I ever played." We continued to walk towards the Temple for several minutes in silence when he added as a postscript: "And my three friends never forgave me for breaking up the foursome!"

"HE NEVER ATE MEAT"

President Smith not only exercised and took care of his body, but he was always very careful with his diet. Towards the end of his life he was also a vegetarian. Although he never told me the reasons for his avoidance of meat, I gained this insight from his personal secretary, D. Arthur Haycock. Arthur told me that the President had an unhappy experience when he was a boy, which led to his avoiding the eating of meat. He was persuaded to go on a rabbit hunt with some of his brothers. On that hunt, President Smith shot his one and only animal. It was a rabbit, and as he walked up to the animal, he found it flopping on the ground and crying, and it seemed to have an accusing expression, as if it were asking, "Why did you do this to me?" He never again killed another animal, and over time began to avoid eating meat. By the time he became President of the Church, he never ate meat.

"A Deep Love for the Temple"

President Smith had a great love for temples, and in particular the Salt Lake Temple. It was a place of great peace for him. He received his endowment in the Salt Lake Temple and was sealed to each of his three wives in that structure. After his son Lewis was killed in action during World War II and following the deaths of his three wives, he retreated to the temple to find solace and comfort. A few months after the death of his son, he was called as the president of the Salt Lake Temple. And of course, as a member of the Quorum of the Twelve and then the First Presidency, he entered the temple weekly for council meetings.

It was while walking to and from the temple with the Prophet that I had some of my sweetest conversations with him.

The temple and temple work always had a central place in President Smith's ministry. In meetings with the counselors in the First Presidency, the Prophet usually deferred to the counselors. They were both much younger men at the top of their game. Both were experienced in Church administration. President Smith knew everything that was going on, but was wise enough to use his two intelligent and able counselors to take the leading oar. He felt no need to be the dominant voice in every matter and was content to let the younger men lead the discussions. The exception was any discussion dealing with the temple. When it came to the temple, his voice was always heard. He had a profound understanding of the temple. He had a deep love for the temple. In all discussions in the First Presidency when the topic of temples came up, he was there, listening intently, directing the discussion, and participating fully with his counselors.

"Next Day He Was Back at His Desk"

President Smith had the most remarkable physical strength of any older man I ever knew. He was tough. He was durable. He was strong. A testimony to that fact is that he was never hospitalized during ten decades of life until a few months after he was ordained President of the Church, when he entered the LDS Hospital for tests due to abdominal pain. However, the next day he was back at his desk early in the morning and attended all of his usual meetings.

"A WIDOWER FOR THE THIRD TIME"

President Smith's third wife, Jessie Evans Smith, died while he was serving as the President of the Church, making him a widower for the third time.

It was interesting to observe the Prophet during this time of grief. President Smith was always an outwardly happy man, but those who knew him well understood that he bore many private sorrows. Here was a man who had been married and widowed three times during his long lifetime. The wife of his youth, Louie Shurtliff, died as a young mother in 1908. His second wife, Ethel Reynolds, died in 1937. His third wife, Jessie Evans died in 1971. She preceded the President in death by almost a year, so he was alone during his final months as the President of the Church.

Jessie Evans Smith was only sixty-eight years of age at the time of her passing. Her death came as a great shock to many, as nearly everyone expected that she would survive the Prophet.

"A QUORUM OF APOSTLES ON FOREIGN SOIL"

A few days after the death of his wife, President Joseph Fielding Smith led a party of General Authorities in attending the first Area Conference to be held in Church history, in Manchester, England. On Friday, August 27, 1971, President Smith attended an historic meeting, held in a conference room in the Piccadilly Hotel in Manchester. It was the first time a quorum of the living Apostles had gathered for a meeting on foreign soil in 130 years! The first such meeting was also in Manchester in 1840. Present in this historic meeting were President Smith; future Church Presidents, Harold B. Lee, Spencer W. Kimball, Howard W. Hunter, Gordon B. Hinckley, and Thomas S. Monson; counselor in the First Presidency, Marion G. Romney; Apostles Richard L. Evans and Boyd K. Packer; future Apostle Russell M. Nelson, and several other General Authorities and others.

"GOD BE WITH YOU, 'TIL WE MEET AGAIN"

At the conclusion of the 1971 Area Conference in Manchester, England, I observed a very touching scene. On the final Sunday, the two final general sessions of the Conference were held at ten o'clock and two o'clock at Kings Hall in Manchester. There was a great outpouring of the Spirit, especially at the end of the last session when the entire congregation remained standing in their places after the Prophet and those with him had left, as if they did not want to leave. Then, spontaneously, the entire assembly burst into song, first singing, "We thank Thee O God for a Prophet," and then, "God Be With You Till We Meet Again." It was a scene never to be forgotten.

In many ways, President Joseph Fielding Smith's participation in the Manchester Conference was a pinnacle of his presidential ministry. After returning to the United States, he often said that it "seemed like a dream." There is no doubt that the Prophet had been magnified and inspired and blessed the lives of many people.

"COMPENSATION FOR A LIFETIME"

President Smith was always unfailingly kind to me, and indeed to all of those who associated with him. A few days prior to the Prophet's death, the Prophet spoke to me as we passed in the hallway. He said, "We certainly appreciate what you do." As he said this, he gave me a friendly pat on the arm. This was almost a compensation for a lifetime!

"HE DIED PEACEFULLY"

On the occasion of the death of Jessie Evans Smith there was a general feeling that the Prophet might not be able to live long without his beloved wife. In the weeks and months following her passing, President Smith seemed quite despondent and even expressed the thought that he ought not to go to Manchester later that month. President Lee and the family ultimately prevailed upon the Prophet to go to England. Meanwhile, the family decided that it would be well for the Prophet to be with one of his children, rather than to live alone in the apartment he had occupied with Aunt Jessie.

In his absence while traveling in England, President Smith's family, at the suggestion of President Lee, moved his clothing and a few of his other personal effects to the home of his daughter and son-in-law, Amelia Smith McConkie and Elder Bruce R. McConkie. There President Smith had a large bedroom and a private bath, which made it more convenient for the family to care for him. The Prophet's oldest son, Joseph Jr., told me that his father had taken the change in good stride and did not appear to be upset by it. To the contrary—he seemed pleased, and a little relieved. President Smith lived comfortably with the McConkies during the remaining months of his life.

On Sunday, July 2, 1972, President Joseph Fielding Smith died quietly at home. He was seated in the same chair in which his wife Jessie died a year before. He had attended sacrament meeting earlier in the day and was chatting with his daughter, Amelia. She stepped out of the room to get something, and upon her return found the Prophet slumped over in the chair.

PRESIDENT JOSEPH FIELDING SMITH

He died as he lived—peacefully and with no fanfare. He was nearly ninety-six years old.

Harold B. Lee

Eleventh President of The Church of Jesus Christ of Latter-day Saints

July 1972 – December 1973

HAROLD B. LEE CHRONOLOGY

March 28, 1899
Harold Bingham Lee is born in Clifton, Idaho, to Samuel Marion Lee, Jr., and Louisa Bingham.

1916
Harold B. Lee moves away from home to attend the Albion State Normal School, where he obtains a secondary teaching certificate.

1916
Harold B. Lee teaches grammar school in Weston, Idaho.

1917
Harold B. Lee is hired as the principal of a grammar school in Oxford, Idaho, at the age of eighteen. He continues in Oxford for three years.

September 1920
Harold B. Lee is called to serve in the Western States Mission.

December 1922
Harold B. Lee completes his mission and returns home.

December 22, 1922
Following his mission, Harold B. Lee speaks at the Ensign Stake conference with Church President Heber J. Grant in attendance.

November 14, 1923
Harold B. Lee is married to Fern Tanner in the Salt Lake Temple.

October 1928
Harold B. Lee is sustained, without prior notice, as a counselor in the Pioneer Stake presidency.

October 1930
Harold B. Lee is called and sustained as president of the Pioneer Stake. At age thirty-one, he is the youngest stake president in the Church at the time.

December 1, 1932
Harold B. Lee is sworn in as a Salt Lake City Commissioner.

1933
Harold B. Lee is reelected to a full term on the Salt Lake City Commission.

April 30, 1935
Harold B. Lee meets with Presidents Heber J. Grant and David O. McKay to brief them on the welfare initiatives he created in the Pioneer Stake.

June 1, 1935
Harold B. Lee presents a general plan to the First Presidency for implementing a Church-wide welfare model.

April 10, 1941
Harold B. Lee is sustained as a member of the Quorum of the Twelve Apostles.

1942
Elder Harold B. Lee accompanies President J. Reuben Clark to attend Church meetings in Arizona. While speaking in a stake conference in Safford, Arizona, President Clark tells the saints that it is likely that Elder Harold B. Lee will one day become the President of the Church.

1944
Elder Harold B. Lee and his wife and daughters spend five weeks traveling in Mexico.

1945
Elder Harold B. Lee gives several radio talks that are later compiled into a book titled, *Youth and the Church.*

1947
Elder Harold B. Lee accompanies Elder Charles A. Callis to create the first stake in the Southern States, in Jacksonville, Florida. He then presides at funeral services for Elder Callis, who dies the day following the stake creation..

1948
During a single week, Elder Harold B. Lee performs twenty-three temple marriages.

March 11, 1956
Elder Harold B. Lee has a special spiritual experience during the dedication of the Los Angeles Temple.

1958
Elder Harold B. Lee and his wife, Fern, tour the South Africa Mission, followed by a three-month tour of South America.

September 24, 1962
President Harold B. Lee's first wife, Fern Tanner Lee, passes away.

June 17, 1963
Elder Harold B. Lee is sealed to his second wife, Joan Jensen Lee, in the Salt Lake Temple.

January 18, 1970
President David O. McKay dies. Elder Harold B. Lee is called as first counselor to President McKay's successor, President Joseph Fielding Smith.

February 1970
President Harold B. Lee convenes a meeting in New York City focused on taking the initiative in media coverage regarding the Church. Included in the meeting are high leaders of the Church and LDS leaders in business and the professions.

August 1971
President Harold B. Lee joins President Joseph Fielding Smith and seven members of the Twelve in attending the first area general conference of the Church, held in Manchester, England.

July 2, 1972
President Joseph Fielding Smith passes away.

July 7, 1972
President Harold B. Lee is ordained and set apart as the eleventh President of the Church.

August 1972
President Harold B. Lee travels to Mexico to preside at the area conference in Mexico City.

September 1972
President Harold B. Lee and Elder Gordon B. Hinckley of the Twelve travel throughout Europe and the Middle East. President Lee's life is miraculously preserved in Jerusalem.

August 1973
President Harold B. Lee heads a delegation from Church headquarters to attend the area conference in Munich, Germany.

December 26, 1973
President Harold B. Lee dies suddenly during a routine medical checkup.

"THE HUMBLENESS OF HIS UPBRINGING"

Many of the great qualities President Harold B. Lee possessed in the years of his great service were acquired as a young farm boy. President Lee was born in the most humble of circumstances, and throughout his life he reflected the humbleness of his upbringing. He was born and raised in Clifton, Idaho, which is a very small farming community in the extreme northern end of the Cache Valley. His ancestors were largely Scottish and Irish, and his people were hardworking.

There was never much money in the Lee household, but he had a remarkable mother, Louisa Lee, who made sure that Harold was raised in a home of culture and refinement. Harold was taught to play the piano as a very young boy and played throughout his life. He also played the trombone, and—like one of his successors, President Howard W. Hunter—he played in a dance band as a young man. In later years, President Lee was often called upon to play the piano or organ in meetings of the First Presidency and the Quorum of the Twelve.

"HAROLD, STAY AWAY FROM THAT BUILDING"

Even as a little boy, President Lee developed a powerful spirituality. I heard him several times relate this story from his early childhood: When he was a very little boy living in Clifton, Idaho, he started to walk one day toward an old abandoned barn or outbuilding on his father's farm. He said that the building had not been used for many years and was in serious disrepair, with the roof beginning to cave in. As he walked toward the building, President Lee said that he heard an audible voice. The voice said: "Harold, stay away from that building!" He looked around, expecting to see his father or one of the neighboring farmers nearby, but found no one. He heeded that warning voice and stayed away from the building. He never knew what danger might have been lurking in the old building, but he learned at a very tender age to recognize and follow the voice of the Spirit.

In my view, this became the prime motivating force in his life—to hear and heed the voice of the Spirit.

"A Reputation as a Brilliant Young Man"

President Harold B. Lee acquired his early education in the grammar school in his tiny hometown of Clifton and then later at the Oneida Stake Academy in Preston, Idaho. In those days there was no government-sponsored education beyond the grammar school grades, and so the Church stepped in to create stake academies. The academies taught all the standard curriculum of a contemporary high school and prepared their students for college or for work in the trades. They also provided religious education.

President Lee was at the stake academy for four years, where he earned a reputation as a brilliant young man. He was a remarkable young man, by all accounts: a top scholar, a student body leader, an athlete, a debater, a writer for the school newspaper, and a musician. Even at that tender age he was what you may call a Renaissance man.

One of the long-lasting friendships President Lee formed at the stake academy in Preston was with future Church President Ezra Taft Benson, who was from another tiny Mormon farming town located not far from Clifton. President Benson was only a few months younger than President Lee, and they became close friends. I find it quite remarkable that two contemporary farm boys from tiny villages in the same remote valley would both live to serve for decades together in the Quorum of the Twelve and then both preside over the Church. It says something for the Cache Valley—and for the many, many other scattered Mormon communities from Canada to Mexico—that it would produce two boys who would grow into men of such stature.

At age seventeen President Lee was admitted to the Albion State School. Albion was two hundred miles from Cache Valley, and President Lee boarded with a Mormon family. It was essentially the first time in his life that he had associated with nonmembers of the Church.

After one semester in Albion, President Lee obtained a teaching certificate, qualifying him to teach grammar school. He soon was hired at age seventeen to teach in Weston, Idaho, a few miles from his hometown of Clifton. On weekends he rode home to Clifton on his horse, where he attended church with his family, and then each Monday morning rode the horse back to Weston.

The following year, President Lee was hired as the principal of a school in Oxford, another little Mormon farming town north of Clifton. He was only eighteen years old, and he had two other teachers working under him. Again, President Lee rode his horse home every weekend to stay with his family in Clifton, where he served as the elders' quorum president in the Clifton Ward.

"An Aura of Light"

Beginning in 1920, President Lee served a full-time mission in the Western States Mission. The mission headquarters were in Denver, where President Lee spent much of his mission serving as a conference president in the largest conference in the mission.

I heard the following story from several sources, and its accuracy was later confirmed to me by President Lee: One of the stalwart members of the Church in Denver, a Sister Harriet Jensen, had a remarkable spiritual experience during the time of President Lee's service there. She said that once during a meeting in Denver when young Elder Harold B. Lee spoke, she saw an aura of light surrounding the young missionary as he stood at the pulpit. After the meeting, this sister sought out President Lee and told him, with great emotion, "Someday you will be the President of the Church!"

"Elder Talmage kindly pulled him aside"

President Lee once shared with me this experience he had during his mission to Colorado, which provided crucial leadership lessons for the young man: During the time when President Lee served as the conference president, he once conducted a baptismal service. As President Lee stood at the pulpit, about to start the meeting, his mission president, John M. Knight, and a visiting Apostle, Elder James E. Talmage, walked unexpectedly into the chapel. The visiting leaders came forward and took seats on the stand. President Lee, who was still standing at the pulpit, was somewhat surprised and mildly flustered, and he immediately began the meeting without recognizing the visiting authorities or first conferring with them, as standard church protocol would dictate.

The meeting proceeded. Several new converts received the ordinance of baptism. As the baptisms were about to proceed, Elder Talmage, the visiting Apostle, suddenly stepped forward to the edge of the font and stood there, carefully watching what went on. Then, after the baptisms, when the confirmations began, Elder Talmage again stepped forward uninvited and said to Harold B. Lee, "Here, young man. I'll confirm this one." President Lee told me that in performing the confirmation, Elder Talmage deliberately reversed the customary order and first said, "Receive ye the Holy Ghost," and then afterward he confirmed the candidate a member of the Church.

After the meeting, Elder Talmage kindly took pulled President Lee aside, put his arm around his shoulder and told him that he had done a marvelous job conducting. Then, having built the young man up, he proceeded to instruct him in priesthood governance. He pointed out the young missionary's error in failing to recognize the presiding authority and checking with him before he proceeded. He also emphasized that there is no set wording to confirm someone a member of the Church.

President Lee told me that this kind but direct tutoring from one of the Apostles was one of the most important leadership lessons he ever learned.

"He Visited Fern Tanner and Joan Jensen"

During President Lee's mission, he met several people who would play important roles in his future life. One of these was Elder James E. Talmage, who carried to the leading councils a good report of the young missionary from Cache Valley. Another important person in his future life was his mission president, John M. Knight, who opened many doors for his young missionary as President Lee began his post-mission life. Other important connections were made with his fellow missionaries. Two others I might mention who played key future roles in President Lee's life were a full-time missionary, Sister Fern Tanner, who had served under his leadership in Denver, and Joan Jensen, a beautiful young woman who was the girlfriend of one of his missionary companions.

President Lee completed his mission at the end of 1922 and traveled first to Salt Lake City, where his mission president had arranged for the young returned missionary to speak in a stake conference in the Ensign Stake. Attending the conference was Church President Heber J. Grant and several other General Authorities. I'm sure that this was a heady and likely an intimidating experience for a farm boy from Idaho—to preach a sermon with the President of the Church seated behind him!

After the conference, President Lee had plans to travel home to Clifton to be reunited with his family for the first time in two years. Before leaving Salt Lake City, however, he visited Sister Tanner and Sister Jensen in their homes, as well as several former missionary companions.

I have always thought that it is an intriguing coincidence that these two young women, Sister Fern

Tanner and Sister Joan Jensen, were both destined to marry President Lee. Sister Fern Tanner, of course, became President Lee's wife less than a year after he was released from his mission. They carried on a long-distance courtship between Cache Valley and Salt Lake City. Joan Jensen, who was dating President Lee's former missionary companion, later broke up with the young man, and she remained single for many decades until she became the Prophet's second wife, after the death of Sister Fern Tanner Lee.

"His Most Distinguishing Characteristic"

I once heard President Lee say that he never had any specific plans in his life other than to follow the dictates of the Spirit wherever they might lead. That is the kind of life-philosophy that might have been followed by Nephi himself. Throughout his life, President Lee listened for the voice of the Spirit and then acted upon the promptings he received. He was a very spiritually sensitive man, perhaps more so than any other man I have ever known. Spirituality, in my mind, was his most distinguishing characteristic.

This habit of listening to the Spirit and then immediately acting was the pattern President Lee followed upon returning home from the Western States Mission. He was not ambitious in a worldly sense, but he was extraordinarily prayerful and diligent. Those early post-mission years were crucial for President Lee. Within only a decade following his mission he had become a well-known, substantial, trusted, and gifted man. But the stature he achieved in that first post-mission decade was not the result of a deliberate program of pursuing a specific set of worldly goals. Rather, President Lee simply followed the Spirit, and the result was that he had, as Shakespeare said, "greatness thrust upon him."

After his marriage to Fern Tanner, the young couple rented a tiny house in the Poplar Grove Ward of the Pioneer Stake, while President Lee taught at the Whittier Elementary School. A short time later, President Lee was sought out and hired as a manager of the Foundation Press. With increased prosperity, the Lees bought a home, also in the Pioneer Stake. President Lee fulfilled a string of significant church callings, including on the stake high council. Then in 1928, only six years after returning from his mission, President Lee was sustained as a counselor in the stake presidency. He was given no advance notice of his call before the stake conference meeting in which he was sustained. President Lee learned of his new calling along with the rest of the stake when the presiding authority read his name! He was only twenty-nine years old at the time. Two years later he was called as the president of the Pioneer Stake, and for some time he was the youngest stake president in the Church.

A short time after his call as stake president, his former mission president, John M. Knight, called President Lee with an interesting and intriguing question. Would President Lee consider an appointment to the Salt Lake City Commission to fill a vacancy caused by the death of another commissioner? President Knight at the time was filling another seat as a Commissioner. President Lee counseled with his wife and prayed about it. The Spirit dictated that he accept, and he did so. He was installed in office in 1935 and a few months later was reelected to a full term. He served in this role until 1935, when he went to work for the Church as the managing director of the Church's new Welfare Department.

His two roles as stake president in one of the largest stakes in the Church and as a city commissioner vaulted President Lee into the spotlight. Without ever setting about on a path to achieve public notoriety, the Spirit had led him into positions of high influence as a very young man.

"He Had a Very Vivid Dream"

President Lee shared with me a significant spiritual experience he had in connection with his call to serve as a stake president at age thirty-one: The Friday before the reorganization of the stake, he received a surprise telephone call asking him to go to the Church Administration building for an interview. President Lee said that he hurried over to 47 East South Temple and was invited into the office of President Rudger Clawson, the President of the Quorum of the Twelve. President Lee was surprised to find a second Apostle, Elder George Albert Smith, sitting in the room. Elder Smith was second in seniority in the Quorum behind President Clawson. Elder George Albert Smith, of course, was destined to become the next President of the Church in a very few years following the death of President Heber J. Grant.

In President Clawson's office, Harold B. Lee was quickly informed that he had been chosen by the First Presidency and the Quorum of the Twelve to be the new president of the Pioneer Stake. President Lee said that this call shocked him to the core, as he was only thirty-one years old at the time. He began to tell the Apostles that he would much prefer working as a counselor to one of the older, experienced brethren in the stake. President Lee told me that Elder George Albert Smith interrupted him and told him very directly that they hadn't invited him in to ask him what should be done, but rather to learn what the Lord wanted him to do. President Lee accepted the call and then asked the two Apostles if they had any suggestions about his counselors. President Lee was again surprised by the response. They told him that they had two specific brethren in mind, but that they weren't going to tell him who they were. They suggested that he pray about it. Elder George Albert Smith told him, "If you are led by the Spirit of the Lord, you will choose the two men whom we have in mind." He was instructed to present the names of his counselors the next morning.

President Lee told me that he was very shaken by this interview and with the prospect of assuming such a heavy priesthood responsibility. He pondered the question of his counselors throughout the rest of the day and evening. During the evening he tentatively chose two men to nominate as counselors. Before retiring to bed for the night he knelt down and prayed with great fervency, but still went to bed in a very agitated state of mind. He said that after falling into a fitful sleep, he had a very vivid dream. In his dream, he commenced his service as stake president with the two counselors he had tentatively chosen. It seemed he was trying to hold presidency and council meetings with them, but misunderstandings and disagreements arose and multiplied, and President Lee awoke from his dream realizing that his first choices were wrong. He lay awake in his bed pondering other alternatives, then fell back asleep. Again, he had a dream in which obstacles and bad feelings arose, and he again awoke. He said that this process went on several times throughout the night, and by morning he felt he was certain whom the Lord wanted to serve in the stake presidency.

Later that day, he met with President Rudger Clawson and Elder George Albert Smith and gave to them the names of two men. The two senior Apostles then told President Lee that these were the two counselors they had in mind all along.

"A MODEL TO HELP THE POOR"

President Harold B. Lee served as a stake president in the Pioneer Stake during the onset of the Great Depression. The Pioneer Stake included many of Salt Lake City's poorest neighborhoods, and the membership was hard hit economically. More than half of the membership of the stake was out of work and reliant upon outside help. Even as a young man, President Lee was a true visionary, and he envisioned a model to help the poor and unemployed in his stake. Rather than simply giving needy members a dole, President Lee taught that members should be expected to work or give service for food or other help they received from the Church. President Lee realized that the idle manpower among his priesthood brethren was a great reservoir upon which the stake could draw. The stake owned a farm, and President Lee put the brethren to work helping with the harvest in exchange for a share of the crops. All the surplus food not divided among the families of the farm workers was canned. The stake bought a warehouse where they made furniture, clothing, and bedding. This warehouse became known as the "storehouse." President Lee devised a system whereby his bishops could make "withdrawals" from the storehouse for their needy members. President Lee also put unemployed brethren to work building a stake gymnasium, which was used for athletic and cultural events. It became the center of Church life in the Pioneer Stake. These far-seeing efforts to lift the people economically received great attention in the Church and in the nation. And behind this great attention was the young visionary leader who had been the architect: Harold B. Lee.

"His Patriarch was living in poverty"

Elder Theodore M. Burton, a long-time General Authority who was raised in the Pioneer Stake during the time President Lee was the stake president, shared with me some of the human background of the creation of the Church welfare program. He told me that early in his service leading the stake, President Lee made the shocking discovery that his stake patriarch was living in abject poverty—without work, income, savings, or even food to put on his table. President Lee immediately gave the patriarch temporal assistance and then began to see to the needs of thousands of other stake members. From this humble beginning sprang the vast, worldwide Church welfare program.

"To Put the Quorums to Work"

On April 30, 1935, President Lee was invited to meet with the First Presidency to explain the welfare initiatives he had created in the Pioneer Stake. The result was that President Lee was asked by President Heber J. Grant to write a proposal whereby the model of welfare assistance he had built in the Pioneer Stake could be extended to the entire Church. He did so, and a year later, on April 15, 1936, the First Presidency called President Lee to head up a new Church Welfare Department. This was a full-time endeavor, and it necessitated his release as stake president and his resignation from the Salt Lake City Commission. From that date until his death, President Lee was engaged in full-time service for the Church.

President Lee shared with me a special spiritual experience he had after receiving the assignment from President Grant to draw up a general plan for the entire Church to implement the initiatives he had created in the Pioneer Stake. After meeting with the First Presidency and receiving his assignment on April 30, President Lee said that he drove up into City Creek Canyon, near downtown Salt Lake City, and walked into a secluded stand of trees, where he knelt down and sought for divine guidance. He said that a great peace came over him, together with this insight: there was no need to create any new organization to care for the poor and the needy, but only to put the priesthood quorums to work.

"A CLEAR IMPRESSION"

President Lee told me of a special experience he had in connection with his call to serve in the Quorum of the Twelve. A few days before he was sustained, he arose from his bed in the morning and received a clear impression that he would be called as a member of the Quorum of the Twelve. He said that the impression was definite and unmistakable. He pondered the impression throughout the day as he went about his work. That evening he received a message to go to the office of President Heber J. Grant, then the President of the Church, where he was called to the apostleship.

"THE DEAN OF THE YOUNGER MEN"

It is clear to me that President J. Reuben Clark exerted an unusually strong influence over President Harold B. Lee, as he did over many other General Authorities. In a sense, President Lee idolized President J. Reuben Clark, as did most of those who worked closely with him—there was a certain awe and almost a reverence toward President Clark. I saw this great respect for President Clark's memory mirrored in most of the leading Brethren of the Church.

When President Lee was called to the Twelve in 1941, he was a very young man in a Quorum filled with old soldiers, and President Clark took him under his wing, so to speak, to school him in his new and sacred calling. Soon after President Lee's call to the Twelve, several of the senior Brethren passed away, and then many other young men were called to the apostleship. These included Elders Spencer W. Kimball, Ezra Taft Benson, Mark E. Petersen, Matthew Cowley, Henry D. Moyle, Delbert L. Stapley, and Marion G. Romney. Because of the contrasting youth of these men, President J. Reuben Clark was fond of referring to them as "the younger men," and he called President Lee, "The dean of the younger men."

President Clark also began to call him "Kid." This was not a sign of disrespect toward the young Apostle. To the contrary, it was a sign of great affection for the aged Apostle to speak to his young Quorum member in this manner. He apparently did the same with most of the other younger Brethren. He did this only in private settings and in a loving manner. For example, President Lee told me that in the early years of the implementation of the Church welfare program, when there was much opposition by many

Church leaders, President Clark came to him and said, "Never mind, Kid. Just stay with it and some day they will all want to climb on the bandwagon."

"When You're Winning, Don't Gloat"

During the years President Lee served as a counselor to President Joseph Fielding Smith, he once told me this fascinating story involving President J. Reuben Clark: As previously mentioned, before his call as a General Authority, President Lee was employed by the Church as the director of the Church's newly implemented welfare program. At the time, President Lee was a very young man with a great deal of responsibility. He was also a Church employee, not an ecclesiastical leader, as were the General Authorities. Because President Lee had pioneered the principles of Church welfare in the stake over which he presided, he knew what he was doing, but he occasionally had differences of opinion with some of the long-time Church employees. On one occasion, President Lee told me, he had a difference of opinion about the welfare program with one of the General Authorities, a man of great Church experience who was much older than President Lee. President Lee respectfully deferred to this man, because he outranked him in authority, but President Lee still considered himself to be in the right. A short time later, President Lee was called to the Quorum of the Twelve, and suddenly he outranked this General Authority. One day, not long after his new call, President Lee was visiting with President Clark, and he made the comment, "Now that I am a member of the Twelve, perhaps this General Authority will pay some attention to me." President Lee said that President Clark was silent and considered this for a few moments, then told President Lee: "Let me give you some advice, Kid. When you're winning, don't gloat." In other words, even though he now outranked this General

Authority, he should show him the courtesy and kindness that this person had failed to show to President Lee.

"A Young Ballplayer with His Coach"

Like President J. Reuben Clark before him, President Lee exerted an unusually strong influence over those with whom he worked closely. There was a quality in his personality that seemed to impel others to want to please him. President Boyd K. Packer once told me that when he was around President Lee he always felt like a young ballplayer with his coach. President Lee was the best of mentors. He was inspiring, but tough. He knew from personal experience what he was talking about. Like young athletes around their coach, everyone wanted to please President Lee. To hear President Lee say, "Well done!" was among the highest of accolades.

"The most Christlike man"

I have already alluded to the special relationship that existed between President Lee and President J. Reuben Clark. President Clark was a great mentor for President Lee, especially in his early years of service in the Quorum of the Twelve. President Lee also spoke often of a second exemplar that affected his life greatly. This was Elder Nicholas G. Smith, who served as an Acting Patriarch to the Church from 1932 to 1934, and then as an Assistant to the Quorum of the Twelve from 1941 to 1945. President Harold B. Lee once told me that Nicholas G. Smith was the most Christlike man he had ever known. President Lee and Elder Smith occupied offices side by side in the Church Administration Building for many years. He told me that they agreed at the beginning that the door connecting the two offices would never be locked. This was emblematic of their relationship, as well. There was never any barrier between the two.

"A DESCRIPTION OF THE SAVIOR"

President Lee had a picture in his office of the Savior, which was given to him by Elder Samuel O. Bennion in 1945, shortly before Elder Bennion's death. President Lee first showed me this picture in 1970, when he asked me to visit with him in his office. Elder Bennion had served for many years as a member of the First Council of the Seventy. President Lee told me that this picture was the most accurate representation he had ever seen, based upon a description of the Savior given by Elder Orson F. Whitney, who saw the Savior in the Salt Lake Temple. President Lee told me that this was the picture that Orson F. Whitney had selected as best depicting the appearance and character of the Savior. President Lee said that based upon Elder Whitney's description and testimony and "other things," he knew that the representations we often see of the Savior are not accurate.

On a later occasion when I was in President Lee's office, after he became President of the Church, he referred again to this same picture of the Savior. He told me that it reflected a character of love, with firmness and strength—a leader capable of driving the moneychangers out of the temple, yet kind and loving enough to hold and bless a little child.

On still another occasion, President Lee told me this story: He said that early in his service as an Apostle, he was traveling with Elder Charles A. Callis of the Twelve. He said that Elder Callis began to tell President Lee of an occasion when the Savior had appeared to him, and they were interrupted, and he was never privileged to hear the account in its entirety, which was a great sadness to President Lee.

"Good job, boy!"

President Lee was called to the Twelve in April of 1941. In January of 1947, while he was still a very junior member of the Quorum of the Twelve, he had one of the most difficult yet spiritually significant experiences of his life to that point. He later shared this experience with me in some detail: President Lee was assigned to assist in the creation of a new stake in Jacksonville, Florida—the first stake of the Church in the Southern States—as the junior companion to one of the senior Apostles, Elder Charles A. Callis. Elder Callis had previously served as a mission president in the South, and was well known and much beloved of the people. When the conference was over, Elder Callis went to President Lee and said with a twinkle in his eye, "Harold, I surely want to thank you for your help, especially because you didn't cross me."

After the conference, Brother Callis insisted that President Lee drive down to Miami with the mission president, Heber Meeks. Brother Callis then said to President Lee grandly, "I want you to see my country as it really is." President Lee and the mission president set out in the car and had traveled some distance through central and southern Florida, when they were stopped by a highway patrolman. The officer informed them that the police had been searching for them all up and down the length of the highway and that there was a "death notice" waiting for their phone call in Jacksonville. They immediately called back to Jacksonville. It was regarding Brother Callis. He had died suddenly back in Jacksonville the day after the creation of the stake.

PRESIDENT HAROLD B. LEE

President Lee was directed by the First Presidency to hold the funeral there in Jacksonville, rather than transport Elder Callis's body back to Salt Lake City. Because of the long distance, none of the other General Authorities attended the funeral, and President Lee had to handle it alone. President Lee told me that this was one of the most difficult experiences he has ever had, particularly because of his closeness to Elder Callis.

The funeral services were held the following Thursday. At the funeral service, President Lee received a telegram from the First Presidency, which they asked be read to the congregation. President Lee said that as he read it, he was instantly filled with such an overwhelming emotion that he couldn't speak, and so he asked President Meeks, the mission president, to read it to the congregation for him. President Lee said that he had seldom felt so alone and oppressed.

Then President Lee told me that later during the service, he suddenly felt a great lifting of the clouds, as it were. A great calm, a great peace, descended upon him. He was flooded by a great feeling of peace and well-being. From that moment forward, he was greatly buoyed up and seemed unusually filled with the Spirit as he concluded the funeral service.

President Lee told me that following the funeral services, he went into a room in the Church house alone to collect his hat and coat. As he entered the room, he seemed to hear the audible voice of Charles A. Callis saying, "Good job, boy!"

When President Lee returned to Salt Lake City, he visited with President Stephen L. Richards, a counselor in the First Presidency. President Richards told President Lee that the Brethren had been thinking of him during the difficult experiences of the past week. Remembering how he had felt unusually buoyed up during Elder Callis's funeral service, President Lee asked President Richards if anything unusual had occurred during the Thursday council meeting of the First Presidency and the Twelve. "Why yes," President Richards said. "President McKay offered a special prayer for you and implored the Lord especially in your behalf. And we all felt a great peace." President Lee told me that as far as he can calculate it, he felt a calm descend upon him in Jacksonville at the precise moment the Prophet and Apostles were praying for him back in Salt Lake City.

President Lee told me that this was one of the most dramatic illustrations of the great power of prayer he had ever experienced.

"A GENERAL FEELING"

President Harold B. Lee was sustained as a member of the Quorum of the Twelve in April of 1941, when he had just turned forty-two years of age. At the time of his call, he was the youngest Apostle by many years and most of his brethren in the Quorum were senior to him by three, four, or five decades.

Because of President Lee's youth, there was a perception in the Church from the very moment of his call that he would serve as the President of the Church one day. This feeling was shared by the highest leadership of the Church. For example, about a year after his call to the Twelve, President Lee accompanied a member of the First Presidency, President J. Reuben Clark, to a stake conference in Safford, Arizona. This, incidentally, was the stake that future Apostle and future Church President Spencer W. Kimball presided over. While speaking in the general session of the stake conference, President Clark told the assembled saints that it was likely that Elder Harold B. Lee would one day become President of the Church.

I am certain that President Lee felt uncomfortable with these kinds of public expressions about his future. He was an innately humble man who did not go out of his way to seek the spotlight. At the same time, I am confident that President Lee himself had a sense of what was to come in his life.

"Possessed with an Evil Spirit"

The following significant story was told to me by my friend, Oscar W. McConkie, Jr., and later corroborated by President Harold B. Lee himself: In 1949 President Lee toured the California Mission with the mission president, Oscar W. McConkie, Sr. Member meetings were held throughout the mission, and President Lee traveled by car with the mission president. As the two of them were driving through Death Valley, the lowest point in North America at nearly 300 feet below sea level, President McConkie shared a vivid dream he had received in which Satan had appeared to him. After pondering this for some time in the car, President Lee offered a private interpretation of the dream. He then told President McConkie about an experience he had with a woman who was possessed with an evil spirit, who said to him, "You are the head of the Church!" In response to this, President McConkie told President Lee that perhaps the evil spirit in the woman had spoken not of the present, but of the future. The implication was that even the evil adversary knew what Harold B. Lee was destined to become during his lifetime.

"A FIRST-RATE INTELLECT"

My first acquaintance with President Harold B. Lee occurred in the late 1940's while I was studying at Stanford University in California. From the outset I was impressed with President Lee's mental powers. He had a first-rate intellect and a penetrating grasp, not only of scripture and doctrine, but also of history, literature, and current world events.

He also had a phenomenal memory. This was illustrated immediately after I began working as the secretary to the First Presidency in 1970. When President Lee first greeted me as I commenced my service, he extended his hand and said, "Brother Gibbons, we met first in Palo Alto, didn't we?" Though it had been nearly twenty-five years since I had first met him, he remembered me. I thought this remarkable, considering the many thousands and tens of thousands of saints President Lee had met during his thirty years of membership in the Quorum of the Twelve.

"HE BLESSED HER EVEN AS HANNAH OF OLD"

As I mentioned, I first met President Harold B. Lee in 1948. My wife, Helen, and I were living in Palo Alto, California, while I was attending law school at Stanford University. We belonged to a study group that included President Lee's daughter, Maurine, and her husband, Ernie Wilkins, who was also a Stanford student. Usually, when President Lee had a conference assignment in the Northern California area, Ernie and Maurine would arrange a meeting of the study group in their home, where we were privileged to receive counsel and instruction from President Lee, then an Apostle, in an intimate, relaxed setting.

At the time, Helen and I were childless, although we had been married for some time. In our patriarchal blessings, we had each been promised both sons and daughters, and so we were very anxious to have a family. But after five years of marriage, we had been unable to conceive.

In early 1950, during one of Elder Lee's visits to Palo Alto, Helen felt inspired to seek a blessing from him. In it, he blessed her that the vital functions of her body would be quickened by the Holy Spirit to begin the processes that would result in motherhood, and he specifically blessed her, "even as Hannah of old," and counseled her to covenant with the Lord in her secret prayers as Hannah had done. He also blessed her with peace of mind and faith, and that if there should be a space of time before she conceived, we should spend that time in service to the Church, in opening our hearts to other children, and proving ourselves worthy of parenthood. He also conferred a special blessing on the doctors who would serve her, that they would be especially inspired in exercising their medical skills in Helen's behalf.

We endeavored, as best we could, to comply with all the conditions Elder Lee had mentioned. We were active in our ward in Palo Alto, filling assignments in Relief Society and Sunday School. We did babysitting for our friends, took Helen's young brother into our home, and even applied to adopt a baby through the California placement service. As far as we can determine, Helen conceived about the time of our visit to the California state agency in San Francisco.

Everything went well with the pregnancy until about three weeks before the expected delivery, when Helen developed a severe pain in her side. The doctor thought her complaints were merely the reaction of a woman pregnant for the first time who did not realize what to expect in carrying a child. Nevertheless, after the complaints continued, he hospitalized Helen to conduct tests, which revealed nothing.

The evening before the baby's birth, the doctor visited Helen in the hospital again and, finding no clues to the root of her trouble, went home. He later told us that he became uneasy as he thought about Helen, and that he felt compelled to return to the hospital. When he arrived and examined her again, he discovered that the baby was in distress, which caused him to decide immediately on a Caesarean section. The doctor contacted me at home to obtain my consent. I barely had time to arrange for a neighbor, Mac Van Valkenburg, to accompany me to the hospital, where we administered to Helen.

After the doctor had taken the baby, he discovered the root of Helen's pain. Somehow, circulation had been cut off to one ovary, resulting in a strangulated ovary. By that time, the lack of circulation had caused the ovary and all the surrounding tissue to become gangrenous, requiring its removal. Had he induced labor as he had thought to do earlier in the evening, or had there been a delay of as much as a half hour in taking the baby, it is almost certain that Suzanne would have been born dead or with serious brain damage because of the lack of oxygen, and Helen would have lost her life.

After the delivery, a nurse told Helen that someone should go to church the next day, Sunday, and thank God that she and the baby were alive and well, which I did, as it was fast Sunday.

A few months after the birth, I wrote President Lee a letter, detailing the circumstances of Suzanne's miraculous birth and of the unusual way in which his blessing to Helen had been fulfilled.

Many years later, and shortly after I began my service to the First Presidency, President Lee came to my office one morning. He said that he had been looking through his "miracle file" and found the letter I had written to him almost twenty years before, telling about Helen's blessing and Suzanne's birth. He asked about Suzanne then, as he often did thereafter; and when she was sealed to Timothy A. Burton in February of 1972 in the Salt Lake Temple, President Lee graciously performed the sealing.

The day before President Lee's death, he called me at home to wish me and my family a Merry Christmas. Almost the last words I ever heard him speak in mortality were to ask, "How is our miracle girl?"

I understand that experiences of this kind were repeated time and again during President Lee's ministry. He was and is a true prophet of God, richly endowed with spiritual perceptions and sensitivities possessed by few of God's servants.

"This Young Man Could Fill Any Position"

Like a coach who works to develop his best players, President Harold B. Lee was constantly aware of the need to train up future leaders of the Church. He would often inquire about the progress of promising young Church leaders in Europe, the Pacific, or Latin America. Perhaps because he had been tapped for high Church leadership at such a young age, he seemed to show a special interest in young leaders who were thrust into significant Church callings at a young age, and he went out of his way to teach them and to help them.

One day a young stake president came in to visit with President Lee when he served as President of the Church. The young man's name was David Stanley, and he was probably the youngest stake president in the Church at the time. He was in his early thirties and presided over the Pioneer Stake, the same stake President Lee had presided over when he was a young man. President Stanley told the Prophet that his stake was suffering greatly because of the loss of the old neighborhoods to industrial development and the new freeway system. The new freeway had bisected his stake, isolating several old neighborhoods. He told President Lee that he was trying to help attract stable families to come live in the Pioneer Stake and wanted the Church to consider buying some abandoned schools, to subdivide them and sell the lots as residential home sites. This would help provide an atmosphere attractive to families, the young stake president said. President Lee listened to this young man with great respect and then granted his request. After President Stanley left the room, President Lee made the comment to those in the room that,

"This young man could fill any position in the Church. We should watch him carefully." President Lee also approved the plan the young stake president had put forth.

About twenty years later this same young man, F. David Stanley, was called as a member of the Seventy.

"With a View to What the Man May Become"

President Lee was a visionary, not only in terms of Church organization, but also with regard to the men and women who he served. I was present over a period of many months as President Lee discussed the calling of a new president of Brigham Young University in 1971. After the resignation of long-time president Ernest Wilkinson, a comprehensive search was undertaken to find a qualified replacement. There were many men of great capacity, experience, and stature who were carefully considered as possible candidates, and a large number of well-qualified educators and administrators were interviewed by the Prophet and others.

Among the names to surface in this long process was twenty-nine-year-old Dallin H. Oaks, who was then a law professor at the University of Chicago Law School. To the surprise of many, this unknown young man was chosen to be interviewed along with a slate of prominent candidates.

I was present when Brother Oaks came in to be interviewed. Following the meeting, after Brother Oaks had left the room, President Lee turned to those present and made this significant, and what I believe to be a prophetic, statement. He commented that resumes and curricula vitae of most of the other candidates greatly excelled that of Brother Oaks, but that "the decision of who to select should not be based upon considerations of what the man now is, but with a view to what the man *may become.*"

Brother Oaks, of course, was selected to lead Brigham Young University, where he served with extraordinary distinction, and he was later called at a relatively young age to the Quorum of the Twelve Apostles.

"The Most Important Moment of His Life"

There was a great feeling of love and unity manifested by President Harold B. Lee and the other leading Brethren of the Church on the occasion of his ordination as the eleventh President of the Church on July 7, 1972. I heard several of the Brethren mention on that day the feeling they had that President Lee had been prepared from the foundations of the world for the position of President of the Church.

President Lee was deeply moved after his ordination and showed great emotion, but immediately got hold of himself. He said it was no time for tears. He said that at the most important moment of his life he had no preachment. On several occasions after his ordination, he spoke of a special moment of spiritual enlightenment when it was revealed to him that the entire Church was like a great family, and that each member of this family must be honored and nurtured and loved as family members.

From the moment of his ordination, President Lee spoke like a Prophet. The mantle had truly fallen upon him. He reminded me of President Brigham Young or of one of the Old Testament prophets. He was indeed a Prophet of the living God. He was a man of great capacity. He was a man of deep spiritual insight. I loved him and still love him and am forever grateful to have been blessed to be brought into close contact with him.

"A MASTER AT PRIESTHOOD LEADERSHIP AND DELEGATION"

President Thomas S. Monson once told me that in his opinion, Harold B. Lee was "the greatest delegator in the Church." He was not alone in this opinion. President Lee was a master at priesthood leadership and delegation. He seldom, if ever, did anything himself that he could get someone else to do. He did this not out of a sense of laziness, but with the knowledge that delegation is how future leaders are trained. This also freed him up to focus upon the duties that only he could perform.

President Lee was very fond of telling this story, which illustrates the principle of delegation: He once visited a special multi-stake conference with one of the senior Apostles. The first meeting of the conference was a leadership meeting for the stake presidencies and bishoprics of the stakes involved. To the great surprise of President Lee and the other Apostle, one of the stake presidents was not in attendance. The two counselors in the stake presidency were there, but not the president. After the meeting, President Lee and the other senior Apostle decided to go to the stake president's home to inquire why he had not attended. They knocked on the man's front door. His wife answered. The Apostles introduced themselves and asked if her husband were home. She replied that he was not, that he had gone to the stake center to help set up chairs for the general meeting. As they left the home, the senior Apostle turned to President Lee and said, "Well, if we have a stake president who insists on doing the work of a deacon, perhaps we should release him and call someone who will fill the role of a stake president."

President Lee never stepped out of his sacred leadership role. I saw him at close hand in two capacities—as a counselor to President Joseph Fielding Smith, and then as President of the Church in his own right. In both capacities he led out with great confidence and firmness, but also with great love. No one ever wondered who was in charge with President Lee at the helm. He was constantly building those around him by giving broad delegations of authority, coupled with a system of making a record of those delegations for follow-through purposes. When President Lee delegated something, you were always anxious to report to him.

I have mentioned that President Packer once told me that he always felt like a player around his coach when he was in President Lee's presence. I felt the same way, and I know that many others did likewise. There was something about President Lee's leadership style and personality—some special intangible quality or special essence—which made you know that you were in the presence of a master spirit, one of God's elect leaders.

"HIS DAUGHTER APPEARED"

Both during the time he served in the Quorum of the Twelve and later as he served in the First Presidency, President Lee was often called upon to perform marriages for young couples in the Salt Lake Temple. One of these couples was our oldest daughter, Suzanne, and her husband, Timothy Burton, who were sealed by President Lee in 1971. During a single week it was not unusual for him to perform ten or twenty marriages. Most of these marriages were performed in the large sealing rooms on the fourth floor of the temple, but he often liked to use a small sealing room located on the east side of the Salt Lake Temple so that he could walk to the temple from his office in the Church Administration Building. He had a key to one of the huge east doors to the temple so that he could slip in and out quickly.

There were many special spiritual experiences that took place during sealing ceremonies performed by the Prophet. Brother Derek Metcalf, who for many years was engaged in temple work for the Church, one day told me that he was on the fourth floor of the temple sorting through some documents when President Lee walked by and stopped to visit with him. President Lee told Derek that he had just performed the sealing for one of his grandsons, who was the son of his deceased daughter, Maurine Wilkins. President Lee, with some emotion, told Derek that during the ceremony his daughter appeared in the sealing room and stood off to the side observing the sealing of her son to his new bride.

"Serve His people"

President Harold B. Lee had a special feeling for the temple. In 1956 he was assigned by the First Presidency to oversee many of the details related to the final construction and then the dedication of the Los Angeles Temple, the largest temple in the Church after the great Salt Lake Temple. One night just prior to the dedication services, President Lee apparently had a powerful spiritual experience, which impacted his future life greatly. On at least three occasions I heard President Lee speak about this special spiritual experience.

The first occasion was in 1970, when I had a long private conversation with President Lee in his office. His office was on the first floor of the Church Administration Building. It was a place of order and peace, with many books on the shelves and pictures and memorabilia hanging on the walls. Prominent among the pictures in his office was a very striking painting of the Savior. As I have mentioned, this picture was given to President Lee by Elder Samuel O. Bennion, a former member of the First Council of the Seventy, shortly before Elder Bennion's death. We sat and talked for an hour or more about a variety of gospel and Church-related subjects. It was one of the most inspiring hours of my life. The conversation turned to personal spiritual experiences. President Lee was very sensitive spiritually, more so than any other man I have known. He was a man who had spiritual experiences and who acted upon them, and through him the Lord manifested His great power.

During this long conversation in his office, President Lee told me that while attending the dedication of the Los

Angeles Temple, he had a vivid, moving dream in the nighttime. In his dream he saw President McKay, who stood at a pulpit in a great meeting, and the aged Prophet, with great emphasis and emotion, said to the congregation, "You do not and you cannot love the Lord unless you serve his people and the Church with full purpose of heart!" At the same time in President Lee's dream, there was a great outpouring of the Spirit in the congregation where the Prophet was preaching. President Lee told me that he saw men and women arise in the vast congregation and speak in tongues. He then told me that he saw other things in his dream which he could not relate to me, but he did tell me that because of the things which he saw, he could attest to the close resemblance between the picture of the Savior he had hanging on the wall of his office and the actual appearance of the Savior.

President Lee then told me that a day or two following this powerful dream, during the actual dedication of the Los Angeles Temple, President McKay was the final speaker at the dedicatory services. He told me that the Prophet's appearance and the words of his sermon were so similar to his dream that he was almost overcome with emotion.

I heard him speak about this special dream on two other occasions. First, he mentioned it a few months after our long conversation while speaking to a small group of brethren and sisters, including Sister Gibbons and me. And finally, he alluded to this dream in his concluding address at the end of the April 1973 general conference, when he bore a very moving testimony. As he had before, he retold the vivid dream he had in Los Angeles. I have never before seen the President as touched emotionally as he was after he finished this talk. He sat with his head leaned back against his chair all during the closing prayer with his glasses off and with tears streaming down his face. It was a rare spiritual experience.

"A FREE INTERCHANGE OF IDEAS"

President Harold B. Lee was, in my opinion, an organizational genius of the first magnitude. He was also a gifted leader of men and women and had the ability to bring out the best in everyone around him. From the very first day of my acquaintance with him, I watched him lift those around him to the highest level of creativity and accomplishment. There was always a free interchange of ideas and concepts in his conversation. He would often devote time discussing principles, organization, policies, and personalities with me and with many others. He often shared special spiritual insights and ideas with those around him.

He would also often ask people to prepare memoranda on a variety of subjects we had discussed. He once asked me to write down my recommendations for improving the organization of the missionary work in the Church. I agreed, and President Lee gave me copies of similar written proposals, which he had received from several others, including President Gordon B. Hinckley. This was one of his favorite leadership tools—to foster the freest kind of interchange of ideas and to glean the benefit of the thinking of many people before reaching a final decision dictated by the Spirit.

"Where would the Savior appear?"

President Harold B. Lee took a great interest in the preparation and spiritual training of newly called missionaries. In those days missionaries did not go directly to a Missionary Training Center, but instead would report to what was called the "Mission Home" in Salt Lake City. There, for two weeks or so, they received training from the missionary department staff and the General Authorities of the Church before going on to their fields of labor or to study their mission languages.

President Lee for many years spoke to each group of departing missionaries in the great fifth floor assembly room of the Salt Lake Temple, with its richly carved pulpits facing both east and west. This special meeting occurred after the missionaries had participated in an endowment ceremony in the ordinance rooms below. Following his instruction, President Lee always asked the missionaries if they had any questions, which they invariably did. He would then carefully answer each question, and he was unusually free in his answers, given the sacred setting. This was a powerful experience for all who participated, and one that I was privileged to witness on several occasions with President Lee. The missionaries all came dressed in white, with their minds focused upon spiritual things, and to then cap off this experience with personal instruction from President Lee, one of the Lord's Apostles, was truly life-changing for the young men and women.

On one occasion President Lee was addressing a large group of missionaries, as usual, when a missionary asked him this question: "Where would the Savior appear if He were to come to this temple?" President Lee considered this question, and then said that since it was the Lord's house, he might appear in any of the rooms of the temple, or even in its hallways. He then said that since the Lord had such a particular interest in missionary work, He most likely would come to the room in which they were then seated because it was used so often for missionary gatherings. At that moment, there was a great emotional outpouring in the room, with many of the young missionaries being moved to tears. President Lee was also moved to tears standing at the pulpit in the assembly room. Finally, without saying a word, he took his seat, where he remained for several minutes. Meanwhile, all was silent in the room, with the young missionaries basking in the spiritual outpouring they were then feeling. Finally, President Lee stood back up and returned to the pulpit. He told the young missionaries that he felt the occasion was too sacred to continue the meeting, but that he wanted them to know that the Savior had been with them that day.

"A Very Gentle and Thoughtful Letter"

One of President Lee's great gifts was the ability to "compose" difficulties. President Gordon B. Hinckley often spoke of learning this principle from President Lee. In the heat of the battle it is best to strive to "compose" disputes rather than to fight them on the field of battle. So, for example, when the Church's attorneys might recommend legal action to assert this or that claim, President Lee's first response was to ask whether it might be best to find a way to "compose" the situation.

This attribute of President Lee met a stern test one day when he received a very brusque and abrasive letter from a woman who deplored the fact that there were not more intellectuals in the local and general leadership of the Church. In his typical way, President Lee wrote the woman a very gentle and thoughtful letter.

A few days later, he received a second letter from this woman. Her tone was very repentant and respectful. She wrote that a few days after mailing her first letter she had fallen and broken her leg. In this she saw divine retribution for what she called her "irascible and intemperate letter" to the Prophet.

"A Song about President Lee"

President Howard W. Hunter told me this amusing story not long after President Lee's ordination. It was reported to President Hunter that a young child came home from Primary and with great excitement told his mother that the children had been singing a song about President Lee at the beginning of each Primary opening exercises. When the mother asked the child what the song was, the child began singing, "Reverent-Lee, Quiet-Lee."

President Hunter shared this story with President Lee, who was delighted by it.

"Preach Optimism, Not Pessimism"

President Harold B. Lee was a man of great optimism. I was once with him in a meeting where several local and general Church leaders were giving presentations. One of the men present began to express his deep pessimism and gloom about the economic future of the United States. President Lee stood up at the conclusion of this brother's presentation and spoke to all present. He did not refer to this brother by name or directly speak about the economic future of the United States, but he remonstrated quite clearly with the tone of the brother's speech. He said that the leaders of the Church have the capacity through their ministry to strongly influence the spirit and tone of our people and of our nation. He then said that Church leaders should preach optimism, not pessimism. He said that those in positions of influence in the Church must look for the strengths and not the weaknesses of the United States and to speak with one voice in building up our nation.

"Spirits from Beyond the Veil"

We have had few teachers in the Church who were as powerful as Harold B. Lee. I have never heard his equal in the pulpit, before or since. In his preaching, he often brought entire congregations to tears, so powerful was the Spirit that his words invoked. On one occasion when speaking to a group of stake presidencies and bishoprics, his talk seemed more in the nature of a prayer to the Lord than a sermon. He invoked the blessing of the Lord upon those in attendance and prayed that the Holy Ghost would bear witness to them during the meeting. He testified of the presence of the spirits from beyond the veil, and implored God, if it were in His wisdom, that they would manifest themselves to the brethren assembled in the room. After this meeting, President Lee confided that the Lord had taken complete control of him during his remarks in a manner that he had never before experienced, and so he could not claim any credit for anything that he said.

"They understood"

In a private conversation in President Lee's home, he shared with my wife, Helen, and me this significant story: He told us of touring the mission and branches of the Church in South America while serving in the Quorum of the Twelve. He had been speaking to a large congregation through an interpreter when he began to notice that many of the saints were nodding assent to what he said before the interpreter finished. During the meeting, a great outpouring of the Spirit occurred, and many, including the interpreter, were overcome with emotion. After the meeting, several of the saints came to him to say that they understood even before the interpreter spoke.

"Experiences too sacred to discuss"

One of my duties as the secretary to the First Presidency was to be the clerk of the General Conferences of the Church. In this capacity, I was privy to all of the preparations that went on behind the scenes, and I sat at a special clerk's desk during each conference session. I can verify that President Harold B. Lee delivered most of his General Conference addresses extemporaneously or only with very simple notes.

This was doubly true with his sermons outside of General Conference. To my knowledge he never wrote out a verbatim sermon, either for General Conference or otherwise. It was contrary to his nature. He was much more effective and uplifting when he spoke extemporaneously. Restricting him to a written talk would have been like caging an eagle. When he could range freely in his thoughts during the sermon, he evoked great spiritual power.

Many of his sermons occupied an hour or more. I recall particularly one sermon he delivered to a large group of Church leaders, which lasted an hour and a half. And yet those that heard him were so doctrinally fed and so spiritually uplifted that it seemed like the briefest of sermons. He concluded this sermon, as with many others, with a very powerful testimony to the effect that he knew with all of his soul that the Church was of divine origin. He testified that he knew this based upon the operation of the Holy Ghost and "experiences too sacred to discuss."

"HE TWICE FELT HANDS UPON HIS HEAD"

In the last years of his life, President Lee appeared outwardly healthy, but privately was struggling with some serious health issues. Not long before he died, President Lee shared with me this special experience: Some time previously, as he traveled to Salt Lake City from the East Coast, he twice felt hands placed upon his head. Each time he turned and saw no one behind him. However, he felt a powerful manifestation of the Spirit each time and knew that some instrumentality from the unseen world was giving him a blessing to preserve his life. Shortly after he returned home, he was hospitalized. His physician told him that he had a very grave internal ailment. His condition was so serious, the doctor said, that had it erupted in flight, he would almost surely have died.

"He didn't look once at the colors"

President Lee's wife, Fern Tanner Lee, died in 1962. The Lees had been married for thirty-nine years. Her passing marked perhaps the greatest trial of President Lee's life.

President Boyd K. Packer told me this touching story from this period in the Prophet's life. When Sister Lee passed away, President Lee could hardly be reconciled. He told the Brethren that he wouldn't attend meetings, and he seemed to have lost all desire to do his work. President Packer told me that President Lee had no hobby to break the tension of his everyday work. He was assigned to go on a mission tour in Europe, which revived him temporarily, but he soon slipped back into a darkness. Then he traveled to a conference on the East Coast. President Packer said that Bill and Ally Marriott took President Lee for a drive to see the beautiful autumn colors in New England. When they returned Ally told Bill, "We might as well not have gone. He didn't look once at the colors."

"I KNOW WHO YOUR HUSBAND WILL BE"

President Lee married his second wife, Joan Jensen Lee, in 1963, more than a year after the death of his first wife, Fern Tanner Lee. As previously mentioned, President Lee had first met Joan Jensen after his mission to Colorado, as Joan was dating one of his former missionary companions at the time. President Lee went on to court and marry Fern Tanner, while Joan Jensen ultimately broke things off with his missionary companion and remained single down through the years.

Sister Joan Lee was a gracious and thoughtful lady, who brightened the life of President Lee following the death of his first wife and through his last years. She was also a woman of great achievement in her own right.

One of the sweetest experiences of my life and the life of my wife, Helen, occurred in the fall of 1970, when we had a long intimate visit with President and Sister Lee in their home in Federal Heights. On a Sunday evening, Sister Joan Lee spoke at a special fireside in the Bonneville Stake, where Helen and I lived with our family. After the fireside, Helen and I drove Sister Lee home. When we arrived, President Lee came out and invited us inside for a visit. We spent a very memorable hour with them.

As we visited, President Lee turned to his wife and said, "Joan, why don't you tell them about our marriage." Sister Lee then related this inspirational story:

Sister Joan Jensen Lee had remained single until she was sixty-five years old. She was a woman of great ability and great faith and knew that married or single the Lord had a great purpose for her. Many years before, she had received a blessing from President Edward J. Wood in

Canada who promised her that she would attain a position in the Church that was far beyond her capacity to imagine. She told us that shortly before her aged mother died, she told her not to be concerned about the future, but to stay close to the Lord and trust in him and that she would receive every blessing pronounced upon her head. So Sister Joan Jensen lived a life filled with faith that the Lord would lead her down the correct path.

Then, when she turned sixty-four years old, about the time Fern Tanner Lee died, Joan Jensen's life changed dramatically. She became engaged to marry a man. One day, not long after her engagement, she went to the home of one of her dearest friends to tell her the big news.

"Guess what?" She began to tell her friend, "I'm getting married."

Her friend interrupted to say, "And I know who your husband will be!"

Joan asked, "Who?"

The friend answered, "Harold B. Lee!"

Sister Joan Jensen was incredulous at this suggestion. However, a short time later, she did in fact break off her engagement with her fiancé for unrelated reasons.

Then one day, some time after she had broken off with this other man, she walked into her home one day to hear the phone ringing. She told us that she knew within herself that it was Brother Lee calling.

She picked up the phone. "Hello?" she said.

"Hello," she heard. "This is Harold Lee calling."

Elder Lee had called to invite her to take a drive to Provo with him. She accepted.

On the day of the drive, Elder Lee pulled up in her driveway and came to the door. They walked back to the car. He held the door open for her. They drove off, and within only a few blocks he proposed!

After Sister Lee told us this story of their engagement, President Lee told us that they had never before told anyone the inspirational circumstances surrounding their marriage.

For Helen and me visiting with President and Sister Lee in their home was without a doubt one of the mountaintop experiences of our lives!

"The Man We Can Least Afford to Lose"

When he was called to the First Presidency in 1970, President Lee was the picture of good health. He had just turned seventy-one years old, and in a Church renown for its octogenarian and nonagenarian leadership, he was still a very young man indeed. He entered into his leadership in the First Presidency with an unprecedented vigor and energy. But there were ominous signs of the hidden health problems that would end his life less than four years later.

The first signs of trouble appeared in late 1972, only a few months after his ordination as the eleventh President of the Church. He suffered a severe bronchial infection, which continued into early 1973. In retrospect, this infection seems very ominous in light of the Prophet's sudden death for bronchial-related symptoms in December of 1973. In late 1972, he developed a very deep-seated cough, which sounded as if he had pneumonia.

By February of 1973, President Lee's cough was still with him, although he had not missed any work. One morning the President invited me to join his counselor, President Marion G. Romney, and Elder Marvin J. Ashton of the Twelve in giving him a special blessing of healing. Elder Ashton anointed the Prophet and the three of us placed our hands on his head as President Romney sealed the anointing. Afterward President Lee said that he did not know of three men on whose faith he would rather rely at that moment in his life. President N. Eldon Tanner, his first counselor, was out of the city at the time. It was a great honor to place my hands on the Prophet's head and to mingle my faith and fervent, silent prayers for his well-being.

President Lee's illness clung to him throughout February and March. In late March he was admitted to the LDS Hospital for some special tests, where he remained for nearly a week. I remember vividly, on the day of President Lee's release from the hospital, I saw President Boyd K. Packer on the steps of the Administration Building, who inquired about the Prophet's condition. President Packer echoed the general feeling of everyone when he said, "We must pray to God for his recovery. President Lee is the man the Church can least afford to lose!"

After his release from the hospital in early spring of 1973, President Lee began to take special treatment at his home, once in the morning and once at night, to try to clear out his lungs. These continued throughout the spring of 1973.

"The two Prophets stood upon Mars Hill"

In September of 1972, two months after becoming President of the Church, President Lee made an extended trip to Europe in the company of President Gordon B. Hinckley, then a member of the Quorum of the Twelve, and their wives, Joan Jensen Lee and Marjorie Pay Hinckley. Their itinerary took them to London, where they were honored at two dinners hosted by Lord Thompson of Fleet—one with the Bulgarian Ambassador, where the Prophet held private discussions about the possibility of preaching the gospel in Bulgaria, and a second dinner with English religious leaders. The wealthy and influential Lord Thompson, who for many years was one of the great friends of the Church in England, also introduced President Lee to influential people from Israel. From England they traveled to Italy, where President Lee spoke to about 250 recent converts to the Church. The Lees and the Hinckleys then traveled to Greece, where diplomatic attempts were made to obtain special "house of worship status" for the Church, allowing us to finally open Greece for the preaching of the Gospel. From Greece they flew to Israel, where steps were taken to improve the Church's relationships with government officials. Finally, they flew to Bern, Switzerland, where President Lee installed a new temple presidency.

When President Lee returned to Salt Lake City, he shared with me this inspirational story. While in Athens, President Lee and President Hinckley walked together early one morning up Mars Hill with their scriptures. The two Prophets stood upon Mars Hill, amid the ancient ruins, as the sun was rising over the Acropolis and the Parthenon.

President Lee then opened his scriptures and read aloud from Acts, Chapter 17:

> Now while Paul waited at Athens, his spirit was stirred in him. . . .
>
> Then Paul stood in the midst of Mars' hill, and said, Ye men of Athens, I perceive that in all things ye are too superstitious.
>
> For as I passed by, and beheld your devotions, I found an altar with this inscription, TO THE UNKNOWN GOD. Whom therefore ye ignorantly worship, him declare I unto you. (Acts 17:16, 22, 23)

"We Have Come to the Land of Miracles"

President Lee's long trip with President Gordon B. Hinckley through Europe and the Middle East took place in September of 1972. This was only two months after the Prophet's ordination as the eleventh President of the Church. This trip was important for the Church in many ways. It greatly strengthened our relationships with friends of the Church in Europe, and it opened the door for the ultimate preaching of the gospel or establishment of the Church in Greece, parts of Eastern Europe, and in Israel. My sense is that it was also very personally significant for both President Lee and President Hinckley.

In about 1982 I had a lengthy conversation with President Hinckley, in which he shared with me these additional insights about this most significant trip.

It was obvious to me from the time I began serving the First Presidency that a strong bond existed between President Lee and President Hinckley. From comments both men made to me, I understand that this bond extended back to the days when they were both staff employees of the Church. Before their calls as General Authorities, President Lee was employed as the Managing Director of the Welfare Department and President Hinckley as the executive secretary of the Radio and Publicity Committee. There are other connections between the two Prophets. It was President Lee who called President Hinckley as a stake president. President Lee later told President Hinckley that when he set him apart, he "saw what was ahead" for him.

Shortly after President Lee was sustained as the President of the Church in July 1972, he went to President Hinckley and asked him to be his traveling companion on a long trip together with their wives, which would take them to Europe and the Holy Land. President Hinckley told me that this was one of the great privileges of his life, to accompany the Prophet in this manner.

President Hinckley said that during the beginning stage of the journey, as the Lees and the Hinckleys visited England, Italy, and Greece, President Lee seemed in perfect health. Then, in Jerusalem, President Lee began having respiratory problems and took ill with heavy congestion in his lungs. The Hinckleys occupied a room adjacent to the Lees in their hotel in Jerusalem. One night there was a knock on President Hinckley's door. It was Sister Joan Lee, the Prophet's wife. Concerned about her husband, Sister Joan Lee asked President Hinckley to come and administer to the Prophet. President Lee in turn invited President Ted Cannon (who was then serving as the mission president in Switzerland with jurisdiction over Jerusalem and who was traveling with them) to come and assist in giving President Lee a priesthood blessing. Brother Cannon anointed the Prophet, and President Hinckley sealed the anointing, giving him a blessing of health.

Later that night, President Hinckley said he heard loud coughing from President Lee's adjoining room, which continued for some time and then stopped. The next morning at breakfast when the Cannons were present, President Lee said nothing about his health. But the following day, after the Cannons had departed, President Lee said privately to President Hinckley at breakfast, "I guess we have had to come to the land of miracles to see miracles in our own lives." He then explained that some time after receiving the priesthood administration from President Hinckley and Brother Cannon, he had taken a severe spell so serious that he felt he was going to die.

Finally, he said, he coughed up a large clot of blood and that the coughing then stopped.

"THE ENTIRE CHURCH WAS A SINGLE FAMILY"

It was a moving experience to observe President Harold B. Lee firsthand in the weeks and months following his ordination as President of the Church in 1972. He had always been a man of great spirituality, but that quality was magnified by the heavy burden that had been laid upon his shoulders. He was transformed in other ways. He now seemed to have taken upon himself a powerful quality of love, kindness, and empathy toward those around him. During his entire presidency he conducted himself as a loving father in the midst of a great family.

I attribute these changes to the special spiritual experience already mentioned, which the Prophet alluded to several times in my presence in 1972. He spoke of this special experience as "a revelation." On the day he was ordained, I heard him say that it had come to him "as a revelation" that the entire church was a single family, and that each member of that family should be loved and nurtured and honored as a family member, each in his or her own place.

"HE SAW THREE MEN SITTING AT A TABLE"

President Harold B. Lee, like all of the Presidents who went before him or succeeded him, was sought out by a multitude of people. There was a constant stream of visitors who came to see the Prophet at 47 East South Temple. Among the most memorable was a delegation of Native Americans from the Arapahoe and Cheyenne tribes. They came in the early days of President Lee's administration. There were many members of this delegation, none of whom were members of the Church. They were all received by the Prophet and his counselors and most of the members of the Twelve in the large council room, with President Lee and his counselors sitting at the head of the table. President Lee explained to these visitors that the Church was directed by a First Presidency of three men and a Quorum of Twelve Apostles, and that when a President of the Church passed away, as had President Joseph Fielding Smith, a new Prophet was chosen, ordained, and sustained from among the living Apostles.

Pleasantries were exchanged, and it appeared the meeting was over. Then one of the men spoke up and asked the Prophet if he could share a personal experience. President Lee told him he would be delighted to listen. The man then told President Lee that several months previously he had a vivid dream in which he saw three men sitting at the head of a table. One of the men, seated in the middle, was very aged. He also saw twelve other men seated at an adjacent table, with six on each side. In his dream, he then saw the most elderly of the three men rise to his feet, and give his place to one of the younger men seated by his side. This man then said that he now knew the interpretation of his dream—that it represented the change in the Mormon First Presidency, which had just been explained to him.

President Lee seemed deeply moved by this experience, and even more so when we learned that this Native American man had been taught the gospel and was baptized in the Salt Lake Tabernacle font a short time later.

"LET EVERY MAN LEARN AND ACT"

President Harold B. Lee was a builder of men and women. His style of leadership was unusually free and inspiring. His philosophy was to inspire them to the highest level of their capacity, and then get out of their way and let them serve with all their might. He often quoted the scripture in the Doctrine and Covenants 107:99, "Wherefore, now let every man learn his duty, and to act in the office in which he is appointed, in all diligence." He then would add this insight—that it is of utmost important that we "let" every man learn and act. We are too inclined as leaders, he said, to attempt to dictate every action of our people. What the Lord wants, he testified, is for us to "let" or permit every man to learn and then perform his duty. Leaders, he said, must act as coaches and not as players in the game of service.

"AN UNSEEN PRESENCE IN THE CIRCLE"

While serving as a counselor in the First Presidency, President Lee shared with me this special spiritual experience, which had occurred years earlier. His memory of this experience was triggered when he drove to Malad, Idaho, in about 1970 to speak at the funeral services for Dr. Thomas Richards. His widow was Hilda Merrill Richards, a daughter of the late Apostle Marriner W. Merrill. President Lee had first become acquainted with Brother and Sister Richards in the late 1940's when Brother Richards served as president of the Central States Mission of the Church.

President Lee recalled to me that he had given a blessing to Brother Richards' wife while he was touring the Central States Mission. Sister Richards was very distraught and despondent over the sudden death of one of their children. President Lee told me that as he and President Richards laid their hands on the head of Sister Hilda Richards, he felt an unseen presence in the circle and he knew it to be her father, Elder Marriner W. Merrill. After the blessing, President Richards told President Lee that he felt the same thing.

"The architect"

Because of the brevity of his service in the prophetic office, President Lee is little remembered today by the membership of the Church. He served only eighteen months as the President of the Church, from July of 1972 until his unexpected death in December of 1973. But his minor renown is in no way indicative of his true legacy.

President Lee was a man of extraordinary vision and leadership ability, who laid the groundwork of many concepts and initiatives that President Spencer W. Kimball saw to full implementation. Among these initiatives were the opening of new doors to the preaching of the gospel, the expansion of temple work, the reorganization of Church administration at headquarters, and the holding of area conferences and solemn assemblies around the world. In many ways President Kimball acted as the "Joshua" to President Harold B. Lee's "Moses." Or, to look at it in another light, President Lee could be likened to the architect who constructed a powerful machine, and President Kimball could be likened to a superior driver who moved the vehicle forward.

"THE MAN TO LEAD GOD'S PEOPLE"

President Lee received a credible death threat in about August of 1973. The day after the threat was received, I had a long visit with the Prophet in his office. I made the comment to President Lee that he was probably experiencing some of the tension and uncertainty that was the Prophet Joseph Smith's portion during most of his adult life. This elicited a ready response from President Lee. He observed to me that this episode might be the means of further disciplining and training him. He then read to me an excerpt from a General Conference sermon delivered in the Tabernacle in 1853 by Elder Orson Hyde, reported in the *Journal of Discourses.* The sermon is entitled, "The Man to Lead God's People." It describes the process through which a man must go in order to prepare him for the prophetic office. Here is the excerpt President Lee referred to:

> It is generally the case, and I think I may say it is invariably the case, that when an individual is ordained and appointed to lead the people, he has passed through tribulations and trials, and has proven himself before God, and before His people, that he is worthy of the situation which he holds. And let this be the motto and safeguard in all future time, that when a person that has not been tried, that has not proved himself before God, and before His people, and before the councils of the Most High, to be worthy, he is not going to step in to lead the Church and people of God. It never has been so, but from the beginning some one that understands the Spirit and counsel of the

Almighty, that knows the Church, and is known of her, is the character that will lead the Church.

How does he become thus acquainted? How does he gain this influence, this confidence in the estimation of the people? He earns it by his upright course and conduct, by the justness of his counsels, and the correctness of his prophecies, and the straightforward spirit he manifests to the people. And he has to do this step by step; he gains influence, and his spirit, like an anchor, is fastened in the hearts of the people; and he is sustained and supported by the love, confidence, and good-will of the Saints, and of Him that dwelt in the bush. This is the kind of character that ought to lead God's people, after he has obtained this good will and this confidence. (Journal of Discourses, vol. 1, p. 123)

President Lee told me that in reading this sermon he almost felt as if he were reading his own biography. He commented on some of the disappointments and difficulties he had encountered during the more than thirty years he had served as a General Authority.

About a week later, with this death threat still on his mind, President Lee again visited privately with me. He again alluded to the many difficulties he had been called upon to endure since being called to Quorum of the Twelve. He then said that he would not have been prepared to lead were it not for "the edifying effect of those experiences."

"Foxes have holes and birds have nests"

In October of 1973 a second, and much more serious threat was made against President Lee's life. In the aftermath of this threat, the Prophet was very calm and seemed to have no real fear or concern. An indication of how lonely the President must have felt at this critical time was this statement that he made. He told me, "I now have a little better understanding of the Master's statement, 'Foxes have holes and birds have nests, but the Son of Man has nowhere to lay his head.'"

"One final conversation"

As Christmas approached in 1973, I had no inkling of the vast changes in the Church that would occur in the space of a few days. I worked in the offices of the First Presidency as usual through Friday, December 21, 1973. At the end of the workday I went to wish President Lee a happy holiday season. He invited me into his office, and then said to me, in substance, "Brother Gibbons, in the language of scripture, I look upon you as a friend and in no sense as a subordinate or servant." When I expressed thanks for my association with him, he answered, "Brother Gibbons, there is no one with whom I feel a closer kinship of spirit than you."

I didn't realize it at the time, but this was the last face-to-face conversation I would have with the Prophet in this lifetime.

I did, however, have one final conversation with President Lee by telephone. Late in the evening on Christmas Day, I received a phone call from President Lee. Among other things, he said to me, "Brother Gibbons, I just wanted to take this opportunity to wish you and yours a Merry Christmas. I had intended," he said, "to come to your house today to pay you a visit, but you can't imagine the turmoil we have had here." He continued, "We did go over to Helen's and Brent's." Then he added, "I have little gifts for you, President Tanner, and President Romney. Since I won't be at the office tomorrow, I will send your gift down there for you." He then expressed appreciation for my service and mentioned the confidence he had in me. He then asked if we had a good Christmas. In answering, I mentioned the fact that we had all been together, including our first grandson. He said, "Is that the child of our special girl?" meaning our daughter Suzanne. When I said, "Yes," President Lee commented on the special circumstances surrounding her birth, which I have previously described.

This phone conversation was the last one I had with this great Prophet. The following day, December 26, 1973, he died at about 9:00 p.m. He had gone to the LDS Hospital in Salt Lake City for his annual check-up. While in the hospital, he apparently experienced some of the same kind of congestion that bothered him so much during the last year of his life. His personal secretary, Brother Arthur Haycock, who called me immediately afterward, was with the Prophet at the time of his death. He said that the President had a mask over his face to help him breathe, when he suddenly seemed to be in distress. A glassy look came into his eyes, and he seemed ready to faint. Arthur summoned a nurse and doctor, but it was to no avail. He was gone with a few minutes of "lung and heart arrest."

Only God knows how much I loved this great man and how much I miss him. God bless his memory.

"No Righteous Man Dies Before His Time"

President Harold B. Lee's funeral was held on Friday, December 28, 1973. The Prophet's body lay in state from 8:00 a.m. to 8:00 p.m. in the foyer of the Administration Building. More than ten thousand people came to pay their respects and view his remains, passing solemnly through the marble foyer. Several of the Prophet's stalwart grandsons were present all during this time, standing beside the casket.

It was a wet and dreary day on which to lay President Lee in the cold ground. The funeral cortege left the Administration Building about 11:30 a.m., following the family prayer. The funeral was held in the Tabernacle. The speakers were President Spencer W. Kimball, future Church President Gordon B. Hinckley, and the two men who served as counselors to Presidents Lee and Kimball, Presidents N. Eldon Tanner and Marion G. Romney.

I recall that President Tanner was highly emotional during his funeral sermon and at times could hardly speak. President Kimball was greatly magnified, and it was evident as he spoke that the prophetic mantle had already fallen upon him.

I was most struck and comforted by something President Gordon B. Hinckley said in his funeral sermon. He said of President Harold B. Lee, "No righteous man dies before his time."

SPENCER W. KIMBALL

Twelfth President of The Church of Jesus
Christ of Latter-day Saints

December 1973 – November 1985

SPENCER W. KIMBALL CHRONOLOGY

March 28, 1895
Spencer Woolley Kimball is born in Salt Lake City, Utah, to Andrew Kimball and Olive Woolley Kimball.

October 21, 1914
Spencer W. Kimball leaves Salt Lake City for the Central States Mission.

December 31, 1916
Spencer W. Kimball returns home after completing his mission.

Fall of 1917
Spencer W. Kimball is drafted into the U.S. Army.

November 16, 1917
Spencer W. Kimball and Camilla Eyring are married in Arizona by Camilla's bishop. They were later sealed in the Salt Lake Temple in June of 1918.

1927
President Kimball forms a partnership with Joseph Greenhalgh, dealing in insurance, bonds, and real estate.

1933
Spencer W. Kimball's youngest son, Andrew, is stricken with polio.

1936

Spencer W. Kimball is elected as the Arizona district governor of Rotary International

1937

Spencer W. Kimball and his wife, Camilla, travel in France, Yugoslavia, Hungary, Austria, Switzerland, Germany, the Netherlands, Belgium, and England.

1937

Spencer W. Kimball is called as the president of the newly formed Mount Graham Stake.

July 8, 1943

Spencer W. Kimball receives a phone call from President Heber J. Grant calling him as a member of the Quorum of the Twelve.

August 26, 1943

Elder Spencer W. Kimball and his family leave their family home in Safford, Arizona, and move to Salt Lake City.

October 7, 1943

Elder Spencer W. Kimball is sustained as a member of the Quorum of the Twelve and ordained by President Heber J. Grant.

September 13, 1946

President George Albert Smith appoints Elder Spencer W. Kimball as chairman of the Church's Lamanite Committee, with instructions to "watch all the Indians in all the world."

May 1948
Elder Spencer W. Kimball suffers his first heart attack while touring the Navajo-Zuni Mission.

September 1948
Elder Spencer W. Kimball resumes his apostolic work after recovering from his heart attack.

December 1949
Elder Spencer W. Kimball suffers more heart trouble, and is ordered by his doctors to rest, returning to his labors in the spring of 1950.

November 1950
Elder Spencer W. Kimball dedicates Central America for the preaching of the Gospel.

1955
Elder Spencer W. Kimball spends five months touring missions in Europe and Great Britain.

December 1956
Elder Spencer W. Kimball and Camilla are in a car accident near the Grand Canyon while driving on an ice-covered mountain road en route to a stake conference in Safford, Arizona. Camilla Kimball is seriously injured.

1957
Elder Spencer W. Kimball undergoes major throat surgery in New York City. He is unable to use his voice for many months, and when he is able to speak, he speaks in a pronounced whisper for the rest of his life.

1959

Elder Spencer W. Kimball and Camilla tour South America for ten weeks, holding meetings in Brazil, Uruguay, Paraguay, Argentina, Chile, Peru, and Bolivia.

1960

Elder Spencer W. Kimball and Camilla travel around the world. They first tour missions in the South Pacific, where President Kimball creates new stakes in Australia and New Zealand. On the return trip to Salt Lake City, the Kimballs visit Southeast Asia, Egypt, the Holy Land, Greece, Italy, Spain, and Portugal.

May 1, 1966

Elder Spencer W. Kimball organizes a stake in Sao Paulo, Brazil—the first stake in South America.

1967

Elder Spencer W. Kimball organizes stakes in Buenos Aires, Argentina, and Montevideo, Uruguay.

1968

Elder Spencer W. Kimball is given apostolic responsibility for the missions in Great Britain.

January 18, 1970

President David O. McKay passes away. Elder Spencer W. Kimball is set apart as the Acting President of the Twelve.

October 1970

President Spencer W. Kimball tours extensively in the Pacific, holding meetings in Tonga, Samoa, Fiji, and Hawaii.

August 1971
President Spencer W. Kimball accompanies the First Presidency to Manchester, England, for the first ever Area Conference.

December 1971
President Spencer W. Kimball undergoes twenty-four cobalt treatments for throat cancer.

April 12, 1972
President Spencer W. Kimball undergoes open-heart surgery. His surgeon, Dr. Russell M. Nelson, says that during the surgery he had the spiritual impression that President Kimball would become President of the Church.

July 2, 1972
President Joseph Fielding Smith passes away. Spencer W. Kimball is sustained as President of the Twelve.

August 1972
President Spencer W. Kimball accompanies the First Presidency to Mexico City for the Church's second Area Conference.

August 1973
President Spencer W. Kimball accompanies the First Presidency to Munich, Germany, for the Church's third Area Conference.

December 26, 1973
President Harold B. Lee dies suddenly during a routine medical checkup and is succeeded as President of the Church by Spencer W. Kimball.

December 30, 1973
President Spencer W. Kimball is ordained and set apart as the twelfth President of the Church, with N. Eldon Tanner and Marion G. Romney as counselors.

April 4, 1974
President Spencer W. Kimball addresses the leaders of the Church at a Regional Representatives seminar, calling for a greater emphasis on missionary work.

1975
President Spencer W. Kimball holds seven Area Conferences in Scandinavia, Sao Paulo, Buenos Aires, Tokyo, Manila, Taipei, and Seoul.

October 1975
The First Quorum of Seventy is reinstated.

June 9, 1978
President Spencer W. Kimball's most significant and enduring contribution to the work is announced—the Revelation on Priesthood. This made the priesthood available to all worthy male members of the church.

September 1979
President Spencer W. Kimball undergoes surgery for a subdural hematoma.

July 1981
President Spencer W. Kimball calls Gordon B. Hinckley as an additional counselor in the First Presidency.

November 1982

Upon the death of N. Eldon Tanner, Marion G. Romney is sustained as President Spencer W. Kimball's first counselor, and Gordon B. Hinckley as his second counselor.

November 5, 1985

President Spencer W. Kimball passes away quietly in Salt Lake City.

"A MAN OF MANY QUALITIES"

President Spencer W. Kimball was a man of many qualities. It is difficult to describe his personality in a few words. He was energetic and forward-looking. He was a true visionary in every sense of the word. In Church leadership he was bold and almost audacious. He was a fighter, a battler. He was like a perpetual motion man, a human whirlwind, or an indefatigable runner. Above all, he was a true disciple of Christ.

"To Name Him 'Roberts'"

President Spencer Woolley Kimball was born in Salt Lake City, Utah Territory, on March 28, 1895, during the Utah Constitutional Convention. His father, Andrew Kimball, was a delegate to the convention.

President Kimball told me once that, according to his mother, his father wanted to name him "Roberts" after B. H. Roberts, who had just given an impassioned speech during the Convention. According to President Kimball, his mother, Olive Woolley Kimball, was not keen on the idea because in his speech Elder Roberts had spoken out against women's suffrage. The views of the wife prevailed over those of the husband, and the baby was named Spencer.

I find two fascinating insights from this story. First, that we very nearly had a Prophet named "Roberts Kimball," and second, that the name "Spencer" may be seen as symbolic of the President Kimball's lifelong passion for lifting up the oppressed and opening doors of opportunity for all men and women.

"THE EPITOME OF PERFECTION"

When President Spencer W. Kimball spoke of his mother, Olive Woolley Kimball, it was in almost reverential terms. I have heard him refer to his mother as "the epitome of perfection." In his eyes she had no faults.

During a fairly brief period in his early teens, young Spencer W. Kimball lost three of his sisters and his mother. The death of his mother hit him especially hard. Even while he served as President of the Church, I could sense that he felt the great loss accompanying her passing.

"A Son of Arizona"

Since I am a native-born Arizonan, I shared a private connection with President Kimball, who was raised in Arizona and lived there for many decades. Though he was born in Salt Lake City, he proudly claimed to be a son of Arizona. In 1898 his father, Andrew Kimball, was called to be the president of the St. Joseph Stake in the Gila Valley of southeastern Arizona. President Kimball was three years old when the family moved there. He was an Arizonan, through and through.

"A TRULY TOUCHING SCENE"

President Kimball had a brother who had been inactive for much of his life. Through all the years, the Prophet remained close to this brother, as he did to his other siblings and their families. But he had a special feeling for this one brother. As plans were laid for the Solemn Assembly in April of 1974 when he was sustained as the twelfth President of the Church, President Kimball invited this brother to attend and made sure that a place was reserved for him on the stand in the Salt Lake Tabernacle.

On the day of the Solemn Assembly, I observed a truly touching scene. President Kimball's brother attended, and we seated him in his reserved place on the stand. Then, as soon as the meeting was ended, President Kimball went directly to him and embraced him. For those of us who witnessed this tender scene, it was a special and touching moment.

"Reminiscing about Uncle Golden"

President Kimball would often recount stories about his granduncle, Elder J. Golden Kimball, who was a member of the First Council of the Seventy. I always perked up my ears when President Kimball would begin reminiscing about "Uncle Golden." Like his grandnephew, J. Golden Kimball was a noted humorist, although the uncle was much saltier than the nephew.

President Kimball once told me that that when the first Assistants to the Twelve were called, "Uncle Golden" had said to him, "Well, I always knew the Twelve were flat tires, but I didn't know they needed spares."

Another time, President Kimball told this story: One Christmas, a generous farmer in Idaho had sent down turkeys to be shared with the General Authorities. They were fresh and had not been plucked and still had long necks. J. Golden Kimball received one of the turkeys and took it home for his Christmas dinner. After Christmas, Spencer W. Kimball was visiting with his uncle and asked how he enjoyed his Christmas turkey. J. Golden Kimball told him, "We enjoyed the turkey, but next year I hope they have them cut off the necks first. The thing looked so much like me that my wife wouldn't eat a bite of it."

"AN IDENTITY PROBLEM"

President Kimball used to delight in telling stories about his early anonymity as a General Authority. Apparently, for many years after his call to the Quorum of the Twelve, he suffered an identity problem among the members of the Church.

President Kimball often told this story: Not long after his call to the Twelve, while attending a stake conference session, one of the counselors in the stake presidency introduced President Kimball as "Ezra Taft Benson." At a later session, the other counselor introduced him as "Richard R. Lyman" (who had recently been excommunicated from the Church). Still later, at the same stake conference, one of the local leaders said apologetically to him, "You know, Elder Richards. I always thought you were Elder Lee."

Early in his ministry, President Kimball even suffered identity problems with his own family. He shared this story with me: While still a relatively new Apostle, he went one weekend to visit his sister, who was then living in Provo. On Sunday morning he went to priesthood meeting with his brother-in-law and nephews. The bishop of her ward, being told that President Kimball was a new Apostle, asked him to speak in sacrament meeting. The bishop announced from the stand that a special visitor from Salt Lake would speak in sacrament meeting that evening and urged all the brethren to come. (That was in the day when priesthood meeting was held in the morning and sacrament meeting in the evening.) On the way home from priesthood meeting, one of President Kimball's nephews was talking about the bishop's announcement and about "the guy from Salt Lake who would speak."

"You sound like a Woolley"

I have heard it said that President Spencer W. Kimball's native stubbornness was inherited not from his paternal Kimball ancestors, but from his mother's side of the family, the Woolleys. The Woolley family has deep pioneer roots and is reputed to be men of woman of an especially headstrong and intractable nature. President Kimball occasionally spoke jokingly about the toughness of one of his Woolley ancestors, saying that if his dead body were thrown into a river, it would surely float upstream.

President J. Reuben Clark also had Woolley ancestry, which he revered. I understand from one of the older Brethren that President Clark was once asked to make an appraisal of Elder Spencer W. Kimball, then in the Quorum of the Twelve. President Clark said, "The Kimball in Spencer will often cause him to hesitate, but when the Woolley in him takes over, he will act with firmness and resolution."

On another occasion I heard this story about President Kimball and President Clark. President Kimball was assigned to divide the old Pioneer Stake. He fulfilled the assignment and named the new unit, the "Temple Stake." When he gave his report to the First Presidency, they had reservations about the name and instructed him to return and give it the name "Temple View Stake" instead. President Kimball then said privately to his cousin, President J. Reuben Clark, "You can be certain that if my last name were Smith or Richards they wouldn't ask me to change the name of the stake." In response, President Clark said, "Spencer, that's the first time I've ever heard you sound like a Woolley!"

"I HAVE FALLEN AMONG CUTTHROATS"

President Spencer W. Kimball underwent extensive surgery on his throat in 1957 while serving in the Quorum of the Twelve Apostles. He traveled to New York for the surgery, which was performed by an eminent physician. President David O. McKay asked future Church President Harold B. Lee to accompany President Kimball. When they visited the doctor before the surgery, President Lee explained Elder Kimball's crucial role as an Apostle and a speaker in the Church and emphasized that his voice must be preserved.

Following the surgery, President Kimball was unable to speak for some time, but gradually regained the limited use of his voice. He called it his "still small voice." I often heard President Kimball speak about his voice, saying that it was a gruff voice. It reminded his listeners around the world, whether in the great Salt Lake Tabernacle or in lowly meeting halls across the world, that the Prophet had suffered great trauma to his voice, and I believe that it caused them to listen more intently than they otherwise would have.

Because he had spent most of his life in Arizona, President Kimball decided to give his first public sermon in his home state after months of recovery. He attended a stake conference in his hometown of Safford, Arizona, where I understand that he told his old friends and neighbors, "I have fallen among cutthroats!"

"A SWEET AND MILD WHISPER"

Following his throat surgery President Spencer W. Kimball's voice became beloved by millions around the world. It sounded like a sweet and mild whisper. On many occasions during his time as President of the Church, he had trouble with his voice. He would be preaching or counseling when, without warning, his voice would seem to break, and he sometimes had to cut his remarks short. He often expressed private concern that his voice was weakening. He regretted that his voice sometimes made it difficult to communicate with the saints. Yet in reality, his mild whisper endeared him to the saints, who came to love that voice, though President Kimball himself may not have fully recognized this fact.

I have an especially heart-rending memory related to President Kimball's voice. During the time I served as the secretary to the First Presidency, I was also President Kimball's home stake president. One day he came into my office to discuss a matter, and while there he told me that one of the stake high councilors had given a great sermon in President Kimball's ward the previous Sunday. He then said to me, "He had a nice, quiet, pleasing voice. It wasn't harsh and ugly like mine." I assured President Kimball that his voice was the sweetest sound in the world to the Latter-day Saints. I'm not sure that he believed me, but it was true!

In about 1975, President Kimball was outfitted with a device that had a tiny microphone, which attached to his eyeglasses. This seemed to help reduce the strain on the Prophet's voice and allowed his voice to be amplified perfectly in any setting.

"A WHOLE CORPS OF DOCTORS"

In the midst of one of his severe physical challenges, I was visiting with President Kimball. One of the General Authorities walked in the room and asked the Prophet how he was feeling. The Prophet told him offhandedly that he was okay. The visitor then proceeded to regale the Prophet about his own health and went into great detail, concluding with the comment that he had been "training a whole corps of doctors in Salt Lake City."

President Kimball merely responded, "You wouldn't mind giving me their names, would you?"

"Spencer, you are not to die!"

President Spencer W. Kimball was no stranger to doctors. Throughout the 1950's and 1960's he was treated for a wide array of ailments—throat cancer and heart disease, chief among them. He suffered some of his greatest health challenges following the death of President David O. McKay. He had prostate surgery in 1970 and then suffered a recurrence of his throat and heart problems. Things looked fairly grave for President Kimball in 1971 and 1972, and for this reason it was almost universally believed that he would never outlive President Harold B. Lee, who was the youngest Church President in many decades.

In 1972 President Kimball faced the greatest crisis of his life. His heart had deteriorated to the point that his longtime cardiologist, Dr. Ernest L. Wilkinson, told him that without surgery he would soon die. President Kimball sought an interview with the First Presidency. Present also were Dr. Wilkinson and heart surgeon Russell M. Nelson, who explained to President Lee the risks of surgery on a man seventy-seven years old.

I remember that President Kimball expressed great reservation to President Lee. He told him that he felt like he was a dying man whose time had come and that he shouldn't risk such a procedure.

At that point President Lee spoke out with great forcefulness. Pounding the table with his hand, he said, "Spencer, you are not to die!" He then counseled that he do all in his power to preserve his life.

"A SPECIAL BLESSING"

Because of his faith in his priesthood leaders, President Spencer W. Kimball elected to have the open-heart surgery. The night before he performed the surgery in April of 1972, Dr. Russell M. Nelson came to President Lee and President Tanner for a special blessing. President Lee blessed him that the surgery would go forward perfectly.

I can attest that during the surgery the members of the First Presidency and Quorum of the Twelve were praying unitedly and fervently for the life of President Kimball. President Lee, in particular, seemed especially moved with the Spirit, and he prayed with great fervency for the life of his friend and fellow Apostle.

I remember being with President Lee when word was received that the operation was a success. Later President Nelson told me that he had never seen an operation in which everything went more perfectly.

"A MODERN-DAY JOB"

President Spencer W. Kimball seemed to face more crises of his health than any other man I have known. He was a modern-day Job. But in the midst of all of these trials, he seldom spoke about them. Many of his personal trials were learned about indirectly or long after the fact.

His list of ailments is almost as impressive as those of Job. Before becoming President of the Church his medical trials included cancer of the throat, open-heart surgery, major abdominal surgery, and Bells palsy. During the time I served him in the office of the First Presidency, he suffered from prostate cancer, cancer of the neck, severe hearing loss in his left ear, excessive internal bleeding, high blood pressure, recurring skin cancer, boils, viral pneumonia, dizziness, cataracts, exhaustion, fainting spells, lesions, stroke, and multiple major head surgeries to relieve the pressure of a subdural hematoma.

During this same period, Sister Camilla Kimball had medical trials of her own, including two major surgeries. But characteristically, the Kimballs tried to keep their private woes to themselves. I remember that once in the mid 1970's at the end of a First Presidency meeting, President Kimball said nonchalantly to his counselors, "I hope you Brethren will forgive me, but I may not stay to the end of the meeting." When asked why by President Tanner, the Prophet said, "Oh, Sister Kimball is just going into the hospital for a little surgery, and I will be going up there with her." This was the first hint the Brethren had that Sister Kimball was not feeling well. This incident is quite typical. To see President and Sister Kimball one would not have thought that they had a care in the world. Theirs was a great example of uncomplaining, dedicated service.

It was as if some malignant force was trying to silence the Prophet's voice and stop his eyes, ears, and heart. But President Kimball barely paid attention to them and continued to work through every obstacle. He seemed able to cast every ailment to the side, like a horse switching away an annoying fly with the flick of his tail.

President Kimball was loath to discuss or even mention his personal ailments. Occasionally the curtain was parted, so to speak, to reveal an ailment, which in another man might provide the topic of complaint and conversation for a lifetime. Not so with President Kimball. For example, I was with President Kimball once when it was reported that one of the General Authorities was recuperating at home after having had a carbuncle lanced. President Kimball was silent for a moment and then mentioned in an offhand way that he once had more than a hundred carbuncles all over his body. On another occasion, word came that one of the other General Authorities, who had been absent for several weeks, had experienced a heart fibrillation. To this President Kimball responded, "I have one of those nearly every day. But I don't pay attention to them. I just go about my business."

He was never at rest, never at ease, even when hospitalized. He continued in constant motion through every treatment, always working, always trying to stimulate those around him to greater faith and devotion, working his whole life to prepare a community of saints worthy to receive the Lord at His second coming.

"A SPECIAL COVENANT WITH THE LORD"

I believe that there was a special spiritual aspect to President Spencer W. Kimball's physical challenges. He on rare occasions would hint at this in private conversations. I believe that he had made a special covenant with the Lord that if he were permitted to live, he would not waste a moment. I know that Elder David B. Haight of the Quorum of the Twelve shared this feeling. Bishop Alfred B. Smith, who was very close to the Prophet, also confirmed this to me. Bishop Smith told me that he had once attended a stake conference with President Kimball. During their travels, Bishop Smith told President Kimball that he was the hardest working General Authority he had ever seen. In answer, President Kimball said, "After my throat operation, I prayed to the Lord and promised Him that if He would bless my voice so I could speak and be heard, I would spend every remaining minute of my life serving Him."

"The Most Stubborn Man"

President Spencer W. Kimball had a unique relationship with his many physicians as he battled one health crisis after another down through the years. I once heard his longtime personal physician, Dr. Ernest L. Wilkinson, say, "President Kimball is without a doubt the most stubborn man I have ever known!" It was this quality of stubbornness that enabled him to endure surgeries and treatments to extend his life.

Another one of his physicians, Dr. Russell M. Nelson, once told me that he had learned one important thing about Spencer W. Kimball while treating him as his heart surgeon—that for President Kimball, the Article of Faith stating, "We believe in being subject to kings, presidents, rulers and magistrates" emphatically did *not* include doctors!

During the prime years of his administration in the 1970's, President Kimball became increasingly fatigued by his relentless schedule. In 1976 Elder David B. Haight of the Twelve accompanied the Prophet on a marathon sequence of meetings in the South Pacific, during which he traveled many thousands of miles and spoke at dozens of meetings. Following this trip, the Prophet returned to Salt Lake utterly exhausted. Elder Haight confided in me that the Prophet had "simply run out of gas." President Kimball soon developed respiratory problems and was hospitalized for viral pneumonia. We hoped that the hospitalization would provide a good rest for the Prophet, but he was soon back at the office, working as hard as ever, plunging ahead with his work as placidly as if he were sailing on a calm sea. When I asked him about his pneumonia, President

Kimball just brushed it off, and told me, "It's all right now," as if it had been a common cold.

Following President Kimball's hospitalization for pneumonia, his doctors, his family, and the Brethren became increasingly concerned for his health. But even though he was greatly fatigued, he refused to slow down. He never missed a day of work and on the weekends continued to fill a heavy travel and speaking calendar.

In the fall of 1977, the Prophet collapsed during a meeting of the Church Board of Education, and paramedics were called. He was hospitalized again. The next day I visited him in the hospital and found him busy at work in his hospital bed, writing letters, outlining plans, and placing phone calls.

On another occasion, in September of 1979, the Prophet was again hospitalized for major surgery. He telephoned me from the hospital and asked me to come up to see him and confer with him about the speaking assignments for the upcoming General Conference. When I arrived at the hospital, he told me that he wanted to speak at the Conference. At the time, it seemed utterly inconceivable to me that the Prophet could even attend General Conference, let alone speak. But the Prophet moved forward with his plans, and about three weeks later he was standing at the pulpit in the Salt Lake Tabernacle delivering a masterful sermon at the final session of Conference. He spoke about the story of Caleb and Joshua and expressed his hope that he would have the same kind of spirit that Caleb had. Several times as he spoke his voice seemed to fail him, but each time he rallied and continued on. It was inspiring to me, having seen his low condition in the hospital only a few days previously, to watch him speak at Conference. Like Caleb, he was praying that God would permit him to live long enough to lead the Lord's people over the Jordan River into a Promised Land.

"Deep compassion"

Not long before he was sustained as the twelfth President of the Church, there was an incident at Church headquarters, which illustrates the deep compassion of President Kimball.

Below the Church Administration block there is a large underground parking garage, which serves a multitude of buildings, including the Church Office Building, the Church Administration Building, the Lion House, the Relief Society Building and the Salt Lake Temple. There is a constant stream of cars moving in and out of this parking garage throughout the day. One afternoon, an ordinance worker who had worked all day in the Salt Lake Temple returned to his car in the parking garage. He sat in his car, closed the door, started the engine, and turned on his headlights. Then he suffered a massive heart attack and died while sitting at the wheel.

There were many who passed by this car and saw this brother slumped over the steering wheel, merely thinking that he had fallen asleep. The first person to stop and check on the man was President Kimball, then the President of the Quorum of the Twelve.

To his very core, President Kimball was compassionate, thoughtful, kind, and considerate.

"A PRETTY FRIGHTENING THING TO FACE"

It was inspiring to observe President Spencer W. Kimball firsthand in the weeks following his ordination as the twelfth President of the Church in 1973. He approached his service with a genuine sense of humility. He spoke in almost reverential terms about President Harold B. Lee, who was younger and apparently in better health than President Kimball. I heard him once refer to his unexpected succession as that of "a pygmy following a giant." On other occasions he used the metaphor of a giant redwood falling in the forest, leaving a great space.

A few days before April General Conference in 1974, the first conference he was to preside over since the death of President Lee, I was in President Kimball's office conferring with him about the agenda for the conference. At one point he turned to me and said, "Brother Gibbons, you know it's a pretty frightening thing to face." I responded to him that the prayers and the faith of millions of members of the Church would uphold him during the Conference.

His humility was deep and honest and in no way feigned. But no one ought to ever confuse his sense of genuine humility with his great confidence and determination. He was unwavering in his devotion to his duty. He was resilient. And he had unwavering integrity.

"He Moved Forward Speedily"

President Kimball's two counselors, Presidents N. Eldon Tanner and Marion G. Romney, had served previously with President Lee. In addition, President Tanner had also served as a counselor to Presidents David O. McKay and Joseph Fielding Smith. Presidents Tanner and Romney were men of significant ability and experience. It might have been natural for a man like President Kimball to defer almost completely to his more experienced counselors. This, however, was not the case. In the months following his ordination, President Kimball took hold of the administration and began to lead with a very strong hand. He listened carefully to his counselors and in the early days often followed their suggestions, but this was done out of his lack of familiarity with the details of the work. He did not abdicate his authority to his counselors, but used them wisely. More and more, as went on, he stepped forward in key aspects of the work with a strong vision and energy. He was a man of great vision, and it was inspiring to see the direction of his ministry soon unfold in a miraculous manner.

A few months after President Kimball began his service, I had a conversation with President Boyd K. Packer, in which he marveled at the inspired ministry of President Kimball. He observed how decisive President Kimball had been from the moment of his ordination, and how he had moved forward speedily and decisively on new initiatives whose time had clearly come.

"The President framed in my doorway"

President Spencer W. Kimball approached his ministry with a practical approach and a unique personal touch. For example, President Kimball was in the habit of simply popping into the offices of the General Authorities or the office staff when he needed something or had a question. A few days following his ordination, I was surprised one morning to look up from my desk and see the President of the Church framed in my doorway. He had simply walked over to my office to discuss something. This occurred over and over. Despite my pleadings to call and let me come to his office, he insisted on coming to my office. This was something of a shock. After serving for nearly four years with Presidents Joseph Fielding Smith and Harold B. Lee, I could count on the fingers of one hand the number of times President Smith or President Lee had come into my office. Now it became an almost daily occurrence.

I was not alone in having the Prophet pop into my office. He did the same thing with members of the Twelve and the other General Authorities and with staff members at Church headquarters. One day Elder Marion D. Hanks of the Seventy was visiting with me in my office when the Prophet came in unannounced. He visited with me briefly about a matter while Elder Hanks waited, then embraced us each in a fatherly way and left as abruptly as he had arrived. After President Kimball left, Elder Hanks turned to me and said, "That's something quite different, isn't it—having the Prophet simply walk into your office?"

It was different and completely in keeping with President Kimball's personality. It beautifully illustrates President Kimball's unique leadership style. He was a pragmatic leader who had a real sense of urgency. To him it made no sense to have a phone call placed by a secretary to invite someone to come into his office. He felt it made more sense to simply walk down the hall or up the staircase to visit the person. I also believe that this habit arose out of President Kimball's deliberate effort to get as much exercise as possible.

"A TRULY UNIQUE LEADERSHIP STYLE"

President Spencer W. Kimball had a truly unique leadership style. Elder LeGrand Richards of the Quorum of the Twelve once told me about his experience accompanying President Kimball to reorganize a stake when they both served in the Twelve. He said that President Kimball would arise very early in the morning to meticulously plan the day and make lists of those whom they would be interviewing. Elder Richards commented to President Kimball that he would have simply called the stake president and asked that he have a clerk or secretary make out the lists. President Kimball responded that he would prefer to simply do it himself. It was not his style to ask someone else to do it. He was very much a hands-on administrator. He wanted to be directly involved in the details.

He was in constant motion. He never really rested. He seemed to have a real sense of urgency in his ministry as an Apostle and later as President of the Church.

He would typically sweep up everything on his desk and appear at meetings with his counselors with his portfolio bulging with correspondence and other miscellaneous documents—some old, some new. He would then plough through them with great focus and diligence. It was his way of working. When he was awake, he never relaxed or shifted into neutral. Every minute of the day or night he was doing something productive. I cannot conceive of President Kimball simply gazing out of the window and reflecting. He would more likely have a pencil in his hand and be scribbling furiously or reading a book. He was a great man who accomplished extraordinary things in a long life. God bless his memory!

"Humble yet supremely confident"

President Spencer W. Kimball's leadership style was really something of a paradox. He was humble, yet supremely confident.

On the one hand, he was truly humble. He was one of the most self-effacing people I have ever known. As I have mentioned, he often referred to himself as a "pygmy following a giant" in reference to his succession of President Harold B. Lee and the other modern prophets.

On the other hand, President Kimball conducted himself as if he had supreme self-confidence. The masterful sermon that he gave to the Regional Representatives in April of 1974, which outlined his vision for the global expansion of missionary work and the strengthening of the Church, was not the product of one who was insecure or incompetent. It was bold and audacious. It was the expression of someone utterly confident in his position and in his leadership abilities. This sermon really set the tone for his entire administration. That administration was among the most aggressive and forward-looking of any in the modern Church. No one hearing that sermon or seeing the Prophet in action could ever doubt that he was a great man with a far-reaching vision.

"Round-the-clock working habits"

President Spencer W. Kimball worked almost every waking hour, and when he couldn't sleep he continued his labors through the night. I began to notice that most of the General Authorities, even those younger by several decades, had trouble keeping up the this indefatigable octogenarian. I was one day visiting with President Boyd K. Packer of the Twelve and Elder Marion D. Hanks of the Seventy. They were comparing notes about their experiences with President Kimball. Elder Hanks told us that he had traveled with the Prophet for a conference assignment, and when he returned to Salt Lake City on Monday, he felt as if he had been gone a month. President Packer said that he had never seen a man work harder than Spencer W. Kimball. He commented upon President Kimball's faithful personal secretary, D. Arthur Haycock, who had recently suffered a heart attack. President Packer said to us, "If anyone in the Church is entitled to have a heart attack, it's Arthur Haycock."

I once heard President Kimball say that some of the Brethren were uneasy serving with him because of his penchant for long, constant work, and for that reason, he said, "some of them will probably be glad when I pass on!"

"A Prophet in perpetual motion"

President Spencer W. Kimball was a Prophet in perpetual motion. He worked incessantly, despite his numerous health challenges. Like the tides of the ocean, he was always working, always doing something. Once he took hold of something, he would never lay it down until he could honestly write *finis* to it. This quality accounted for the milestones he reached during his administration: the reorganization of the Seventy, universal priesthood for all worthy men, emeritus status for General Authorities, and the reorganization of the system of the Church to respond to the unprecedented growth in membership. These, and other accomplishments, were things that had been under consideration for years. For President Kimball, however, they were not merely ideas to be bandied about, but were projects to be achieved. One by one, he persistently began to work, and strive, and struggle with them. Endless hours were spent in counseling, in studying, in fasting, and in praying as he sought information, inspiration, and confirmation. When everything was in order, and when he felt at peace and satisfied, then he acted decisively and without any hesitation.

Continuous, applied work was not a passing fad with President Kimball, but a way of life that permeated and infused his entire administration. President Kimball was a very tough-minded man, not to be deterred by any difficulty or obstacle. If ever he took hold of a matter, he would never lay it aside until it had been concluded to his satisfaction. And once he had decided upon a course of action, he seemed unable to rest until it was completed. If someone else were ever given an assignment to carry out a decision, he would ask again and again if it had been done, and if it hadn't been done as promptly or as thoroughly as he thought it ought to have been done, he would simply do it himself.

"HE ABHORRED VACATIONS"

I learned very early in my association with President Kimball that he never really took time off. He abhorred vacations as such. It was interesting over the years to observe the efforts of his counselors to persuade the President to rest now and then. The Church owned a small beach house in Laguna Beach, California, which had been used occasionally by Presidents of the Church dating back many years. Presidents Tanner and Romney were constantly urging President Kimball to use this house for a few days of rest now and then.

In the winter of 1974 the President had flown to Los Angeles to consult with an ear specialist about his hearing and then was supposed to rest over the weekend at the beach cottage in Laguna Beach. However, it was soon learned from other sources that the Prophet had spent the entire weekend placing phone calls to cheer up various old friends who were in need of counsel and comfort. One of these calls was made to the mother of a lifelong friend, who was suffering from Parkinson's disease and had been very despondent. Then on Sunday, President Kimball had insisted on being driven to nearby Camp Pendleton, where he spoke to a group of LDS servicemen in the post chapel.

A couple of years later, the counselors again persuaded the Prophet to take a short vacation in Laguna Beach. But word soon filtered back that President Kimball was not resting at all. Percy Fetzer, one of the temple presidents, reported that President Kimball called him twice during the week about matters pertaining to his call as president of the Swiss Temple. Also, Emil Fetzer, the head architect for the Church for many years, reported that President Kimball called him about plans for a small temple Emil had been working on. These were surely only the tip of the iceberg—the Prophet was likely spending his entire days making phone calls, reading memoranda, writing instructions, and making plans.

Even in a quiet, little beach house, freed of the constant, daily pressure of his calling, he would not or could not relax or slow the tempo of his activity. He merely turned it in another direction. President Kimball was moved constantly by an inner, overpowering compulsion from which he could not escape. And he insisted that those around him be always on the move. The evidence of his implacable will to keep moving and to keep everyone around him moving was on every hand, including the sign he displayed on his desk reading, "Do it! Now!" He mentioned several times in my hearing that he looked forward to the day when the temples of the Church would operate around the clock.

When the Prophet returned from a lengthy foreign trip to the Pacific and the Far East in 1975, I noted that the Brethren who accompanied him seemed deeply fatigued. Most of them commented on the frenetic pace of the President, and that he seemed to thrive upon it. He seemed almost determined to die with his boots on, so to speak. He was like perpetual motion during all his waking hours. He seldom stopped or rested. And when he did rest, his mind was working, probing, searching.

"A PENCIL IN HIS HAND"

I seldom saw President Spencer W. Kimball at Church headquarters without a pencil in his hand. He often had a yellow pad with him as well, and he constantly made notes as he spoke with people, noting down what was said and things that he wanted to follow up on.

This was the President's style. He worked incessantly, discussing, reviewing, and planning. He seemed at a loss unless he had a pencil in his hand and a piece of paper to write on. It is hard for me to visualize his sitting alone and just thinking. His nonstop, perpetual motion habits hardly permitted him to cease moving or at least writing notes in his portfolio or on a yellow notepad.

"I DON'T WANT TO BE SAVED"

I once heard President Spencer W. Kimball say that if he had any preeminent virtue, it was the capacity to work. And work he did! His incessant work habits became an increasing sense of concern of those around him, who feared that he was overworking his tired and weakened frame. His personal secretary, D. Arthur Haycock, was especially concerned about the health of the Prophet, and tried to do more and more to clear the path for the Prophet. Arthur told me that on one occasion after he had taken it upon himself to do several little things for President Kimball, the Prophet told him he wanted to continue to do them for himself. When Arthur tried to persuade him, the Prophet said, "I know you are trying to save me—but I don't want to be saved, I want to be exalted."

"Never stand still"

President Spencer W. Kimball disliked vacations and had his own "rest theory," which he frequently expounded upon in public and in private. As he explained it to me, he believed that the "rest of the Lord" referred to in the scriptures is not *relaxation*, but the feeling of joy and satisfaction which one receives from doing his *duty*.

I was once in a meeting with President Kimball when the hymn, "Come Let Us Anew," was sung. President Kimball stood up a few moments later and referred to the line, "and never stand still till the Master appear," and commented, "This is good doctrine!"

"To Die in the Harness"

As President Spencer W. Kimball's age advanced and the ravages of his physical infirmities took an ever-mounting toll upon his strength and energy, he continued to push himself to the limit. In this he became an inspiration to many. In his late seventies he visited a nursing home and spoke to the residents, many of whom were in their sixties and early seventies. He later shared with me his impression that while they may have been decades younger than he, they were actually *old, old*, because they had given up and had ceased being active. When the Prophet reached age eighty, his pace seemed to increase to almost a fever pitch. He drove full speed ahead. He rejected out of hand any suggestion to ease up or to provide any latitude in his schedule. He seemed to have the absolute determination to spend himself in service, to die in the harness.

One evening the Prophet stopped by our home. He had in his hand some letters pertaining to the creation of an Area in Europe. He had stopped by President Tanner's home and gotten his signature on the letters and wanted to get them immediately in my hands to send out into the field. By an action of this kind, he dramatically showed that his motto, "Do it! Now!" was no idle gesture.

I honestly marveled at the heavy schedule the Prophet maintained. He was an octogenarian, but was outrunning men twenty, thirty, forty, or fifty years his junior. He seemed absolutely determined to run at full pace until he dropped in his tracks. I felt that my own determination to work hard was magnified by his tremendous example. He lived up to his oft-repeated admonishment to "Lengthen your stride." His body and mind were running at a pace that men half his age would have difficulty keeping up with.

"A KEEN SENSE OF HUMOR"

President Spencer W. Kimball had a keen sense of humor. I believe his native cheery disposition was one of the tools he used to overcome adversity in his life and to keep his perspective. In times of pain or trial, he maintained his good humor. It made it both delightful and inspiring to be in his presence. And even amidst all of his life's challenges, the Prophet maintained his native sunny disposition.

His sense of humor also enabled him to remain humble. He always took his prophetic calling seriously, but never himself. His good humor also endeared himself to those around him and to the people.

"Are you willing to share?"

I was once part of a conversation the Prophet had with Homer Ellsworth, who had recently moved from Salt Lake City to a small farm in Utah County. It beautifully illustrates the delightful give-and-take of President Kimball's sense of humor. The conversation went something like this:

"Homer, is it true you have moved to Lehi?"

"Yes, President, that's true," Homer answered.

"And is it also true you have acreage there on which you raise part of your sustenance?"

"That's right, President," Homer said.

"And Homer," the Prophet continued. "Do you have your year's supply safely stocked and stored?"

"Yes, Sir," Homer responded.

"And Homer," the President continued, "Do you by chance have a little surplus food that might be made available for others in time of need?"

"Yes sir."

"And are you willing to share?"

"I certainly am," Homer said.

At that, President Kimball reached into his famous portfolio, which he always carried with him, and brought out his note pad and asked, "Homer, can you tell me your address?"

"You Didn't Kill This, Did You?"

One day I was visiting with President Boyd K. Packer in his office. There was an animal skin lying on a table, which had been given to President Packer by the saints in South Africa. President Kimball had recently given a conference address condemning the needless killing of animals and birds. President Packer told me that the Prophet had recently come into his office and seen the animal skin on the table. After they had conversed for some time about Church business, the Prophet stood up to leave, and on his way out he pointed to the animal skin and asked President Packer, with a twinkle in his eye, "You didn't kill this, did you?"

"WOULD YOU GENTLEMEN LIKE A COCKTAIL?"

One of the members of the Twelve told me this delightful story about President Kimball: The two were flying on an airplane during a long series of meetings abroad when the flight attendant, a beautiful young woman, approached their row and asked them, "Would you gentlemen like a cocktail?"

"No, thank you," said President Kimball.

"Well, would you like some tea or a coffee?"

"No," said the Prophet.

"How about a Coke?"

"No, thank you," said President Kimball.

Finally, the flight attendant said, "Gentlemen, isn't there *anything* I can get for you?"

President Kimball thought a moment, and then asked, "Do you have a little lemonade?"

"No," the flight attendant said, then pausing she added, "But I could squeeze *you* a little."

The member of the Twelve told me that President Kimball raised his hands in mock defense and said, "Don't you dare touch me!"

"Do Not Fail to Give Me a Ticket"

President Kimball continued to drive himself in his own car even after he became the President of the Church. It was really something to be in the Church parking lot early in the morning and see the Prophet drive up, park his car, and get out with his portfolio. There were security men and other assistants readily available to drive the Prophet anytime to any destination, but he simply liked to drive himself. A time or two, he even drove by our home to drop off letters and other documents.

A trooper in the Utah Highway Patrol who was a faithful member of the Church shared the following true story with me about the Prophet's driving. This occurred in the mid 1970's, when the Prophet was about eighty years old.

One evening after dark, the trooper was driving along State Street in Salt Lake City when he saw a car driving without headlights approaching in the opposite direction. The officer made a U-turn and turned on his lights and siren. He quickly pulled the car over and approached the vehicle.

Leaning down to look in the driver's window, the trooper immediately saw that the driver was the President of the Church! Sister Camilla Kimball was seated on the passenger side, clutching her purse and looking nervous.

"Sir," the trooper said. "Did you know you were driving with your lights off?"

"Yes," the Prophet answered. "I just noticed it."

"President Kimball," he said, "Please let me see your driver's license for a moment."

"I was hoping you wouldn't recognize me," President Kimball said.

"I was hoping it wouldn't be you," the trooper said.

The trooper took President Kimball's license back to his patrol car and wrote out a warning ticket. He then walked back to the Prophet's car and handed it to President Kimball.

President Kimball looked at the warning ticket, and said, "Now, young man. Do not fail to give me a ticket, if I deserve one, merely because of my position in the Church."

The trooper said, "All right, President Kimball, if you insist."

"I don't insist," President Kimball said.

The trooper told me that all the while this was going on Sister Kimball sat chuckling on the passenger side of the front seat.

"His delicious sense of humor"

Near the end of his life, when old age and infirmity had slowed President Kimball down physically and mentally, his delicious sense of humor remained strong.

The Prophet and Sister Kimball lived for several years in special suite of rooms in the Hotel Utah. Since the hotel was next door to the Church Administration Building, it was convenient for the Prophet to live there, so that when he attended meetings he had only a short distance to travel. The suite was comfortable and airy with views of the Salt Lake Valley, but I'm sure that, compared with their old house and yard, it often felt very confining for President and Sister Kimball. I would often visit the Prophet in his hotel suite, sometimes in company with President Gordon B. Hinckley, who was then a counselor in the First Presidency.

On one such visit, a few months before the Prophet passed away, he showed that his old keen sense of humor had not left him. When we entered the suite, President Kimball addressed President Hinckley with this question: "Gordon, did you know that the Kimballs have been in jail?"

Some time later, on one of the rare occasions when President Kimball came over to the office, President Hinckley greeted him and said, "It's good to have you here."

President Kimball responded with a twinkle in his eye, "How good?"

"To Go to the Front of the Line"

There was a quality of genuine humility and self-deprecation in President Spencer W. Kimball. A few days after his ordination as the twelfth President of the Church, he went over to the Lion House for lunch and stood in line with the rest of the paying public and refused to go to the front of the line, as he was urged to do by those in front of him.

"WITH ALL THE LOVE OF WHICH I AM CAPABLE"

Elder David B. Haight, who was called to the Quorum of the Twelve by President Kimball, had a deep affection for the Prophet. President Kimball seemed to take a special interest in Elder Haight, and on several occasions he shared these insights with me:

When President Kimball called Elder Haight to the Twelve, instead of sitting across the desk and issuing the calling, he embraced Elder Haight and, looking him in the eye, said, "With all the love of which I am capable, I call you as a member of the Twelve!"

President Kimball often carried a thick portfolio around with him at Church headquarters, which was literally stuffed to overflowing with papers. Elder Haight told me that shortly after his call to the Twelve, the Prophet saw the new Apostle carrying a very slim leather portfolio in his hands. Motioning toward Elder Haight's portfolio, the Prophet said, "David, are we overworking you?"

Elder Haight also told me that shortly after he was called to the Twelve, he was in a meeting with the Brethren when President Kimball called for a vote on an issue. Elder Haight, unfamiliar with the procedure, and perhaps awed by being in the circle, failed to raise his hand. President Kimball spoke up and said, "David, are you with us?"

"How is Henry?"

For many years I was close with the eminent scientist, Dr. Henry J. Eyring, who was a neighbor of ours and who served with me in leadership roles in our home stake. Brother Eyring was the brother of Camilla Eyring Kimball, and hence the Prophet's brother-in-law.

There was a special relationship between Brother Eyring and President Kimball, which I was able to observe both at Church headquarters and on a more private basis, as President Kimball was also a neighbor and a member of our stake.

Henry Eyring once told me that, in his opinion, Spencer W. Kimball had the greatest integrity of any man he had ever known. He was wholly without pretense. What you saw in public was the same man he had always known in private. Henry told me that in all the years he had known President Kimball, he had never known him to show even a hint of impatience.

In the months and weeks leading up to Henry Eyring's death in 1981, I was able to observe the close relationship that the two men had. Particularly touching to me was the following little interchange I observed:

One day after a long meeting, President Kimball took my arm and asked me to help him back to his office. At the time the Prophet was very weak and needed a helping hand from time to time to get around. When we got back to his office, I asked the Prophet how Henry Eyring was doing. Immediately he said, "Let's call Camilla and find out." I dialed the number and handed the receiver to the Prophet. He took the receiver in his hand, and, standing behind his desk with his head half bowed, he said to his wife, "Mother, how is Henry?" I could hear Sister Kimball's voice clearly across the desk when she answered, "He's in intensive care," though the Prophet did not hear this clearly because of his weak hearing, so she repeated the information a little louder: "Henry's in intensive care in the hospital." The Prophet understood the second time and nodded his head. I then heard Sister Kimball say in a loving, kindly voice, "Maybe we can go up and see him tonight." He answered her in an equally kind and endearing voice, "Thank you, darling!"

It was a tender moment for me to see such an outpouring of love in that family. At the moment, I felt such an overpowering love for this kindly, aged man that I wanted to walk around the desk and take him in my arms!

"Remember, I love you"

President Spencer W. Kimball was very affectionate with his family and those who worked closely with him. When greeting me, he would invariably embrace me in a fatherly way and often kiss me on the cheek. He would often say, "I love you," or, "You don't know how much I love you." This would occur several times each week! It was a blessed experience, as one can imagine!

President Kimball did the same with the General Authorities, with other church leaders and staff members, and with visitors who came to see him. I remember particularly one newly called mission president whom the Prophet embraced in a great bear hug and kissed on the cheek after his call. This brother was so overcome with emotion afterwards that he could scarcely speak. On another occasion, two of our great friends, Max and Donna Clark, came one day to visit me in my office. While they were there, the Prophet walked into the room to see me. Before leaving, he deposited a kiss on each of our cheeks. Max and Donna seemed overwhelmed at the thought of being kissed by a Prophet of God!

In the final years of his life, when his activities were severely limited, the Prophet spoke very seldom in public or to his brethren, but when he did so, his chief message was invariably one of love and appreciation. I recall with special fondness an experience I had with President Kimball not long before his death. I was walking from the temple with the Prophet to his waiting cart, where a security man waited to drive him to his office. As he got into the cart, he kissed me on the cheek and almost as if saying goodbye for the last time, he whispered, "Remember, I love you!"

"A VISIONARY, NOT AN ADMINISTRATOR"

President Kimball was very wise in his choice of counselors. Both President N. Eldon Tanner and President Marion G. Romney were men of significant administrative ability. President Kimball was a visionary, not an administrator. He was a true minister of the gospel. He was the inspiration, but he left the nuts and bolts of administration to his counselors and those around them.

There was a spiritual quality about President Spencer W. Kimball's leadership. He conducted himself as a true disciple, not as a businessman. He was content to let his able counselors shoulder almost the entire burden of the temporal administration of the Church. It was the spiritual things that President Kimball's mind was focused upon. He had the ability to set distant goals and to motivate the members to reach them. If he had a weakness, it was administration. The counselors, especially President Tanner, filled that lack.

This contrast between the administrative styles of the Prophet and his counselors was evident in an amusing incident I observed. The Church auditors would occasionally come in to report on financial matters to President Kimball and his counselors. Wilford Edling was the chairman of the Church Finance Committee, and one day he presented a rather long and detailed report to the Brethren.

After Brother Edling and his associates left the room and the meeting was over, President Kimball turned to his counselors and apologized to them for repeatedly falling asleep during Brother Edling's presentation. He said, "There was just something about the monotonous tone of his voice and the dryness of the subject matter which made it almost impossible for me to stay awake."

In response, President Tanner and President Romney both mentioned how much they had *enjoyed* Brother Edling's presentation. President Tanner was especially high in his praise, saying that the matters reported on were his "lifeblood" and that he practically "hung on every word" of Brother Edling's presentation!

"Plowing new ground"

President Spencer W. Kimball launched the Church in new directions almost immediately after becoming President of the Church. He may be more remembered in time for his innovation than for his energetic expansion of missionary work. This willingness to move the Church in new directions remained with him throughout his presidency. I remember that not long after his call of Gordon B. Hinckley as an additional counselor in the First Presidency, a novel request was presented to the Brethren for consideration. President Hinckley commented to the Prophet that to follow the suggested action would be "plowing new ground." President Kimball responded to President Hinckley, "There is nothing wrong with plowing new ground."

"THE INSPIRATION OF DREAMS"

In matters of Church administration, President Kimball always relied more upon the Spirit than upon his own intellect. When faced with an especially thorny problem, President Kimball often observed that he must do "a good deal more praying about it." The Prophet was a "visionary man." He believed in the inspiration of dreams and visions.

I remember on several occasions, particularly in the late 1970's, that President Kimball spoke about dreams he had received concerning temples and temple work. I remember that on several occasions he spoke of seeing the Kirtland Temple in his dreams. Another time, early one morning, he shared with me that he had "dreamed all night long about the temples and temple work."

"Kaleidoscopic Sermons"

President Spencer W. Kimball was fond of delivering what can be called kaleidoscopic sermons—sermons touching upon a vast array of topics of importance to the saints. He would often weave a multitude of topics into one sermon: cleaning up our homes and farms; the importance of voting in elections; warnings against polygamist cults; the Word of Wisdom; the evils of Sabbath shopping; the dangers of card playing; food storage; the virtues of work; frugality; living within our means; the evils of blasphemy and profanity; avoidance of pornography; the destructive effects of abortion and adultery; the disturbing trend toward sameness in the appearance of the sexes; and the shrewd and evil influence of satanic forces. Other favorite themes of President Kimball included the role of the family, the urging of members to keep journals and family histories, and the need for increased fellowshipping, especially toward people from different cultures and races. The Prophet was also not afraid of broaching uncomfortable or unpopular subjects. He spoke frequently of the doctrine of repentance. He came down hard on the transgressors. He called his hearers to repentance according to the ancient tradition of his apostolic calling.

Many of the subjects covered in his sermons had not been touched on for many years by a President of the Church. I believe that it signaled to the Church and to the world a firm determination to adhere to the high standards of conduct for which the Church has become noted. President Kimball's pattern of delivering these kaleidoscopic sermons continued to the end of his active ministry.

"Unprepared sermons"

President Kimball was most effective in delivering unprepared sermons. Almost all of his preaching, aside from major sermons delivered at general or area conferences, was essentially extemporaneous. It showed a sense of relaxation and self-confidence, coupled with a deep spirituality.

I recall hearing the Prophet speak extemporaneously at a stake conference. He told the story of the woman who ate cheese and crackers during an entire voyage, saving her money for a final meal, when she planned to "eat in style." It was only then, at the conclusion of a long voyage during which she had practically starved herself, that she learned that the cost of all her meals was included in the cost of her ticket. President Kimball then developed the idea that all the blessings of the gospel are immediately available to anyone who will prepare for and attend the feast that is prepared for us each day.

"The Day of the Lamanite"

President Spencer W. Kimball had a special feeling for the original inhabitants of North, South, and Central America, whom the Latter-day Saints traditionally refer to as "Lamanites." From the beginning of his apostolic ministry, President Kimball labored extensively with Native American peoples and was their strong advocate at Church headquarters.

In the mid 1980's, near the end of my service as a General Authority, I had a long discussion with Elder F. Melvin Hammond of the Seventy. We talked about the astounding success the Church was experiencing in Central and South America, where we had both labored as General Authorities. I mentioned to Elder Hammond that in 1954 President McKay traveled to Santiago, Chile, and was met at the airport by Bill Fotheringham and his wife, who were then the only two known members of the Church in Chile. We marveled at what had happened in Chile during the space of only thirty years. At the time there were hundreds of thousands of members in Chile alone, with a beautiful new temple in Santiago.

Elder Hammond then shared with me this significant event in the life of President Kimball: In 1956, Brother Hammond was permitted to attend the dedication of a chapel in Duncan, Arizona, where Elder Spencer W. Kimball, then a member of the Quorum of the Twelve, presided. In the talk that he delivered at the dedication service, Elder Kimball prophesied that the day of the Lamanite had arrived, and that from that day forward the work would flourish among the Lamanites. This was less than two years after President McKay's trip to Santiago when there were only two Latter-day Saints in all of Chile.

"The Apostle to the Lamanites"

Throughout his life, President Spencer W. Kimball thrust himself forward as a friend to the friendless, an ally of the powerless, and an advocate for the saints from the nations of the world, particularly in Latin America. He was a lifelong advocate for the poor and the downtrodden and was known as "the Apostle to the Lamanites" because of his loving concern and advocacy for the peoples of Latin America. I often heard him speak about the role of the Lamanites as recorded in the Book of Mormon and the phenomenal growth of the church in Mexico, Central America, and South America.

"Baptizing illegal aliens"

President Kimball was especially sensitive to the plight of Native Americans and Hispanic immigrants in the United States. During President Kimball's presidency, there was much talk about the politics of illegal aliens in the United States, and the question naturally arose concerning whether illegal aliens should be baptized into the Church. Soon after President Kimball became the President of the Church, he approved a policy allowing illegal aliens to be baptized. However, over time there was a growing sentiment among some in the Church that the policy ought to be changed.

I vividly recall being with the Prophet in a private setting when he listened to a prominent member of the Church argue passionately that it was wrong to baptize illegal aliens. This member felt that the Church policy of permitting baptism flew in the face of the twelfth article of faith, which states that, "We believe in . . . obeying, honoring and sustaining the law." He said that a convert who is in the country illegally cannot be obeying the law, and hence is unworthy to be baptized. The Prophet listened patiently without interruption or comment, never attempting to question or contradict what was said. After the conversation, when the man had left, he said quietly to me, "There's nothing wrong with baptizing illegal aliens."

"To Raise Up Strong Leaders"

His vision of lifting up the members of the Church from foreign nations became almost an obsession with President Kimball. He talked a great deal about the appointment of members of the Seventy from Latin America and other areas of the world. It was a subject that filled President Kimball's mind and conversation. At times he seemed so caught up in the prospect of a Church led by an international leadership that he discussed little else. There was a consuming sense of urgency in this vision.

In his later years, President Kimball once told me that he had struggled and prayed that the Lord would permit him to live, and afterwards he seemed to have only one thought in mind—the appointment of new Seventies from Mexico, Brazil, and other places in the world. President Kimball expressed his desire to make the Church truly international in character by having General Authority representation from many countries.

This became an important thrust of the Prophet during the last months of his active presidency—the desire to raise up strong leaders, even General Authorities, from the various nations of the world, and particularly from Central and South America. The President came back to this subject time and again in the last years and months of his service.

"He motioned to Brother Martins"

While I was serving as a General Authority, my wife and I resided in South America for three years, from 1986 to 1989. During that time I became very close with Brother Helvecio Martins, then president of the Brazil Fortaleza Mission, and later the first General Authority in this dispensation of African descent. Elder Martins eventually served as my counselor in the Brazil Area Presidency. On several occasions, Elder Martins shared with me some significant events surrounding his receipt of the priesthood, involving President Kimball.

I first had a long discussion with Elder Martins about the 1978 Revelation on Priesthood while he was serving as a mission president. We were at the mission home in Fortaleza, in a private setting, and I related to him some of the circumstances surrounding the 1978 Revelation on Priesthood (which I will discuss later). I mentioned President Kimball's long preoccupation with the question of priesthood for all worthy members, dating back many months before the June 1978 announcement. I also told him about the experience in the temple in early 1978 involving Elder LeGrand Richards, when President Wilford Woodruff appeared in the upper room of the Salt Lake Temple.

President Martins then told me about two incidents in his life which help to further bring this historic event into focus:

First, in the late spring or early summer of 1977, Presidents Spencer W. Kimball and Marion G. Romney were in Sao Paulo, Brazil, for an event connected with the construction of the new temple. Elder James E. Faust, then a member of the Seventy, was with them. Brother Martins was in the audience. Before the meeting began and while people were still taking their seats in the congregation, President Kimball made eye contact with Brother Martins and motioned for him to come up to the stand. However, the Prophet used the North American custom of hooking the right index finger back and forth with the hand facing upward. This gesture is unintelligible to a Brazilian. When Brother Martins seemed not to understand that President Kimball was motioning for him to come forward, Elder Faust motioned to him in the Brazilian manner with the hand turned downward, wiggling all four fingers. It was only then that Brother Martins realized, to his shock, that the Prophet wanted him to come forward for a private conversation! When Brother Martins came to him, President Kimball said, with Elder Faust interpreting, that if Helvecio were faithful and remained firm in his faithfulness, he would ultimately receive all of the blessings of the gospel. As he said this, the Prophet placed his hand on Brother Martins' arm and gripped it strongly. Helvecio told me that he often pondered this promise and wondered how it could ever come to pass, since at the time he was ineligible to receive the priesthood.

Helvecio later told me about a second experience which he had regarding his receipt of the priesthood. In November of 1977, shortly after Elder James E. Faust had been called to the Twelve, Brother Martins attended a stake conference in Rio de Janeiro, where he lived with his family. Elder Faust was the visiting General Authority, and after the conference he invited Brother Martins to accompany him to the airport. At the airport, he drew Brother Martins aside and told him that President Kimball had asked him to confer with Brother Martins again to make sure he had understood what President Kimball told him a few months before in Sao Paulo. Brother Martins told Elder Faust that he had understood quite clearly—if he were faithful and remained firm in his faithfulness, he would ultimately receive all of the blessings of the gospel!

I do not know this for a fact, but I have the strong feeling that President Kimball's contact with Helvecio Martins, a faithful, patient black man, is one of the things that drove President Kimball to his knees repeatedly, seeking revelation about the policy regarding priesthood.

"A MAP OF AFRICA CAME INTO HIS MIND"

Elder David B. Haight of the Twelve later shared these additional details with me about President Kimball's subsequent keen interest in the life and service of Brother Helvecio Martins:

Elder Haight set apart Helvecio as a counselor in a stake presidency not long after the 1978 Revelation on Priesthood. Elder Haight told me that while his hands were on Helvecio's head, a map of Africa came into his mind in full color with its boundaries clearly delineated. In the blessing, Elder Haight promised Brother Martins that the Lord had a great work for him to perform, and that he would provide important leadership in the future, although he did not mention Africa. He later reported the incident to President Kimball. Elder Haight told me that President Kimball asked him to repeat the experience to him carefully. After he had done so, the Prophet asked him, "Do you see him as a General Authority?"

Elder Haight answered, "Yes."

"Is he ready now?" asked President Kimball.

"No," answered Elder Haight, "but in the future he will be."

"BLACKS AND THE PRIESTHOOD"

Aside from President Kimball's interaction with Helvecio Martins, there were several other key events preceding the 1978 Revelation on Priesthood.

In early March of 1978, President Kimball began discussing the question of blacks and the priesthood with his counselors. He said that his mind was caught up on the subject because of the impending completion and dedication of the Sao Paulo Brazil Temple, a temple that would be serving a numerous people in a great nation where there was a long history of very significant intermarriage between those of South American, European, and African ancestry. I recall that President Kimball made reference to Exodus 20:2 as a point of departure as he discussed this significant issue: "I am the Lord thy God, which have brought thee out of the land of Egypt, out of the house of bondage."

President Kimball said that the only proper basis upon which the Brethren should make a decision opening the doors wide for priesthood blessings for those of all nations would be a revelation from God to the Prophet. President Kimball asked his counselors to begin fasting and praying about the matter as he strived to learn the mind and will of the Lord on this matter.

"A WAKEFUL NIGHT"

A few days after first broaching the subject, President Kimball said he had spent a wakeful night wrestling with the issue of blacks and the priesthood. He said that he felt that the restrictions should be lifted. My recollection is that this was on March 22, 1978.

The Prophet did not elaborate on the basis for this feeling, nor did he discuss any intention to make any announcement. He did ask his counselors how the membership of the Church might react to such a significant change. The reaction of the counselors was interesting. President N. Eldon Tanner told the Prophet that he thought the membership would embrace such a change. President Marion G. Romney said that it would make no difference how the people reacted. He said that should President Kimball receive the inspiration that the time had come to make such a change, that it would be right and that the change should take place regardless of the consequences.

"The native Brazilian missionaries"

In early April of 1978, I was with President Kimball and Elder James E. Faust of the Quorum of the Twelve when the Prophet discussed the dedication of the Sao Paulo Temple. President Kimball told Elder Faust that he wanted to invite all of the native Brazilian missionaries to attend the dedicatory services. Though he did not mention to Elder Faust the fact that he was wrestling with the question of priesthood for those of African ancestry, that was the implication. Elder Faust responded positively to this suggestion, then posed a significant question. He asked, in essence, "How do we generate the spiritual strength to bring down the Iron Curtain and the Bamboo Curtain and take the gospel to all nations?"

I believe that this question posed by Elder Faust deeply impressed President Kimball.

"A MANIFESTATION OF THE WILL OF GOD"

In late April of 1978, President Kimball first broached the subject of the historical priesthood restrictions with all of the Apostles. He then asked all of the Brethren to bend their prayers that he would be able to receive a clear manifestation of the will of God on the matter.

A short time later, I heard President Kimball remark that in all of his service as an Apostle or as President of the Church, he had never exerted his spiritual powers as he was then doing in, as he put it, trying to find his way out of this "labyrinth."

From this point forward, President Kimball began meeting privately with members of the Twelve to hear their views and feelings on the matter.

I believe that in this event in the Prophet's life, we see a dramatic illustration of the application of the so-called "Oliver Cowdery test" set forth in Doctrine and Covenants 9:8: "But, behold, I say unto you, that you must study it out in your mind; then you must ask me if be right . . ."

President Kimball was following this counsel as he wrestled with this significant question.

"A SPIRITUAL PERSONAGE IN THE ROOM"

The following sacred experience occurred on May 4, 1978, in the Upper Room of the Salt Lake Temple a few weeks before the announcement, which is now the subject of Official Declaration 2 in the Doctrine and Covenants. The Upper Room is another name for the Council Room of the First Presidency and Quorum of the Twelve, located on the fourth floor of the Temple. This is the room where the Brethren meet for many hours each Thursday to discuss the governance and direction of the Church.

I feel comfortable in sharing this special experience, because one of the key participants, Elder LeGrand Richards, himself, shared this same experience to Lucile Tate, his biographer, and allowed it to be published in 1982.

On May 4, 1978, President Kimball met with his counselors and all members of the Quorum of the Twelve in the Upper Room of the Temple. I recall that during the meeting President Kimball was most inspiring in his counsel. He said that the Lord is our friend, that everything will work out in the end, and that the Lord will fight our battles for us. He then said, in essence, that when we go down in death, we should have finished our lives "fighting for the rights of the people of the Church."

At the conclusion of the Prophet's testimony, Elder LeGrand Richards of the Twelve asked President Kimball if he could say a few words. This was highly unusual, since in the Church we traditionally allow the presiding authority to speak last, but President Kimball invited Elder Richards to speak.

Elder Richards said that he wanted to relate a spiritual experience, which he had during the meeting. He said that while he sat and listened to President Kimball's testimony, he saw a spiritual personage in the room. He said the personage was seated in a chair above the organ in the corner of the room. He then said that the man had a beard and was dressed in a white suit and looked exactly like President Wilford Woodruff. Elder Richards said that he was not a visionary man, but that what he saw was as plain as anything he had ever seen in his life. He then said that perhaps the reason he saw the personage and no one else in the room saw him was because he was the only person in the room who had met President Woodruff in life. Elder Richards said he remembered President Woodruff. As an eight-year-old boy, LeGrand Richards was in the Salt Lake Temple on the day it was dedicated by President Wilford Woodruff.

I believe that this electrifying spiritual experience had a deep impact upon President Kimball as he sought the will of the Lord. President Woodruff, like President Kimball, was wrestling with a similarly perplexing question—the issue of plural marriage—and he prayerfully sought the will of God. The appearance of President Woodruff in the Salt Lake Temple thus had a very comforting effect upon President Kimball. I believe it confirmed to him that he was doing the will of God in extending the blessings of the priesthood and the temple to all worthy members of the Church, regardless of race or color.

"ALONE IN THE UPPER ROOM"

A week after the appearance of President Wilford Woodruff, I was alone with the Prophet in the Upper Room of the Salt Lake Temple following the conclusion of another meeting. I typically accompanied the Prophet back to the Church Administration Building, and so lingered to wait for him, but on this occasion he told me that he wanted to remain alone in the Upper Room for a while and told me to go ahead without him. I felt certain that he wanted to remain alone to pray and meditate about the question of priesthood for those of African ancestry, which had been on his mind so much during the early months of 1978. He had been talking extensively with members of the Twelve to learn of their feelings on the question. I am sure he realized that this was the most difficult and significant issue that he would face during his service as President of the Church, and he wanted to make sure that what was done represented the mind and the will of the Lord.

A few days after this experience, President Kimball told his counselors that he had spent several hours alone in the temple asking the Lord for guidance and inspiration.

"He Had a Good, Warm Feeling"

On May 30, 1978, President Kimball read a tentative statement to his counselors, removing all priesthood restrictions from those of African ancestry, except for the restrictions of worthiness that apply to all alike. After he read this statement, he said that he had a good, warm feeling about the course of action.

The following day, June 1, 1978, the Prophet asked all of the members of the Twelve to express themselves on the subject of the long-held practice of priesthood restrictions for those of African ancestry. Reference was made to numerous scriptures that affirm that the blessings of the Lord are intended for all unconditionally, except those who fail to keep the commandments of God. It was also noted that there have been times in the past when, in the wisdom of God, the priesthood and its blessings have been withheld from whole classes of people, as in the case of non-Levites in ancient Israel or the Gentiles during the Savior's earthly ministry. President Boyd K. Packer expressed the thought that there was special significance in the appearance of President Wilford Woodruff to Elder LeGrand Richards, saying that this was surely a confirmation that Prophet was doing the will of God in solving this dilemma. There was complete unanimity among the Twelve that the time had come to lift all restrictions upon those of African ancestry.

"Unanimity among the Brethren"

President Kimball's way of addressing the issue of priesthood restrictions on those of African ancestry says much about the man and about the quality of his leadership. It is evident to me that he had already received the confirmation to move forward with this significant change as early as March of 1978, when he first raised the issue to his counselors, and perhaps much sooner. It was in the late spring or early summer of 1977 that he made the startling promise to Helvecio Martins that if he were faithful and remained firm in his faithfulness, he would ultimately receive all of the blessings of the gospel.

As President of the Church, it was his prerogative to move forward with this vast change at any time. But instead, he waited until he had counseled privately with all the leaders of the Church, and only then, when there was true unanimity among the Brethren, did he move forward. He was a wise and careful leader, filled with great compassion and love for the people and for all mankind.

"THE PRAYERFUL STRUGGLE IN THE TEMPLE"

I have already mentioned President Kimball's personal attention to detail. This inherent trait expressed itself in a most revealing and touching manner during the days leading up to the announcement of the Revelation on Priesthood in 1978.

On Wednesday, June 7, 1978, the formal decision was made by the First Presidency and the Quorum of the Twelve to lift all priesthood and temple restrictions from those of African descent. A formal announcement was planned for the following day, June 8, 1978.

Elders Gordon B. Hinckley, Boyd K. Packer, and Bruce R. McConkie of the Quorum of the Twelve, at the invitation of President Kimball, had each previously prepared separate draft statements announcing the decision. President Kimball asked me to review these three drafts and then prepare a final draft, which became the final letter to be issued by the First Presidency and is now contained in Official Declaration 2 in the Doctrine and Covenants.

After receiving this assignment, I returned alone to my office to carry out this most significant assignment. Within an hour and a half, President Kimball came into my office to discuss the statement. He asked that the letter make special mention of the prayerful struggle he had gone through in the temple before receiving an answer.

Accordingly, as I prepared the final draft of the letter on Wednesday afternoon, I included the words, "we have pleaded long and earnestly in behalf of these, our faithful brethren, spending many hours in the Upper Room of the Temple supplicating the Lord for divine guidance" (*see* Doctrine and Covenants, Official Declaration 2).

Later in the afternoon, I took the fourth draft into President Kimball's office, where we read it over together. He expressed satisfaction with it and said that later in the day he would review it with his counselors before Thursday's meetings. The following day the letter was prepared in final form and signed. President Kimball came to my office to sign it. He expressed relief to me that the matter was about to be concluded.

There is a certain poignancy about the way the Prophet concluded this historic action. Instead of signing the official letter in his own office, or in the imposing First Presidency's Council Room on the main floor, he simply walked down the hall to the office of his scribe and signed the letter.

"I HAVE NEVER SEEN A MORE HISTORIC DAY"

On a personal note, I have never seen a more historic day than when President Kimball announced the Revelation on Priesthood. Through this action, the doors to all nations were flung open. When the gospel has been offered to all people without hindrance or let, can the end be near? I bear witness to my family and to all who may hear or read these words that God truly spoke to His Prophet by the power of the Holy Ghost.

Ezra Taft Benson

Thirteenth President of The Church of Jesus Christ of Latter-day Saints

November 1985 – June 1994

Ezra Taft Benson Chronology

August 4, 1899
Ezra Taft Benson is born in Whitney, Idaho, to George T. Benson, Jr., and Sarah Dunkley.

1918
Ezra Taft Benson contracts influenza while in military training in Logan, Utah.

July 1921
Ezra Taft Benson is set apart as a full-time missionary to Great Britain.

1924
Ezra Taft Benson transfers to Brigham Young University following his return from his mission.

Spring of 1926
Ezra Taft Benson graduates with honors from Brigham Young University and is voted Most Popular Man on campus.

July 12, 1926
Ezra Taft Benson and Flora Amussen announce their engagement.

September 10, 1926
Ezra Taft Benson and Flora Amussen are sealed in the Salt Lake Temple by Elder Orson F. Whitney of the Quorum of the Twelve.

July 1927
Ezra Taft Benson and his wife return to Whitney, Idaho, after spending a year doing postgraduate work in agriculture at Iowa State University.

Spring 1928
Ezra Taft Benson and his family move to Preston, Idaho, where he is appointed as agricultural agent for Franklin County.

1929
Ezra Taft Benson moves his family to Boise, Idaho, where he becomes an agricultural economist at the University of Idaho and a specialist for the State of Idaho.

1936
Ezra Taft Benson is given a fellowship grant to study at the University of California at Berkeley. He is appointed to the high council in California, though he had not been released from serving in the stake presidency in Boise.

November 27, 1938
Ezra Taft Benson is sustained as president of the Boise Stake.

January 1939
After counseling with the General Authorities of the Church, Ezra Taft Benson accepts an appointment as the executive secretary of the National Council of Farm Cooperatives in Washington, D.C. This necessitates his release as stake president in Boise.

March 26, 1939
Ezra Taft Benson is released as president of the Boise Stake to enable him to move to Washington D.C. with his family.

June 1940
Ezra Taft Benson is called as the first president of the Washington D.C. Stake.

July 26, 1943
While traveling through Salt Lake City, Ezra Taft Benson is told that President Heber J. Grant wants to visit with him. At a cabin in Emigration Canyon, President Grant calls President Benson as a member of the Quorum of the Twelve.

October 7, 1943
Elder Ezra Taft Benson is ordained and set apart as a member of the Quorum of the Twelve.

March 5, 1944
Elder Ezra Taft Benson is released as president of the Washington D.C. Stake and resigns as the executive secretary of the National Council of Farm Cooperatives. The Bensons then move to Salt Lake City, where he begins his service in the Quorum of the Twelve.

January 29, 1946
Elder Ezra Taft Benson leaves Salt Lake City to serve for eleven months in Europe to help oversee relief efforts given to Church members in the wake of World War II.

August 1947
Elder Ezra Taft Benson gives a talk to the American Institute of Cooperation, which brings him into political prominence with members of the national Republican Party.

1948
During the 1948 U.S. Presidential campaign, New York Governor Thomas E. Dewey seeks advice from Ezra Taft Benson on farming and other matters.

November 1952
U.S. President-elect Dwight D. Eisenhower asks Elder Ezra Taft Benson if he will accept an appointment as Secretary of Agriculture in his new administration.

October 18, 1963
Elder Ezra Taft Benson is called to preside over the European Mission. He spends two years in Europe.

December 1973
When President Harold B. Lee dies unexpectedly, Elder Ezra Taft Benson becomes the President of the Quorum of the Twelve.

November 5, 1985
President Spencer W. Kimball passes away.

November 10, 1985
President Ezra Taft Benson is ordained and set apart as the thirteenth President of the Church.

August 1992

President Ezra Taft Benson's wife, Flora Amussen Benson, passes away in Salt Lake City.

May 30, 1994

President Ezra Taft Benson, thirteenth President of The Church of Jesus Christ of Latter-day Saints, dies at age 94.

"A Portrait of President Benson"

It is not difficult for me to create a word portrait of President Ezra Taft Benson, who was one of the most fascinating, complex, whole-souled, and genuine people I have ever met.

I first met Elder Ezra Taft Benson on Thursday, April 9, 1970. On that day I had been greatly surprised to be invited to meet in the early morning hours with the three members of the First Presidency of the Church. At the time I was a Salt Lake City attorney with a very busy law practice. I walked over to the Church Administration Building alone that morning before going to my law office for the day. I was ushered into the council room and introduced to the First Presidency: Joseph Fielding Smith, Harold B. Lee, and N. Eldon Tanner. I then had the most significant interview of my life, the upshot of which was that I was asked by the First Presidency of the Church to give up my legal career and commence serving immediately as the secretary to the First Presidency. I told them I would, and my life was forever changed.

A few minutes later I walked to the Salt Lake Temple with the First Presidency and went with them to the fourth floor Council Room. As the four of us walked into the room, the members of the Quorum of the Twelve stood in front of their upholstered chairs, which were arranged in a semicircle facing the west, where there stood the empty chairs of the First Presidency and a desk for the secretary to the First Presidency. I was then taken around the circle by President Harold B. Lee and introduced to each member of the Twelve, shaking hands with them as I went. Second in seniority in the Twelve was Elder Ezra Taft Benson, then seventy-one years of age.

My first impressions of Ezra Taft Benson were profound, and they altered several false preconceptions I had about him. It is interesting how a close association with a man or woman has the power to alter the opinions we might have about them beforehand. Before my close acquaintance with President Benson, I had always viewed him as a rather austere, no-nonsense man with a perpetually serious expression on his countenance. This may have been due to the serious, never humorous, content of his public sermons. When I first met him on April 9, 1970, he shook my hand warmly and looked with great kindness into my eyes. Indeed, on that occasion President Benson showed toward me an attitude and demeanor that characterized all of our personal relationships during the succeeding decades—he was open, friendly, and cordial. There was nothing feigned or phony or forced in his interaction. He was genuine and whole-hearted. Indeed, over the years I have come to believe that the major quality in President Benson's makeup is that he is genuine and whole souled.

So that is a portrait of one of the most unique and fascinating men I have ever met—a man whom I love and sustain as a Prophet, Seer, and Revelator!

Over time, my impressions of President Benson sharpened and deepened. As I began to observe him at close hand—day by day, over a period of months, then years, then decades—I saw that he was actually a man of great humility. This caught me by surprise, as he had served in the leading councils of both the Church and the U.S. government. But despite this, he was wholly without pretension. He was very friendly and outgoing. In private settings he never showed the stridency and austerity that seemed to come through when he preached in public on doctrinal or on political themes.

"His birth was a great miracle"

President Ezra Taft Benson often spoke with awe of his mother, Sarah Dunkley Benson, who bore him on August 4, 1899. President Benson was the oldest of eleven children born by his mother. In his long life she took on something of the quality of a saint or a guardian angel.

President Benson almost didn't survive. His birth was a considered a great miracle in the Benson family. He was delivered by a local medical doctor, with his two grandmothers assisting as midwives. The future Prophet and his mother both almost lost their lives during the delivery. He was so large at birth—almost twelve pounds—that the doctor almost despaired of saving the mother. Crude birthing instruments, such as were used in the nineteenth century, were employed and did much damage both to mother and child. After the long and excruciating delivery, the big baby boy emerged bloody and lifeless. The doctor set the infant's body aside, thinking that he had not survived the birth, and turned all his attention upon the mother, who was hemorrhaging terribly. The two grandmothers took the lifeless baby boy into the next room where they bathed him alternately in warm and cold water. Soon the doctor was surprised to hear lusty cries from the next room.

"Two Prophets Walked Out of the Same Farmland"

President Benson was born and raised in the tiny Mormon settlement of Whitney, Idaho. Named after Mormon Apostle Orson F. Whitney, it had a population of only a few hundred people. A few miles away in the equally tiny village of Clifton, another future Prophet—President Harold B. Lee—had been born a few months before President Benson's birth. It is remarkable that in this vast worldwide Church, two future Church Presidents should have been born in the same year and in the same remote and obscure farming community. Two Prophets walked out of the same farmland, as it were. Both boys in their teen years attended the Oneida Stake Academy located in Preston, Idaho. There they became great friends. In those days President Benson went by the nickname "T" and President Lee went by the nickname "Hal."

"T" and "Hal" had much in common aside from their common birth and upbringing in rural Idaho. Both of them went on to serve missions in England. Both married remarkable women who brought out the best in their husbands. Both had a flair for public life and served in political office, President Lee as a Salt Lake City Commissioner and President Benson as the U.S. Secretary of Agriculture. And both were called at relatively young ages to the Quorum of the Twelve, where they went through a decades-long process of refining and tutoring in the presence of great men.

"He Became a Man at Age Twelve"

As the oldest of eleven children, President Benson had to grow up fast. His early life was filled with farm duties—caring for horses, cows, chickens, and pigs; and hoeing, planting, irrigating, weeding, and harvesting. He followed his father around the farm like a little shadow, always willing to work and to learn. And amid all of this labor, there was the daily chore of milking the cows. Milking was either a never-ending burden or a delight. For young Ezra Taft Benson it was a delight, and never a burden. Little Ezra Taft Benson took to farm life naturally. He always said that he loved hard work. As a boy, his only life aspiration was to become a successful farmer, like his father before him.

When Ezra Taft Benson turned twelve, his father was called as a full-time missionary to labor in the Northern States. This was not uncommon in the period, to call a mature married man to leave his family and occupation to serve in the ministry, though the practice placed heavy burdens upon the families left behind. As the oldest child in a large family, Ezra Taft Benson assumed the workload of a grown man when his father departed. He assumed the daily responsibility of caring for the family's dairy herd. He became a man at age twelve.

"Bunkmates on Either Side of Him Died"

When the United States declared war on Germany and the other Axis powers in 1917, Ezra Taft Benson felt an immediate urge to join the military. He counseled with his parents, and it was decided that he should leave the Oneida Stake Academy and enroll in a military training program at Utah State University in Logan, Utah. He signed the necessary papers and traveled to Logan to begin his training. He lived in a military-style barracks on campus with other new recruits, most of whom were from farming communities in the Cache Valley.

In the fall of 1917, the directors of the military camp decided to give the recruits a two-week leave to return home to their farms to help with the harvest. An announcement was made to the recruits.

The day before the recruits were to return home, Ezra awoke in the morning with a powerful spiritual prompting that he should go home immediately and not wait for the next day. He resisted the prompting and went about his training and military duties as usual, but had the prompting a second and then a third time. He went to his training officer and asked for special permission to return home a day early. Permission was given to him. He left the military camp and caught a ride north to Whitney, where he arrived home about noon.

Later the same day, young Ezra developed a very high fever, and he became delirious. The doctors diagnosed that he was stricken with influenza, which was then sweeping the world in a deadly epidemic. For several days he lay in bed, drifting in and out of consciousness. In one of the moments when he was conscious, he heard the doctor saying that everything had been done medically for the boy, and that only the power of God could save his life. He was then aware of his father and grandfather laying hands upon his head to anoint and bless him.

After receiving a priesthood blessing, President Benson's fever broke, and he began to recover. He later learned that the day he left the military camp, an influenza outbreak had affected most of his fellow recruits. His bunkmates on either side of him died. He lost many friends, including his cousin, George B. Parkinson. Ezra Taft Benson always believed that the spiritual prompting he had received to leave the camp a day early had saved his life.

"A BEAUTIFUL GIRL IN A SPORTS CAR"

After President Benson recovered fully from the influenza in 1918, he enrolled full time as a student at Utah State Agricultural College. He had saved his money and, with the support of his parents, he made preparations to move back to Logan for the school year. While on a visit to the campus to make his final preparations, he was with a group of friends, walking along the street. A beautiful girl drove by in a sports car. The boys watched the girl drive away, and then were surprised when "T" Benson, as he was called then, turned to his friends and announced that this was the girl he would marry some day! They laughed at him because the girl was Flora Amussen, a member of a very wealthy family who was also one of the most popular and beautiful girls at the college. The thought that "T" Benson, a farm boy from Whitney would stand a chance with the beautiful and accomplished Flora Amussen was beyond imagination.

Not long after seeing Flora Amussen for the first time, Ezra was shocked when she appeared in his Sunday School class in little Whitney, Idaho. Flora was the weekend guest of his cousin, Ann Dunkley. Then Ann's father asked Ezra if he would mind driving the two girls on an outing to Lava Hot Springs that afternoon. Ezra agreed immediately, and then arranged to have someone handle his evening milking chores. During the drive to and from Lava Hot Springs, Ezra and Flora got acquainted. Ezra discovered that despite an upbringing of privilege and wealth, Flora was outgoing, modest, and humble. He became very interested in this girl.

Once Ezra settled in Logan for the school year and started his studies, he began to date Flora Amussen, and their relationship blossomed over the next two years. Then Ezra received a mission call to serve in Great Britain in 1921. After being set apart for his mission, he traveled with his fellow missionaries from Salt Lake City to Ogden, Utah, where the main train lines ran. Flora Amussen traveled with them, and on the train trip they had a talk about their future. During his mission they had what was then called an "understanding." They understood that, in all likelihood, they would one day be married.

"Our Benson"

Ezra Taft Benson served his full-time mission in England at a time when the Church faced great opposition. For example, a lurid silent film entitled *Trapped by the Mormons* was released in 1922 and then shown throughout England by ministers of the Church of England to deter their parishioners from giving the young Mormon missionaries a listening ear. The movie portrayed the young missionaries as degenerates who were trying to lure women to Utah for immoral purposes.

I have often thought that this unprecedented spirit of opposition was a great training ground for young Ezra Taft Benson, as it would also be for his fellow Cache Valley farm friend, Harold B. Lee. It taught him that the work could move forward despite fierce opposition. It also taught him patience in the face of unrelenting personal attacks.

In the mission field Ezra Taft Benson fell under the sway of two great leaders of the Church. His first mission president was Elder Orson F. Whitney of the Quorum of the Twelve. The older Apostle was to have a great influence upon the spiritual life of the young missionary. Ezra Taft Benson was electrified when he heard Elder Whitney's testimony of having seen the Savior in a vision. It had a profound effect upon the young man's life. Later Elder Whitney. would perform the marriage ceremony of young Elder Benson to his wife, Flora Amussen.

President Whitney first assigned Ezra Taft Benson to labor in the city of Carlisle in the Newcastle District. A short time later, President Whitney was released and replaced by a young mission president, David O. McKay. President McKay transferred Ezra Taft Benson from Carlisle to

Sunderland, where he served as the conference clerk and branch president in the Sunderland Branch. President McKay was a second great leader who was to have a lasting impact upon Ezra Taft Benson's life. In Sunderland, under the leadership of President McKay, Elder Benson began teaching the saints the then-novel concept of "every member a missionary." He also began counseling the saints not to immigrate to America, but to remain in place in their branches in England to build up the Church locally. Ezra Taft Benson completed his mission serving as branch president in Sunderland and was much beloved by the British saints, who often called him, "our Benson!"

"The Young Couple"

Following his return from the mission field, President Benson received permission to tour for a month in Europe with another missionary, and then returned home. Passing through Salt Lake City on his way home to Whitney, Idaho, he received a special blessing from the Church patriarch, who promised him that he would live to a "goodly age" and that his name would be held in "honorable remembrance" throughout all time.

Back in Logan, he picked up his studies at Utah State and also his relationship with Flora Amussen, who had waited for him during his mission to England. Interestingly, the young couple decided against marrying at that point, and instead decided that Flora should serve a full-time mission of her own. She was called to the Hawaii Mission, and President Benson now took his turn waiting for her to return. During her mission he transferred to Brigham Young University, where he graduated with honors in 1926, the same year in which he married Flora upon her return from Hawaii.

"A STRIKING CONTRAST"

There was a striking contrast between the backgrounds of President Ezra Taft Benson and Sister Flora Amussen Benson. Sister Flora Benson was the daughter of Carl Christian Amussen, a wealthy Salt Lake jeweler. Her father died when she was still a baby, but left her mother, Barbara Smith Amussen a substantial legacy, and little Flora grew up amid wealth and comfort. She was raised in an urban home of privilege, culture, and refinement. She enjoyed many of the good things of life. For example, when President Benson first laid eyes upon his future wife, she was driving a little sports car around the college town of Logan, Utah. She was an expert tennis player, winning Utah State University's women's singles titles. In short, she was everything that the country boy, "T" Benson, was not—well educated, cultured, and refined. He had been raised on a farm, the oldest in a large family, where all had to work hard merely to survive.

President Benson often commented upon his wife's superior upbringing and jokingly made mention of the fact that he had "married up." But despite his humble upbringing, President Benson was a man of great native ability who had the potential to be molded into someone of achievement. In that sense, Sister Benson was in no way superior to her husband, but she became the catalyst for him to reach toward heights of education and culture he might not otherwise have sought. This impression that President Benson was a man of superior native ability was universally shared by those in the Church who knew and loved him.

"An Exemplary Latter-day Saint Family"

President Benson did post-graduate work at both Iowa State University and at the University of California at Berkeley. Later, he accepted a position with the National Council of Farm Cooperatives in Washington D.C. During each of these moves, Flora and his children accompanied him. In each place they lived, they lived the standards of an exemplary Latter-day Saint family, with family prayer, family home evening, and daily scripture study being strictly observed.

In each place they went, Ezra Taft Benson was also called upon for significant Church service. For example, he served as a counselor in a stake presidency and then a stake president in Boise, Idaho, and then as a stake president in Washington, D.C.

"The Scoutmaster shaved his head"

The wards of the Oneida Stake at the north end of the Cache Valley were among the earliest sponsors of the Boy Scouts of America. Ezra Taft Benson was a boy scout as a young man and a lifelong proponent of the program for boys and young men. He later became the scoutmaster in the Whitney Ward and was what we may call a "youth man," always willing to help the young people of the Church in their activity programs.

As an old man, the subject of scouting was seldom mentioned without his reminiscence about serving as a scoutmaster with the boys from Whitney. He was especially fond of recalling a special troop outing that included a hike over the mountain to Bear Lake. The hike was a reward for the boys' winning a singing competition. Because of a dare, all of the boys wore their hair short in what was then called a "crew cut," while the scoutmaster, Ezra Taft Benson, shaved his head completely for the trek. The camaraderie he built with the boys of his troop lasted a lifetime.

As one of the senior leaders of the Church, Ezra Taft Benson was a tireless proponent for the Church's continuation of its sponsorship of the Boy Scouts of America, and he received some of scouting's most distinguished awards.

"THE CABIN ITSELF WAS A SACRED PLACE"

During the hottest weeks of the summer, President Heber J. Grant often traveled up Emigration Canyon to a small cabin, where he spent many happy and pleasant days. The cabin was rustic, with a stone fireplace heating a large living room. There was a small bedroom adjoining the living room, where President Grant slept. Here the Prophet was not far from downtown Salt Lake City and could transact Church business during daylight hours and receive visitors, and at night he could enjoy the utter peace and quiet and the invigorating coolness of the mountains.

On July 26, 1943, President Grant was staying in his cabin in Emigration Canyon when he invited forty-four-year-old Ezra Taft Benson to visit him in the canyon. There, in a private room, he extended a call to the younger man to serve in the Quorum of the Twelve. President Benson often spoke about the sacredness of this moment when he was interviewed privately by the Prophet and called to the Apostleship. For President Benson, the cabin itself was also a sacred place—a place where his entire life was changed and reshaped.

A few months after he was called and ordained as the thirteenth President of the Church, President Benson made arrangements to visit the old cabin in Emigration Canyon where President Grant had called him to the Twelve. The cabin was then owned by the Cannon family, and they invited President Benson and his family to visit. President Benson went alone into the little bedroom adjoining the living room. He closed the door and spent some time alone. He then invited his family to join him, and they sat for a long time reminiscing about how the call from President

REMEMBERING SEVEN PROPHETS

Grant had altered the lives of the Benson family during the nearly forty-five years that had intervened since his call in 1943. Those years had taken President Benson around the world in the service of the Church, to Washington, D.C., where he served in the highest councils of government, and back home to Salt Lake City, where he ultimately became President of the Church.

"Cities Leveled by Intense Bombing"

For nearly a year following World War II, President Benson lived in Europe, where he directed the administration of relief to Latter-day Saints affected by the war. He established a headquarters in London, England, and then made numerous trips throughout Europe. He often spoke of his shock at the devastation that had occurred in Europe as a result of the war, particularly in Germany. All of the major cities had essentially been leveled by intense Allied bombing, and hundreds of thousands, even millions, of people were displaced. He organized the Church's efforts to distribute welfare commodities shipped from the United States to the destitute and scattered saints. He also worked to supervise the finding of lost members of the Church and to strengthen and train local leaders and missionaries.

In later years, President Benson spoke often of his hatred of dictatorships, which arose from what he observed firsthand in Europe in 1946 to 1947. It explains much about his great, energized attacks upon Communism in the years ahead. It was also during this period that he came to the attention of prominent Republicans in Washington, D.C. It was this prominence that caused his name to surface in 1952 as a possible member of President-elect Dwight D. Eisenhower's Cabinet.

"YOU OUGHT TO ACCEPT"

After General Dwight D. Eisenhower. was elected as the U.S. President in November of 1952, Elder Ezra Taft Benson was asked if he would accept an appointment as the Secretary of Agriculture. Because Elder Benson served as a member of the Quorum of the Twelve, he counseled with President David O. McKay about the request. President Benson told me that President McKay was initially hesitant about the request, and suggested that he wait to decide until he had met with President-elect Eisenhower in person. The counsel the Prophet gave to Elder Benson was that "if the invitation comes in the proper spirit, you ought to accept."

Elder Benson subsequently flew to New York, where he had a private interview with President Eisenhower. President Eisenhower told Elder Benson that should he accept the appointment, he would never be asked to promote any policy with which he disagreed. Given the spirit in which the appointment was made, Elder Benson accepted.

"Joseph in Pharaoh's Kingdom"

I, along with many thousands of other Latter-day Saints, watched with great interest in the weeks following the election when President Eisenhower named Elder Ezra Taft Benson of the Quorum of the Twelve to a post in his Cabinet as Secretary of Agriculture. Many members of the Church watched Elder Benson's career in Washington with great interest. Many people shared his conservative views and admired his integrity, intelligence, and hard work. He and his family were good exemplars of a Latter-day Saint family, and generally the Church membership basked in the glow of Elder Benson's service and reputation.

Brother D. Arthur Haycock, who served as a private secretary to several Presidents of the Church, also served for several years on Elder Benson's staff in Washington, D.C., during the years of the Eisenhower Administration. Arthur had some significant insights into President Benson's years in Washington, D.C., which he often shared with me. According to Arthur, Elder Benson began his service as the Secretary of Agriculture with the thought that he was in a sense a modern-day Joseph, elevated to a high position in Pharaoh's Kingdom, to fill the granaries of the United States against the day of famine.

"To Open Doors for the Church"

My sense is that President Benson's years in Washington, D.C. had a profound impact upon the man. It opened up avenues of worldly influence to him that had never before been open to a Mormon, let alone to a General Authority. While in Washington, President Benson made hundreds of contacts, including contacts with foreign heads of state, which would ultimately be of great help to the Church in the years to come.

President Benson was aware of his influence, and he used it carefully for the blessing of the work. He knew that politics and influence could open doors for the Church. Even decades after his withdrawal from government service, the topic of politics and government leaders, past and present, continued to occupy his conversation. In about 1971, a few months after I began my work with the First Presidency of the Church, Elder Benson invited me to pay a visit to his office. He was pleased to show me the chair, the government flags, the photographs, and other memorabilia brought from his office in Washington. He spoke of his time with President Dwight D. Eisenhower and about the man's character. He called my attention to a picture of Eisenhower's Cabinet and discussed it for a long time, commenting on the personalities of the various members. All this he did without an air of condescension or pride, but in a matter-of-fact manner. This experience of sitting in the leading councils of both the Church and the U.S. government was simply a part of President Benson's makeup. It was a part of "who he was."

Years after this first visit to President Benson's private office, I gained further insight into the effect of his years of service in the U.S. Cabinet. There was an aura of stature and notoriety that this service gave to President Benson and the Church, which lingered for many years. He was a celebrity, both in and out of the Church, and he knew very well how to make good use of his celebrity. He seemed determined to use his experience and status as a former Cabinet member for the good of the Church. For example, he was always ready to use that card to open doors to people of significance who might help the cause of the Church. He seemed to feel that the Lord had placed the tools of status and influence into his hands, and he was determined to use it to advance his work as a minister of the gospel and a representative of the Church.

An example of this special influence occurred in the late 1960's, almost a decade after President Benson concluded his service in the Cabinet. Former Israeli Prime Minister David Ben Gurion contacted Ezra Taft Benson in Salt Lake City and invited the Apostle to pay him a visit in Israel. David Ben Gurion had heard of Orson Hyde's dedication of the Holy Land for the return of the Jews in 1841. He wanted a copy of the dedicatory prayer for a history of Israel he was writing, and to discuss it with a Mormon of stature who could explain it to him. President Benson paid the great Israeli patriot a visit in Israel and had a lengthy discussion with him. David Ben Gurion told President Benson that the Mormon people seemed to understand the Jews better than anyone else on earth.

On another occasion, in the late 1970's, President Benson was asked to make contact with some of his long-time Egyptian contacts on behalf of the Church in an effort to obtain recognition for the Church there. All of this opened doors for the Church in both Israel and Egypt and in many other parts of the world, due in part to the former government service and reputation of Ezra Taft Benson.

"HE CULTIVATED A SENSE OF FAMILY"

As the Secretary of Agriculture, Ezra Taft Benson directed one of the largest departments in the U.S. government, with tens of thousands of employees located around the world. In order to survive administratively, he had to become a master leader and to delegate broadly. He brought this skill of strong administration with him when he became the President of the Quorum of the Twelve and then later as the thirteenth President of the Church. His ability to delegate freed him from administrative detail and gave him freedom to see the broad direction of the Church and to chart a safe course. It also allowed his Brethren to develop as they grew under the weight of delegated responsibility. With this skill, he also cultivated a sense of family among those who worked with him. He treated all of his fellow laborers as family. He took a genuine interest in those who made up his inner circle, often expressing his love and appreciation for them and going out of his way to perform thoughtful acts of service.

"HE LEARNED TO THINK ON HIS FEET"

President Benson was one of the most eloquent speakers among the General Authorities of the Church. His speaking skill was first honed when he served as a young missionary in England. There he learned to think on his feet as he spoke to unruly crowds on street corners. He also gained extensive experience in public speaking as he served in various teaching and executive positions in the Church. Then during his Washington years as a member of the U.S. Cabinet, he learned poise under pressure as he jousted with Presidents, Senators, Congressmen, bureaucrats, and lobbyists in the Capitol, and with politicians out on the hustings. Regardless of the forum in which he spoke, he was always earnest, sincere, and articulate. He conveyed the impression of being absolutely honest and above board. He could be very blunt sometimes, especially when he was speaking about communism or moral transgression. Usually, however, he was very positive and upbeat in his speaking.

"HE OCCASIONALLY TOLD A GOOD STORY"

Despite his formal and earnest manner as a speaker at the pulpit, in private settings President Ezra Taft Benson was warm, friendly, and even humorous. Unlike many popular Church speakers, President Benson seldom, if ever, used humor in speaking. But in private he enjoyed a good laugh and occasionally told a good story. Here are three of my favorite stories shared by President Benson:

On one occasion, President Benson shared this story in private to a small group of his close associates: When a man boasted to his wife that he had been promoted to vice president in his company, she seemed unimpressed. "Why, there is even a vice president in charge of prunes at the supermarket," she said. Doubting her word, the husband later called the supermarket and asked to speak to the vice president in charge of prunes. "Packaged or bulk?" asked the voice.

President Benson shared this story one day at the dinner table: He told about the man who insisted that his wife serve only margarine at the table because butter had become too expensive. Once, while guests were being treated to butter at the family table, one of the sons, weary of margarine, went into the kitchen and brought in a plate of butter, which he then helped himself to, spreading it lavishly on his bread. Startled, the boys' father, hoping to restrain and instruct his son, observed that the butter cost sixty cents a pound. Undeterred, the boy answered, "For butter, I would say it's very well worth it."

President Benson once told me this very amusing story: When a man who had died presented himself at the Pearly Gates, the attendant there asked to see his temple recommend. The man promptly excused himself and said he would be right back. He was gone a very long time and when he returned the attendant asked what had taken so long. "I have been looking all over hell for my bishop," the man answered.

"WE'LL SEE IF YOUR SPIRITUAL ANTENNA IS UP"

In 1970 I had a memorable personal spiritual experience involving Elder Ezra Taft Benson, who was then a member of the Quorum of the Twelve. I recount it because it shows the miraculous way in which the Spirit works with the leading Brethren of the Church, and it also reveals something of the character of President Benson.

At the time of this experience Russell M. Nelson, now a member of the Twelve, was then the President of the Bonneville Stake where my wife and I resided with our family. It was stake conference weekend, and the General Authority visitor was Elder Benson. During the general session, I was sitting with my wife, Helen, and our children in the chapel. President Nelson stood up and announced that Elder Benson now had a special matter of business to transact. At that moment, I had an impression that Elder Benson would call Harold Bennett, a long-time member of our stake, as a stake patriarch. Impulsively I leaned over and whispered that impression to Helen who was seated beside me, who looked at me skeptically and responded, "We'll see if your spiritual antenna is up this morning." I'm sure that part of her skepticism arose from the fact that we already had a stake patriarch and there was no reason to expect a second to be called, sustained, and ordained. Elder Benson walked to the pulpit and amid gasps of surprise and murmurs of approval from the congregation, presented the name of Harold Bennett as an additional stake patriarch. Helen and I exchanged a meaningful glance. We both knew that for some reason the Spirit had given me a true flash of inspiration about this surprise call.

Later in the same meeting, the new patriarch, Harold Bennett, was called on to speak by President Russell M. Nelson. In his remarks, the new patriarch told, in substance, this story: "Several years ago as I rode home alone from work one evening, a voice spoke to me and said, 'LeGrand Richards will be called as the new member of the Twelve.' When I got home, I went into the kitchen where my wife Emily was preparing the evening meal. I hugged her and then said, 'Emily. I know who the new member of the Twelve will be.' 'Oh?' she answered. 'Who is it?' I told her it would be LeGrand Richards. 'Oh, you must be mistaken, Hal,' she responded. 'LeGrand Richards is the Presiding Bishop. The Brethren surely wouldn't call him.' I told her, 'Well, that's what the voice said.' LeGrand Richards was, indeed, called to the Twelve as the voice had told me. Then this morning, in the interval between the time the phone rang at our home and the time I answered it, that same voice said to me, 'You will be called by Elder Ezra Taft Benson as a patriarch.' On the line was President Russell M. Nelson who said that Elder Benson wanted to talk to me privately at the stake center. When I came here, Elder Benson called me as a patriarch."

This experience occurred not long after I was called to work as the secretary to the First Presidency. A few days following this incident, I happened to be at work visiting with Elder Benson, and I mentioned the impression I had had at the previous Sunday's stake conference. He listened with great interest, and then told me, "The decision to call another patriarch was not made until early Sunday morning. There were several men under consideration. Then the clear prompting came to me that it was to be Harold Bennett." Elder Benson told me that this was an illustration of the truth of the work. It shows that the Spirit is at work both among the leaders of the Church as well as with ordinary saints. He said that it reminded him of the teaching of the Prophet Joseph Smith, that "God hath not revealed anything to Joseph, but what he will make known unto the Twelve, and even the least Saint may know all things as fast as he is able to bear them" (*Teachings of the Prophet Joseph Smith*).

"Two Future Church Presidents"

During President Kimball's final months of life, when President Gordon B. Hinckley was the only physically active member of the First Presidency, President Benson developed a special relationship with President Hinckley. It was a powerful lesson to see President Benson give such deference and respect to his position as a counselor in the First Presidency. At the same time, President Hinckley had the wisdom to counsel often with President Benson, who he knew at any moment could become the senior Apostle upon the death of President Kimball. It was an interesting time to observe this, and it strengthened my estimation of the qualities of followership and leadership in President Ezra Taft Benson.

President Gordon B. Hinckley directed the Church by delegation of authority for many months while Presidents Spencer W. Kimball and Marion G. Romney were not well. He handled it efficiently but not without trauma. One aspect of the work that troubled him especially was considering the cases of cancellation of temple sealings, divorce clearances, and the restoration of blessings. Ordinarily these matters were heard by the full First Presidency, but with President Kimball and Romney physically unable to be in the office, President Hinckley sat alone in the consideration of these heavy matters, with only me at his side as his scribe and secretary. He often told me how uncomfortable he felt in handling these matters alone and sensed the need for additional counsel in deciding them. At that point he began to invite President Benson to join us each Tuesday morning for this purpose. This practice continued for many months until the time of

President Kimball's death. Although seven years older than he, with almost twenty years of seniority in the Apostleship and with vastly greater experience in international affairs, President Benson was always perfectly subordinate to President Hinckley through all the months of this unusual relationship. President Benson showed that same deference when counseling with the Twelve and with the other General Authorities.

President Hinckley also looked to President Benson for leadership and direction in other areas during this same time period. With both President Kimball and President Romney often unwell and out of the office, it was only natural, as President Benson was senior to him in the Apostleship and would likely become the next President of the Church. For example, President Hinckley called in President Benson for counsel in purchasing properties for future temples.

This cooperation between two future Presidents of the Church, Ezra Taft Benson and Gordon B. Hinckley, was a great testimony builder for me. It showed the wisdom and leadership of both men, as well as their Christlike attributes of kindness and patience. This manner of leadership and followership adds great stability to the administration of the Church and demonstrates the wisdom of a policy whereby the senior Apostle succeeds to leadership on the death or disability of the Prophet.

"THE PROPHETIC MANTLE"

Those of us who worked closely with President Ezra Taft Benson at the time of his ordination as the thirteenth President of the Church were all inspired by the way in which the prophetic mantle quickly fell upon him. From the day of his ordination, he was greatly magnified.

It is interesting that many of the themes President Benson emphasized during his tenure as President emerged in his private conversations and in his public sermons in the earliest days and weeks after his ordination. For example, in every conversation or discussion and in every sermon he gave in those earliest days, I heard him give special emphasis to *The Book of Mormon*. He also went to great lengths in expressing love for everyone. I had witnessed the same phenomenon occur following the ordinations of Presidents Harold B. Lee and Spencer W. Kimball.

"No Empty Chairs"

President Benson had powerful feelings for his family. He was intensely loyal to his family. It was said if you challenged one of the Bensons, you should be prepared to take on the whole family. In times of trial, in times of illness, in times of emergency, they spoke as with a single voice. When job promotions or advancements or moves to this city or that were being considered, the entire family was consulted. An achievement of one member became a cause for celebration by the entire family. And when one of them faced a special task, all joined in to lend support. So when President Benson rose to speak in General Conference, the one sitting at the end of the Benson bench would whisper, "Pray for Dad." That message would be passed from one to the other down the row until all were united in praying for the family patriarch as he stood at the pulpit in the Tabernacle. And if a family friend were seated on the row, he would be temporarily admitted into the Benson prayer chain. A favorite wish expressed by President Benson was that in the hereafter there would be "no empty chairs" in the Benson family circle.

President and Sister Benson enjoyed an unusually close relationship. This became especially evident during the 1970's when Sister Flora Benson began to experience some health problems. I remember that one day Sister Benson was hospitalized, and President Benson called me, asking that her name be placed upon the special prayer roll of the First Presidency and Quorum of the Twelve. He told me that she was feeling very uneasy in the hospital, being separated from President Benson. "She is all right while I am with her," he told me, "but she dreads being alone."

It was President Benson's powerful feeling for his family—past, present and future—which prompted him to direct that he be buried in the little country cemetery overlooking his hometown of Whitney, Idaho. When Sister Flora Benson died in 1992, he had a large headstone prepared which contained all the relevant facts for both of them, except the date of his death. And unlike any other headstone I have ever seen, it also had the names of all of their children carved in stone.

It reminded me of the Prophet Joseph Smith's statement, made at a funeral in Nauvoo:

> I will tell you what I want. If tomorrow I shall be called to lie in yonder tomb, in the morning of the resurrection let me strike hands with my father, and cry, 'My father,' and he will say, 'My son, my son,' as soon as the rock rends and before we come out of our graves. . . . And when the voice calls for the dead to arise, suppose I am laid by the side of my father, what would be the first joy of my heart? To meet my father, my mother, my brother, my sister. (*History of the Church,* 5:361-62).

"WHAT'S BEST FOR THE KINGDOM?"

I often heard President Ezra Taft Benson pose this rhetorical question, when faced with questions of importance in the administration of the Church: "What's best for the Kingdom?" If there were ever a significant question about missionary work, temples, family history, Church Welfare, or a myriad other issues, President Benson would often pause before speaking, and ask, "What's best for the Kingdom?" Sometimes the answer he received led to surprising results. After asking this question, he very often laid aside his first, impulsive course of action, and chose something of more lasting value.

This question became a kind of touchstone by which he guided not only the Church, but also his daily walk as a man and a disciple of Jesus Christ. I am confident that he became a better man, husband, father, grandfather, disciple, Church leader, and President of the Church by constantly asking himself, "What's best for the Kingdom?"

"I LOOK UPON YOU AS A TRUE FRIEND"

In the days before I ended my service as the secretary to the First Presidency and was subsequently called to the Seventy, I was privileged to spend several hours with President Benson alone. At the time, President Benson was just commencing his service as the thirteenth President of the Church. During one of our meetings he said to me, in substance, "Brother Gibbons, I am so grateful for what you have done for me. I look upon you as a true friend." On another occasion, I expressed to him the hope that one day I would be able to write his biography, as I had already written biographies of a dozen Presidents of the Church. At the time there was only a single biography of President Benson in print, written by Sheri L. Dew. He referred to this one biography and protested that anyone would ever want a second biography of him. When I expressed the opinion that over time there would be several biographies of him written, he indicated he would be honored to have me write his biography.

"Poise and Self-Control"

If I were asked to name President Benson's salient characteristics, I would give this list in order: integrity, perseverance, faith in God and the Church, love of family, and patriotism.

Poise and self-control also appear high on the list. In more than twenty years of personal association with him, in conversations with others who knew him well, and in reviewing voluminous documents about his life while writing his biography, I found or learned of no instance when he allowed his temper or anger to dominate his conduct. I know of many instances when he was heavily provoked, but in no case did he ever lose his temper. He was always in control of himself. His feelings were kept in check. And some of his feelings ran very deep. Elder Joseph Anderson of the Seventy, whom I succeeded as secretary to the First Presidency, told me that he had seen several occasions when Ezra Taft Benson was provoked by strong personal attacks. Elder Anderson said these attacks would have angered and upset almost any man, but they left Ezra Taft Benson completely unruffled.

"No weapon that is formed against thee"

President Ezra Taft Benson was a thoughtful, introspective man. He lived very much within himself. My sense is that he had deep-seated thoughts and aspirations that he nourished inside, but which were seldom, if ever, divulged to others, except, perhaps, to members of his own family. And I would not doubt that there were some sacred things that he told to no one, even to his own wife and children.

I gained some insight into his inner world during a three-hour conversation I had with him shortly after his ordination as President of the Church. During that time, he confided to me that he had long carried around in his wallet a piece of paper on which is quoted this scripture:

> No weapon that is formed against thee shall prosper; and every tongue that shall revile against thee in judgment thou shalt condemn. This is the heritage of the servants of the Lord, and their righteousness is of me, saith the Lord. (Isaiah 54:17 and 3 Nephi 22:17)

HOWARD W. HUNTER

Fourteenth President of The Church of Jesus
Christ of Latter-day Saints

June 1994 – March 1995

HOWARD W. HUNTER CHRONOLOGY

November 14, 1907
Howard W. Hunter is born in Salt Lake City, Utah, to John William Hunter and Nellie Rasmussen Hunter.

April 4, 1920
President Howard W. Hunter is baptized in Boise, Idaho at age twelve.

June 1926
President Howard W. Hunter graduates from high school in Boise, Idaho, and begins a career as a professional pianist and bandleader. He puts together a five-man combo called "Hunter's Croonaders."

January 5, 1927
President Howard W. Hunter and "Hunters Croonaders" embark from Seattle, Washington, on the *SS President Jackson*, a cruise ship, for an extended tour of the Far East, with the band providing evening music for the entertainment of the passengers.

March 1928
President Howard W. Hunter decides to move to Los Angeles, California, and begins taking night classes at the American Institute of Banking while continuing his musical career. He also meets his future wife, Clara May Jeffs, in his LDS ward in Los Angeles.

June 6, 1931
President Howard W. Hunter plays his last engagement as a professional musician. That night he packs up his professional band instruments and never uses them again. Four days later, on **June 10, 1931**, he is married and sealed to Clara Jeffs in the Salt Lake Temple.

October 1934
President Howard W. Hunter's first son, Howard William Hunter, Jr., dies when he is seven months old.

September 1935
President Howard W. Hunter is admitted as a law student at Southwestern University.

June 1939
President Howard W. Hunter graduates *cum laude* from Southwestern University College of Law. Soon thereafter he sits for and passes the California bar exam.

1940
President Howard W. Hunter rents an office and opens a solo law practice.

August 1940
President Howard W. Hunter is surprised to be called as bishop of the El Sereno Ward. He serves for six years.

November 1946
President Howard W. Hunter is called as the president of the stake high priests quorum.

1948
President Howard W. Hunter buys a new home in Arcadia, California.

February 1950
President Howard W. Hunter is called as president of the Pasadena Stake. He serves for nine and a half years.

October 9, 1959
President Howard W. Hunter is surprised to be called as a member of the Quorum of the Twelve by President David O. McKay. He is sustained **October 10, 1959** and ordained and set apart the following Thursday, **October 15, 1959**.

October 1959 to April 1961
President Howard W. Hunter winds down his law practice in California, traveling by train or plane each week to Salt Lake City to attend the Thursday council meetings of the First Presidency and Quorum of the Twelve.

April 1961
President Howard W. Hunter and his family move into an apartment in Salt Lake City.

Late 1961
President and Sister Hunter travel to the Middle East with President and Sister Spencer W. Kimball. They visit Iraq, Egypt, the Holy Land, Europe, and Great Britain.

July 22, 1963
President Howard W. Hunter and his family move into a newly constructed home in the Oak Hills subdivision of Salt Lake City.

January 1964
President Howard W. Hunter becomes president of the Genealogical Society.

January 1965
President Howard W. Hunter is appointed president and chairman of the board of the Church's Polynesian Cultural Center in Hawaii.

June 22, 1966
President Howard W. Hunter dedicates the newly constructed Granite Mountain Record Vaults of the Church in Little Cottonwood Canyon near Salt Lake City.

August 1969
President Howard W. Hunter directs the World Conference on Records held in Salt Lake City.

January 1970
President Howard W. Hunter is appointed Church Historian and Recorder following the death of President David O. McKay.

November 1975
President Howard W. Hunter creates fifteen stakes out of five in a single weekend in Mexico City, Mexico.

1981 to 1982
President Howard W. Hunter's wife, Clara May Jeffs Hunter, suffers several cerebral hemorrhages and is moved to a nursing care facility where she spends the remainder of her life.

October 1983

President Howard W. Hunter's first wife, Clara May Jeffs Hunter, passes away after a long illness.

November 1985

President Howard W. Hunter becomes Acting President of the Quorum of the Twelve upon the death of President Spencer W. Kimball. A few years later, after the death of President Marion G. Romney, President Hunter is set apart as President of the Quorum.

October 1986

President Howard W. Hunter undergoes quadruple-bypass surgery.

October 1987

President Howard W. Hunter delivers his first sermon in General Conference while seated in a wheelchair.

May 20, 1988

President Howard W. Hunter becomes President of the Quorum of the Twelve Apostles following the death of President Marion G. Romney.

May 1989

President Howard W. Hunter travels to the Holy Land to attend the dedication of the Jerusalem Center.

April 10, 1990

President Howard W. Hunter is married and sealed to his second wife, Inis Stanton, in the Salt Lake Temple.

September 12, 1992
President Howard W. Hunter dedicates Austria for the preaching of the Gospel.

February 1993
President Howard W. Hunter is threatened by an assailant in the BYU Marriott Center in Provo, Utah.

May 30, 1994
President Howard W. Hunter becomes the senior Apostle upon the death of President Ezra Taft Benson.

June 5, 1994
President Howard W. Hunter is ordained and set apart as the fourteenth President of the Church.

1994 to 1995
Shortly after succeeding to the Prophetic office, President Howard W. Hunter presides over ceremonies in Nauvoo, Illinois, commemorating the 150th anniversary of the martyrdom of Joseph and Hyrum Smith. President Hunter creates the two thousandth stake of the Church in Mexico City, and he dedicates temples in Orlando, Florida, and Bountiful, Utah.

January 1995
President Howard W. Hunter is hospitalized with bone cancer.

March 3, 1995
President Howard W. Hunter passes away at his home in Salt Lake City.

"A HOME OF BOOKS"

President Howard W. Hunter grew up in Boise, Idaho, in a loving home environment. His father was not a member of the Church, while his mother was a believing Latter-day Saint. My impression is that President Hunter learned qualities of faith from his mother and independent thinking from his father. As a boy, President Hunter was disposed to go his own way and keep his own counsel. President Hunter's father would not allow his son to be baptized at age eight, but insisted he wait longer to make sure the boy was certain about the course of action he wanted to take. The father finally relented when he saw young Howard's disappointment in not being advanced to the Aaronic Priesthood with his friends at age twelve.

President Hunter grew up in a home of books with a piano in the center. He once told me that his father loved books, and their home in Boise was filled with good literature. There was also a piano in the home, which President Hunter was encouraged to play. Both of these resources—a home library and the family piano—became crucial tools for the growth and development of young Howard W. Hunter. He became a reading man very early in his life, and this inclination stayed with him throughout his youth, his legal and business career, and his life as an Apostle and ultimately President of the Church. The piano also was a crucial tool—in fact, President Hunter's first dream was to pursue a career in music. He learned to play several other instruments besides the piano, and as a teenager embarked on the life of a professional performing musician. Though he later abandoned this path, he was a lifelong lover of music, and even into his high old age he could play the piano with great skill and feeling.

"WE DON'T RAGTIME MUSIC"

Sister Gibbons and I once had dinner with President Howard W. Hunter and his wife, during which he shared these revealing anecdotes related to his youth:

President Hunter told us about the band he formed after finishing high school and his efforts to make his way as a professional musician for several years. This was in the late 1920's and early 1930's, and he was very skilled on the piano and also very much into the popular music of the day. He told us that one evening he was at a gathering of young Latter-day Saints in the home of a Brother Ursenbach, who lived in his home ward in Boise, Idaho. President Hunter was the life of the party, as he sat at the Ursenbach's piano and played popular songs while the youth and young singles gathered around, singing along with him and applauding him. Apparently this rankled the very staid and conservative Brother Ursenbach, who, at the end of the evening, said to President Hunter: "We enjoy having you in our home, but we don't appreciate your playing ragtime music on our piano!"

During this period the young President Hunter traveled throughout the Pacific and Far East with his band called "Hunter's Croonaders." Later, he returned home to pursue his education and find his niche in the world. But President Hunter told us that he continued to play with his band at professional gigs for several years to help fund his education. He would play dance music in clubs until late at night, then study during the day. This was during the period when he was courting and ultimately preparing to marry his first wife, Clara May Jeffs. He told us that after the wedding had been set and all the preparations made to travel to the Salt Lake Temple to be sealed, President Hunter played one final gig with his band. The group played at a dance until about 2:00 in the morning. Afterward, he went home, carefully cleaned and stored his band instruments, and then never used them again, except on rare special family occasions.

"CHURCH LEADERS WHO WERE LAWYERS"

Of all the Prophets I have known personally and worked with, President Howard W. Hunter had the most unique personality. Perhaps part of this difference arises from the fact that he is the only lawyer among all of the Presidents of the Church. I have often thought that some of the early brethren, Brigham Young in particular, might have expressed dismay that a lawyer had risen to the Prophetic office. As a lawyer, President Hunter had a unique training, not shared by any other President of the Church. To be sure, there have been other prominent Church leaders who were lawyers, including First Presidency counselors Presidents J. Reuben Clark, Hugh B. Brown, Henry D. Moyle, Stephen L. Richards, and James E. Faust. Other lawyers in the highest echelons of Church leadership have included Elders Bruce R. McConkie, Dallin H. Oaks, D. Todd Christopherson, and others. But up until now, we have had only a single lawyer serve as the President of the Church—President Howard W. Hunter.

"HIS CALL TO THE APOSTLESHIP"

Over a period of sixteen years I had the almost daily privilege of observing President Hunter in his work at Church headquarters. However, I gained additional insight into his character and personality when he was assigned in the early 1970's as a conference visitor in the Bonneville Stake, over which I presided. It was most interesting to spend time with him away from headquarters.

After he received the conference assignment, he visited with me about the preparations for the conference. During that discussion I told him that it was conceivable that both President Spencer W. Kimball and President Marion G. Romney might be in attendance, as they both lived within the boundaries of the stake. Hearing this, President Hunter joked, "I hope they don't come!" He then told me that it must be tough presiding over a stake where the Prophet and so many other General Authorities resided. "You must have the feeling that they are constantly looking over your shoulder," he said.

During the weekend of stake conference, I had a long and relaxed visit with President Hunter. He related to me the circumstances of his call to the Apostleship.

Before his call as a General Authority, President Hunter had been a stake president in Pasadena, California, where was a prominent practicing attorney and businessman. He thus came from a background far removed from Church headquarters, but traveled each General Conference to attend the sessions as a stake president. He told me that he flew to Salt Lake City in the morning with one of his counselors, Daken K. Broadhead. They checked into the Hotel Utah and were able to attend the last part of the morning session. After the morning session, President Hunter lingered in the Tabernacle to visit with some acquaintances and then returned to the hotel to freshen up before the afternoon session.

When President Hunter arrived at his hotel room and began to unlock the door, his counselor, Daken Broadhead, who occupied an adjoining room, came out into the hallway and said, "Claire Middlemiss, President David O. McKay's secretary called. She is looking for you!"

"All right," said President Hunter, not feeling any particular excitement about the phone call. "I'll call her."

Daken said, "Aren't you at all excited or curious about this?"

"Why should I be," asked President Hunter.

Daken answered, "There's a vacancy in the Quorum of the Twelve, you know."

"Oh come on, Daken!" said President Hunter.

A short while later President Hunter presented himself at 47 East South Temple and was immediately ushered into President David O. McKay's office. He said that the Prophet took President Hunter into his arms and said, in substance, "Brother Hunter, the Lord has spoken. You have been called as a member of the Quorum of the Twelve. Your ministry will now extend to the entire world!"

President Hunter told me that he couldn't remember anything the Prophet said after those initial shocking words. In fact, he said, he remembers very little of anything that transpired between receiving his calling and being sustained in General Conference the following day. He did remember attending a basketball game with his son that evening and then wandering in a daze on a long walk through the streets of downtown Salt Lake City and up

Capitol Hill, where he sat and meditated for hours on the grounds of the State Capitol.

President Hunter told me that he had no premonition of any kind of his call to the Twelve.

"Think"

President Howard W. Hunter was a reading man. I understand that his boyhood home was filled with books, as were his homes in California and Salt Lake City. His office at 47 East South Temple was also filled with books of Church history and biography, as well as the classics of world literature. The scriptures were invariably open upon the desk in his office.

I remember being with President Hunter in his office one day when I remarked upon something I had often noticed on his credenza—a little plaque that had the word, "Think" engraved upon it. I asked him about the significance of this. He told me that as a young man and a practicing lawyer he had always been greatly impressed by the writings of James Allen, the popular author of *As a Man Thinketh,* and Napoleon Hill, the author of *Think and Grow Rich.* This accounted for this visual reminder, which he always had on his desk. More than any of the Brethren I was blessed to know, President Howard W. Hunter knew how to "think."

It is interesting to contrast this little office motto with that of President Hunter's predecessor, President Spencer W. Kimball. President Kimball had a similar plaque on his office desk with the motto, "Do it." I think that these mottos say something about the personal style and focus of these two great Prophets of God! Both careful thought as well as concrete action are important.

"Sweet, hopeful, and uncomplaining"

In the late 1970's President Howard W. Hunter began to suffer from various physical problems. I remember that the first indication of his coming physical ordeals appeared when he contracted the mumps. President Hunter was on the receiving end of a great deal of good-natured kidding and banter among the leading Brethren of the Church when this happened—after all, mumps is an illness we typically associate with children, not men in their seventies! However, it soon became apparent that the mumps were no laughing matter for President Hunter, and he developed serious complications. President Hunter received several administrations from the First Presidency during this time and became the subject of daily, fervent prayers spoken in his behalf.

After several months, President Hunter underwent abdominal surgery to remove a benign tumor. Then, while he was recovering from the surgery, he suffered a heart attack. Over the next several years President Hunter endured a litany of physical ailments: continued heart problems, the deterioration of his spinal discs, bleeding ulcers, and the loss of much of the use of his legs. All of this he endured with a sweet, hopeful, and uncomplaining attitude.

"A LOVING HUSBAND"

President Howard W. Hunter's first wife, Clara May Jeffs Hunter began to suffer severe headaches and memory loss in the early 1970's, when she was still a relatively young woman. She was the subject of many blessings during that time, and her name was a near-constant fixture on the special prayer roll of the First Presidency and Quorum of the Twelve for their regular Thursday meetings for the last decade of her life. Sister Hunter's condition worsened over the years, and ultimately she became virtually incapacitated. In the early 1980's she suffered several cerebral hemorrhages, and it was necessary for her to have twenty-four hour care in a nursing facility from that time forward. She ultimately passed away in October of 1983.

It was inspiring to observe President Hunter during these years. He visited Claire faithfully each day while she was in the nursing home, and sometimes twice a day. When he was with her, he would sit and talk quietly with her. Even though she could not speak, she could express herself through facial expressions or the squeeze of a hand. I understand that she was generally unresponsive to her nurses or other family members or friends who visited her, and that she only responded to President Hunter.

"His Wisdom and Vision Were Vindicated"

President Howard W. Hunter was a true visionary and also a bold administrator, even in the face of doubters. In November of 1975, during the administration of President Kimball, President Hunter, then in the Twelve, was assigned to travel to Mexico City to divide the five fast-growing stakes located there. He was given broad discretion by the First Presidency to divide the stakes as he saw fit, but it was envisioned that this might result in an increase of three, four, or perhaps five new stakes. However, once he was on the ground, President Hunter made the decision to create fifteen stakes out of five! This he accomplished with the help of Elder J. Thomas Fyans, an Assistant to the Quorum of the Twelve, and several Regional Representatives.

When word came back to Church headquarters that President Hunter had created fifteen stakes, there were mixed feelings on the part of some of the Brethren. A few felt that he had overstepped his bounds and spread the organization too thinly. However, President Hunter's wisdom and vision were vindicated, as all fifteen of the new stakes thrived, and in fact had to be divided again in less than two years.

"He was uniformly kind to everyone"

When I first met President Hunter I was immediately impressed by his warmth and friendliness. He was very open and approachable. He did not seem to have an inflated sense of his own importance. Though I was in a subservient position, he always treated me with the utmost respect and dignity. He was uniformly kind to everyone—to both those above him and those below him. He was highly intelligent, but not necessarily an intellectual. He was positive and quick in his actions and very pleasant and open-faced in his dealings. It was evident to me from the outset that here was a man of deep faith who could be trusted.

"Junior member of the Twelve"

I first met Howard W. Hunter in the Upper Room of the temple on April 9, 1970. That was the first day I attended a meeting of the Council of the First Presidency and the Twelve in the Upper Room of the Salt Lake Temple. Earlier that day I had attended my first meeting of the First Presidency in the Council Room on the main floor of the Church Administration Building. At the time I was a practicing attorney in Salt Lake City and had the surprising experience of being invited that Thursday morning to meet with the Prophet and his counselors. During that meeting, it was decided by the First Presidency that I was to replace Elder Joseph Anderson as the Secretary to the First Presidency.

The First Presidency, consisting of Presidents Joseph Fielding Smith, Harold B. Lee, and N. Eldon Tanner, left the Administration Building just before 10:00 that morning. Joseph Anderson and I accompanied them, and we walked to the temple through the tunnel beneath Main Street.

When we got to the temple, we took the elevator up to the fourth floor and had entered what is called the "Upper Room," or the Council Room of the First Presidency and the Quorum of the Twelve. There, each Thursday for more than a century, the First Presidency and the Twelve have met to guide the Church. Prior to the construction of the Salt Lake Temple, the Brethren met in other places, dating back to the days of Joseph Smith in Nauvoo, when weekly prayer meetings were held with the Twelve and other Church leaders each Thursday.

As we entered the Upper Room, the Twelve, who had been in session there since 8:00 a.m., stood in order to shake hands with the Brethren. President Lee took me around the semi-circle and introduced me personally to each member of the Twelve. I had previously met only two of them—Elder Delbert L. Stapley, whom I had known in Phoenix, and Elder Richard L. Evans, whom I had known from my service as a guide on Temple Square and who had recently ordained me as the Bishop of the Yalecrest Ward in the Bonneville Stake. The others, of course, I knew by reputation.

At the time I first shook hands with President Howard W. Hunter, he was the fourth junior member of the Twelve, being senior only to Elders Gordon B. Hinckley, Thomas S. Monson and Boyd K. Packer. Elder Packer, incidentally, was ordained and set apart as a member of the Twelve later in the meeting.

As I shook hands with President Hunter, he greeted me warmly with a genuine smile. I learned later he had questioned taking me away from the legal profession at such a relatively young age when I had reached the point of greatest influence and productivity as an attorney. Being an attorney himself, he would have appreciated my status and situation more than any of the others.

"How Prophets are raised up"

Not long after commencing my duties as the secretary to the First Presidency, I accompanied the Brethren to St. George, Utah, where a Solemn Assembly was held in the St. George Temple. We all rode down on a chartered bus. En route, we stopped in Provo, where Brother Dallin H. Oaks, the future Apostle, was installed as the new president of the Brigham Young University. By then, President Hunter had been appointed as the Church Historian and Recorder. This was a position he cherished, as he had been an avid record keeper since the days of his youth when he commenced to keep a diary in Boise, Idaho. On the way to St. George, I noticed him making careful notes, perhaps for his own diary or for the official church record.

In St. George, the night before the Solemn Assembly was to begin, the party was served dinner in one of the local ward recreation halls. Afterward the Brethren went to their own quarters, either to sleep or to prepare for the morrow. Instead of going to bed immediately, I decided to take a walk up Main Street. On the way back, I met President Hunter, who also was out for a constitutional. We fell in together and spent about a half hour visiting as we walked. It was the first time I really had a chance to talk to him on a personal basis. I found him to be open, friendly, and devoid of any sense of self-importance or arrogance. There was no guile in him. In the years ahead I saw and heard nothing that was inconsistent with these first impressions of Howard W. Hunter.

During this same trip, I had a long private conversation with Elder Gordon B. Hinckley in Fillmore, Utah. He told me about his grandfather, Ira Hinckley who built Cove Fort and who later was the President of the Millard Stake with headquarters in Fillmore. It was a coincidence that on this the first trip I took with the Brethren I had private conversations with two members of the Twelve who would later become Presidents of the Church.

It is interesting to consider the vastly different backgrounds of these two future Presidents of the Church: President Hunter was born in Boise, Idaho, of a father who was not a member of the church and who would not allow Howard to be baptized until he was over twelve years of age. Even then he relented only because President Hunter was crushed because he could not pass the sacrament with his friends. On the other hand, Elder Hinckley's father, Bryant S. Hinckley, and grandfather, Ira Hinckley, were both stake presidents. And his father was a confidant of President Heber J. Grant, wrote his biography, handled some of his personal correspondence, and made behind-the-scene contacts for him.

Encouraged by his family, Elder Hinckley graduated from the University and filled a mission while at the same age President Hunter organized a band called "Hunter's Croonaders" and took it on an extended luxury ship cruise of the orient. He later had to complete his university legal studies by attending night school while working full time. It is a classic example of how Prophets are raised up from widely different environments but with the same dedication to the Lord and His Church.

"Three Stake Presidents in Agreement"

While I served as a stake president in Salt Lake City, I had an interesting interchange with President Hunter. Marvin Curtis, president of the Monument Park Stake; Lamonte Peterson, president of the Salt Lake Central Stake; and I as president of the Bonneville Stake had conferred about recommending boundary changes affecting the three stakes. What we had come up with was to transfer the Monument Park Second Ward and that portion of the Monument Park First Ward below the Boulevard from the Monument Park Stake to the Bonneville Stake; and to transfer the Douglas Ward, the Thirty-Third Ward and the North Thirty Third Ward from the Bonneville Stake to the Salt Lake Central Stake. Interestingly, the effect of these changes was to transfer President Kimball and President Romney from the Monument Park Stake to the Bonneville Stake and to transfer President Tanner from the Bonneville Stake to the Salt Lake Central Stake.

In any event, when these recommendations were submitted to Church headquarters, President Howard W. Hunter was assigned to study the matter and to make a report and recommendation. President Hunter conferred with the three of us, reviewed the maps and the documents, and concluded it was the thing to do. When he made his report in the temple meeting, where the changes were approved, he said in substance, "Because this is the first time I have seen three stake presidents in full agreement on a matter, I recommend the application be approved without question."

"A SWEET AND KIND A SPIRIT ABOUT HIM"

I have mentioned elsewhere that the First Presidency and the Quorum of the Twelve hold a council meeting each Thursday in the Salt Lake Temple. The Brethren sit in fifteen large chairs in a circle during these meetings, in order of seniority, with the members of the First Presidency sitting at the head of the circle, and the Twelve Apostles sitting around the circle in order of seniority. Beside the chair of the junior Apostle is a small writing desk, which I was privileged to occupy during these meetings, taking shorthand minutes of the proceedings. These meetings were usually many hours long, often lasting from early morning into the early or even late afternoon. Following each meeting the Brethren ate a meal together in a special dining room on the fourth floor of the temple. This meal was served "family style," with the food laid out in large serving dishes in the center of the table, which the Brethren helped themselves to or passed around as you might do in a simple evening meal in any Latter-day Saint home. It was another one of my great privileges to join the fifteen members of the First Presidency and the Twelve for these weekly luncheons in the temple. The members of the First Presidency and Twelve invariably took their seats around the large dining room table in order of seniority.

For many years President Howard W. Hunter sat beside Elder LeGrand Richards in meetings of the Twelve or in conference settings, and also at this dining table on the fourth floor of the Temple. Elder Richards was quite elderly during the time I knew and served with him, while President Hunter was still in his early sixties, a generation younger than the older Apostle. It was inspiring for me to observe President Hunter in his interaction with Elder Richards and the other Apostles at these dinner settings. President Hunter had as sweet and kind a spirit about him as any of the Brethren I have ever known. At the luncheons following the council meetings, President Hunter was invariably the first one in the dining room, where he began pouring ice water in the glasses of the arriving Brethren. He was also very solicitous of Elder Richards, who sat next to him at the table, to make certain that his needs were cared for.

"Very Cordial and Quite Passive"

After my call as a General Authority, I was assigned to travel to a stake conference as a junior companion to President Howard W. Hunter. The stake presidency was reorganized during the conference we attended together. During the interviews we conducted, he was very cordial and quite passive. He did not lead out aggressively in the conversations, as some are prone to do. Instead, he allowed them to develop and to proceed in a normal way. Indeed, when one left the room he probably would not have known he had been interviewed, except for the fact he had been told he was coming for an interview.

During the time we were together, I sought to draw President Hunter out to gain helpful insights into him and into other General Authorities with whom he had worked. I was especially interested in President Hunter's anecdote about the Apostle, Elder Joseph F. Merrill, who was a conference visitor to the Pasadena Stake while President Hunter was the stake president. After the conference, Howard accompanied the visitor to the depot to catch his train. When Elder Merrill started walking toward a chair car, his host tried to steer him toward the Pullman. The apostle continued toward the chair car, explaining, "I always take the chair car to Las Vegas then transfer to a Pullman. Doing this saves the church $11.50." This is typical of other stories I have heard about the frugality and honesty of Elder Merrill.

"HE TOOK GREAT DELIGHT IN CHILDREN"

President Howard W. Hunter always took great delight in children and had a special feeling for the young people of the Church. I recall while he served as a member of the Twelve he delighted in sharing stories about children in the Church, which he heard as he traveled about the world. For example, during the administration of President Harold B. Lee he took special pleasure in recounting the story of a Primary child, who told his mother that the children had been singing a special song about the Prophet at the commencement of Primary each week. When the mother asked what the song was, the child began singing, "Reverent-Lee, Quiet-Lee!"

On another occasion President Hunter shared this delightful story: An announcement was made in a stake where President Hunter was to hold a conference that "Apostle Hunter" would be attending and speaking. A little boy who heard this announcement in Primary went home and excitedly told his parents that "A Possum Hunter" would be speaking at stake conference!

On still another occasion, President Hunter told of this experience. He was greeting the saints after a particularly long meeting, when he saw a young boy lingering in the chapel waiting for his parents. President Hunter caught the eye of the boy and called to him, asking him how he enjoyed the meeting. The boy's honest answer delighted President Hunter. "Well," he said, "When I sit so long, I don't hear so good."

"Unity Among the Highest Leaders"

Early in my association with President Hunter, I had a long discussion with him about the extraordinary operation of the leading councils of the Church. At the time, President Hunter had been a member of the Twelve for over a decade. He confided in me that in all his time at Church headquarters he had never seen a dissenting vote on any matter that came before the First Presidency and the Twelve for decision. He went on to say that this was no indication of a lack of diversity of opinion. To the contrary. He said that the members of the Twelve and the First Presidency were all very strong men with firm opinions. But, he said, as matters were discussed and debated by the Brethren, one was able to judge how the consensus of opinion was lining up, and this was how the Brethren voted. It was, he said, a testimony to the unity that exists among the highest leaders of the Church.

"A MAN WHOLLY WITHOUT GUILE"

I was in the home of President Howard W. Hunter only once. It was in about 1980, when President Kimball was recuperating from one of his many illnesses. I had accompanied Presidents Tanner and Romney to President Kimball's home, where a First Presidency meeting was held. At the time, President Hunter also was recuperating from an illness, or perhaps it was a surgery. Since the Hunters' home was only a few blocks from the Prophet's residence, we decided to call on him before returning to the office. President Hunter's wife, Claire, was then in a full care facility, so he was home alone. We had called ahead to make sure it would not be inconvenient to visit him. We found President Hunter dressed in slacks, a shirt open at the collar, stockings and house slippers, and a handsome house robe. The house was immaculate. Nothing seemed out of place. The airy living room where we chatted was tastefully decorated in light hues. Crystal chandeliers could be seen in the adjoining dining room and a large piece of statuary occupied a prominent place in the living room. As always, President Hunter was cordial and gracious. He had a pleasant smile, and when he was amused, he had a subdued but genuine chuckle. We visited, talking shop, asking about his health, and reporting on the condition of the Prophet, then left. The visit confirmed my impression of President Hunter as a man wholly without guile, humble, and sincere, yet a man assured of his own self worth. There was a sweet spirit in his home, a spirit of peace and contentment.

In council meetings, President Hunter said little, unlike other members of the Twelve, who spoke out on almost every issue. When President Hunter did speak, however, his words had impact and were listened to. In reporting assignments, he related only positive things. Like a good lawyer, he chose his words carefully. And he used them with telling effect.

His most enduring contribution to the Mormon community was his admonition to live Christlike lives, to be loving and kind to each other, and to make the temple the earthly object of our energies and devotion.

"THE CHURCH IS A FRIEND TO ISLAM"

President Hunter was a very tolerant and open-minded man. An example of this occurred during the 1970's, when he befriended three young Arab students who were living in Salt Lake City and attending the University of Utah. One day President Hunter invited these three students and their advisor to 47 East South Temple and introduced them to President Spencer W. Kimball, then President of the Church. The three young men were very eloquent and well spoken and made a favorable impression with President Kimball. I was with Presidents Hunter and Kimball as they visited with these young men, who were pleading with the Prophet for a more balanced stance of the Church toward Muslims generally, and Palestinians in particular. President Kimball and President Hunter told them that the Church is a friend to Islam and its people and takes seriously their divine commission to preach the gospel to all, including Muslims.

It was inspiring to see these two servants of the Lord testify to these young men about their apostolic commissions to carry the gospel to all nations, including to the nations of Islam.

"ABSOLUTE FAITH IN THE PRIESTHOOD"

In the mid 1970's President Hunter told me this remarkable story:

During his apostolic service, President Hunter toured the South Pacific and visited a remote island where a stalwart group of Latter-day Saints lived. He said the conditions on the island were very primitive, but the people seemed happy beyond measure and possessed with a deep spirituality and hope in the promises of the gospel. One day near the conclusion of his visit to this island, a Latter-day Saint couple approached President Hunter and asked for a special blessing. Through a translator, the wife explained to the Apostle that she had been barren for many years and unable to bear children, but that she and her husband had hopes of having a child to raise in the gospel. President Hunter complied with their request and gave the woman a blessing.

Nine months after his return to Salt Lake City, President Hunter received word through the mission president that this woman had conceived and borne a child. Four years later he received the news through another source that this woman had conceived again and bore a second child. About this time, Elder Marvin J. Ashton of the Twelve visited this same island and this same woman asked him for a blessing. He complied, and word later came to President Hunter and Elder Ashton that this believing woman had conceived a third time, and nine months later bore a set of twins.

President Hunter seemed deeply moved by this story. He said it was a powerful illustration in the principle of faith. This sister had absolute faith in the blessings of the priesthood, and she was blessed for it.

"The Timetable of the Lord"

In late 1983 President Hunter traveled on Church business to the Middle East in company with Elder Mark E. Peterson of the Quorum of the Twelve. During this trip, the Brethren were involved in a terrible automobile accident near Cairo, Egypt, and Elder Peterson was gravely injured. It was undoubtedly as a result of these injuries that Elder Peterson's life was shortened. He ultimately died in January of 1984.

President Hunter later shared with me these details about the accident: President Hunter and Elder Peterson were traveling together with several others in two vehicles. At the last moment before their departure, President Hunter was about to enter one vehicle with Elder Peterson, when he urged him to ride in the second vehicle. A short while later, a drunken motorist crossed over the median strip of a divided highway and crashed almost head-on into the car in which Elder Peterson was riding.

This experience is a good illustration of the truth that we never know the precise timetable of the Lord, but have faith that if we are faithful we are in His hands, both in life and in death. President Hunter did not ascribe any special Providence to this experience, but I can't help but feel that the Lord had his hand in preserving the life of this future President of the Church.

"LeGrand will return!"

In the early 1980's, Brother William O. Nelson, who served for many years as an assistant secretary to the Quorum of the Twelve, told me this story about President Hunter:

Two or three years before he died, Elder LeGrand Richards of the Quorum of the Twelve was gravely ill and not expected to live. In fact, his doctors told Elder Richards' family that the end was very near and that they should prepare themselves. This grave diagnosis was reported to the members of the Quorum of the Twelve, and in one of their meetings the Brethren spent a significant period of time talking about Elder Richards and extolling his virtues and past contributions. President Hunter was next to Elder Richards in seniority, and so always sat next to him in council meetings. Bill said that some of the Brethren expressed regret that Elder Richards would no longer be with them.

During all this time President Hunter sat quietly by, sitting in his arm chair next to Elder Richards' empty seat, but finally spoke up and said quietly, "Brethren, LeGrand isn't dead yet." This comment was ignored, and the other Brethren continued their eulogies. Finally, President Hunter brought his hands down on the arms of his chair in an unusual show of forcefulness, and pointing to the empty chair beside him said, "Brethren! LeGrand will yet return and sit in this chair!"

Within a short time Elder Richards recovered fully and returned to very vigorous service in the Twelve and continued on for several years. In fact, it was after this experience that Elder Richards experienced the remarkable appearance of President Wilford Woodruff in the Upper Room of the Temple in connection with the 1978 revelation on Priesthood.

This experience reveals both the spirituality of President Hunter as well as his quiet strength.

Gordon B. Hinckley

Fifteenth President of The Church of Jesus Christ of Latter-day Saints

March 1995 – January 2008

Gordon B. Hinckley Chronology

June 23, 1910
Gordon Bitner Hinckley is born in Salt Lake City, Utah, to Bryant S. Hinckley and Ada Bitner Hinckley.

June 1928
President Gordon B. Hinckley graduates from LDS High School

November 9, 1930
President Gordon B. Hinckley's mother, Ada Bitner Hinckley, dies.

June 1932
President Gordon B. Hinckley graduates from the University of Utah.

1933 to 1935
President Gordon B. Hinckley serves as a full-time missionary in England.

August 1935
President Gordon B. Hinckley, upon his return from his mission, is hired as the executive secretary of the Church Radio, Publicity, and Mission Literature Committee.

April 29, 1937
President Gordon B. Hinckley marries Marjorie Pay.

1937 to 1946
President Gordon B. Hinckley serves on the Sunday School General Board.

May 1941
President Gordon B. Hinckley completes construction on a new home in East Millcreek.

January 1945
President Gordon B. Hinckley moves his family to Denver, where he works for the Denver and Rio Grande Railroad.

Fall of 1945
President Gordon B. Hinckley moves his family back to Salt Lake City.

November 14, 1948
President Gordon B. Hinckley is called as first counselor in the East Millcreek Stake presidency.

October 28, 1956
President Gordon B. Hinckley is called as president of the East Millcreek Stake.

April 6, 1958
President Gordon B. Hinckley is called as an Assistant to the Quorum of the Twelve.

June 5, 1961
President Gordon B. Hinckley's father, Bryant S. Hinckley, dies.

September 30, 1961
President Gordon B. Hinckley is called and sustained as a member of the Quorum of the Twelve.

September 1972
President Gordon B. Hinckley travels to the Holy Land with President Harold B. Lee.

July 15, 1981
President Gordon B. Hinckley is called as an additional counselor in the First Presidency by President Spencer W. Kimball.

May 6, 1982
President Gordon B. Hinckley is admitted to the hospital for the first time in his life.

November 27, 1982
President N. Eldon Tanner passes away.

December 2, 1982
President Gordon B. Hinckley is set apart as second counselor in the First Presidency.

November 10, 1985
President Gordon B. Hinckley is set apart as first counselor in the First Presidency under President Ezra Taft Benson.

June 5, 1994
President Gordon B. Hinckley is set apart as first counselor to President Howard W. Hunter.

March 12, 1995

President Gordon B. Hinckley is ordained and set apart as the fifteenth President of the Church.

January 27, 2008

President Gordon B. Hinckley dies in Salt Lake City at the age of 97.

"Son and Grandson of Stake Presidents"

My sense is much of President Hinckley's self confidence comes from his father's influence and a heritage rich in Church service. He was the son and grandson of stake presidents. His father, Bryant S. Hinckley, was the president of the Liberty Stake for many years, a well-known speaker and writer, and a confidant of President Heber J. Grant and other General Authorities. Bryant S. Hinckley was the son of Ira Hinckley, who also was a stake president, and the brother of Elder Alonzo A. Hinckley, who was a stake president and later a member of the Twelve. Another of Bryant's brothers, Arza Hinckley, also served as a stake president. And before President Hinckley was called as a General Authority, he also served as a stake president. Interestingly, both of President Hinckley's sons have served as stake presidents, putting an exclamation mark upon the rich heritage of significant Church service in the Hinckley family. From his youth, therefore, Gordon B. Hinckley knew that he came from a line of solid Mormon leaders who had inspired the confidence of men in high places. The Hinckley family were all men and women of intelligence and substance who were his exemplars and role models. Young Gordon B. Hinckley admired them and sought to emulate them. And it is apparent he was amenable to their instruction and example. A notable example of this occurred shortly after Gordon entered the mission field. He was not having much success and was discouraged. He wrote home and told his father he was wasting his time and the father's money and that he ought to go home. The father answered in a brief letter, which said in substance: "Dear Gordon. I have received and read your letter. Forget yourself and go to work." Love, Father." I heard President Hinckley tell this story to a group of missionaries in Quito, Ecuador. He said it was the best advice he had ever received and that he could think of no better advice than this to pass on to the missionaries.

"Known Among All Nations"

President Hinckley always spoke with deep respect and of his father, Bryant S. Hinckley. I first sensed this when I took a long walk with President Hinckley in Fillmore, Utah, in the fall of 1975. We were en route to the rededication of the St. George Temple, traveling in a large bus with most of the General Authorities and their wives, and we stopped in Fillmore for lunch and a rest. President Hinckley, knowing that I loved to walk, suggested that the two of us take a long walk together to stretch our legs. This was a rare experience for me, as President Hinckley was in an expansive mood and spoke at great length about his family heritage, which has deep connections with Fillmore and Millard County.

As we walked that day, President Hinckley told me that his grandfather was the first stake president there in Fillmore, having first founded Cove Fort, in the nearby mountains. President Hinckley also talked much about his father, Bryant S. Hinckley, and his uncle, Elder Alonzo A. Hinckley. His father, Bryant, was a very well-known man in the Church, a writer, and the president of the Liberty Stake in the Salt Lake Valley. The brother, Alonzo, was less well known as a young man.

Alonzo Hinckley was also called as a stake president, like his father and brother, serving in the Deseret Stake, which included the western half of Millard County. President Hinckley told me that shortly after his Uncle Alonzo was sustained as stake president, a Brother Ashman who was then the stake patriarch came to him and said that he felt impressed to give Alonzo Hinckley a patriarchal blessing. Among other things, the patriarch told Brother

Hinckley that if he would continue with the same zeal he then manifested, he would one day serve as a member of the Quorum of Twelve and that "the name Hinckley will become known among all nations."

President Hinckley said that his uncle received this special blessing in about 1912. More than two decades later, in 1934, Alonzo was indeed called to the Quorum of the Twelve, fulfilling the first promise uttered in the blessing by Patriarch Ashman. The fulfillment of the second promise, however, was not so clearly fulfilled, as Alonzo A. Hinckley only served in the Twelve for two years, dying in 1936. Because of the brevity of his apostolic service, he was not well known even in his own lifetime, and today his name is hardly a footnote in the consciousness of the Latter-day Saints.

It is interesting to note that Elder Alonzo A. Hinckley's blessing never promised that *he* would become well known, only that *the name Hinckley* would become known among all nations.

For many years during the 1960s and 1970s my sons, Mark and Daniel, and I were assigned as the home teachers for Angie Hinckley Solomon and her family in the Yalecrest Ward in Salt Lake City. Angie was a daughter of Elder Alonzo A. Hinckley, and on one or two occasions she showed me the blessing given to her father, which President Hinckley alluded to during our walk together in Fillmore. It was Angie's feeling that her cousin, Gordon B. Hinckley, then a newly called member of the Twelve, would one day become the means of fulfilling that part of the blessing about the Hinckley name becoming known throughout the world.

That promise, uttered in 1912 by a patriarch in an obscure stake in the Church, has surely come to pass through the great service of Alonzo A. Hinckley's nephew, President Gordon B. Hinckley.

"THE EXAMPLE OF ROBERT LOUIS STEVENSON"

President Hinckley's father was a well-known writer of religious works, including biographies and works of Church history. Growing up in such a home., President Hinckley was well trained scholastically and in Church doctrine and procedure. He graduated from the University of Utah in English and English literature before serving his mission in England. He apparently did very well in his studies. At least the skill he displayed as a young missionary in both writing. and speaking the English language strongly imply this. His bent in this direction was influenced by his father who was an eloquent man and highly literate. During his university years, these qualities pointed Gordon B. Hinckley toward a career as a professional writer. President Hinckley told me once that as a young man he aspired to become a writer, and that he had gone so far as to lay plans to spend a year or so on a South Sea Island where he could study and write about the native culture. He told me that he was influenced by the example of Robert Louis Stevenson.

"A PATRIARCHAL BLESSING"

President Hinckley told me that when he was eleven he received a patriarchal blessing in which he was told that he would preach and bear testimony in the nations of the earth. After his mission in Great Britain, he and Elder G. Homer Durham toured in Europe together, and in the process he had the opportunity to preach at meetings in both Germany and France. He felt afterward that since he had spoken in four different countries—the United States, England, Germany and France—this part of his patriarchal blessing had been completely fulfilled. Little did he know what was in store for him down the road. Since then, of course, he visited and spoke in most of the nations of the earth except for Tibet, Mongolia, and a few other nations in Africa and Eastern Europe.

"CLOSE ASSOCIATION WITH TWO APOSTLES"

Aside from his association with his great father, President Hinckley's first real Church training occurred in the mission field. While serving in England., he worked at mission headquarters, where he was on the staff of the *Millennial Star*. This brought him into close association with two Apostles, who served successively as President of the European Mission: Elder John A. Widtsoe and later Elder Joseph F. Merrill. From these two Apostles young Gordon gained important insight into the apostolic calling and Church administrative skills.

Among the great blessings of President Hinckley's mission was the beginning of his lifelong friendship with two of his missionary companions, Elder G. Homer Durham and Elder Richard L. Evans. Many years ago I heard Elder Widtsoe comment that the fame and influence of most great men depended upon the existence of devoted and able disciples. Such was the case with Joseph Smith. I think that if Elder Widtsoe ever occupies a place of commanding importance in Church history, it will be through his "disciples" who were his missionaries while he presided in Great Britain, including Gordon B. Hinckley, Richard L. Evans, and G. Homer Durham. Elder Evans, of course, served in the Quorum of the Twelve and Elder Durham in the Seventy.

After his mission, Elder Durham married the daughter of Elder John A. Widtsoe, who had been his mission president.

"We will give you 15 minutes"

In 1973, President Hinckley and I had a long conversation as we sat together on a flight from Munich to Frankfurt, Germany, during which he told me about some significant events which occurred at the conclusion of his mission to England. He told me that as he worked on the staff of the *Millennial Star,* he had become very close to Elder Joseph F. Merrill of the Twelve, who was then the president of the European Mission. Elder Merrill relied heavily upon President Hinckley, and in fact wrote to the First Presidency requesting that Gordon B. Hinckley's mission be extended for an additional six months. This request was turned down by the Brethren in Salt Lake City, and President Hinckley told me that Elder Merrill was very upset. In anger and with great emphasis, the Apostle told the young missionary, "The Brethren just don't understand our situation. I want you to explain it to them when you return home." He then wrote back personally to President Heber J. Grant, asking that young Elder Gordon B. Hinckley be permitted to visit with the First Presidency when he returned home to Salt Lake City from England.

President Hinckley told me that when he went in to keep this specially arranged appointment with the First Presidency, President Grant told him, "We will give you 15 minutes." However, as the discussion proceeded, the Brethren asked him a number of questions, and Elder Hinckley remained with them for an hour and a half.

Shortly following this interview, President David O. McKay called President Hinckley and invited him to come to his office for an interview. At that time he called the young Elder Hinckley to become the secretary to a newly formed committee comprised of six members of the Twelve and chaired by President Stephen L. Richards. The committee was organized to explore ways to expand the outreach of the Church using not only print media, but radio and film.

President Hinckley obviously made quite an impression on the Brethren, as their contacts with him resulted almost immediately in his employment as a member of the Church administrative staff. The interesting thing is that except for a short interval during World War II when he was employed by the railroad, President Hinckley was continuously at Church headquarters from the time of his mission until his death at age 97, serving either on the staff or as a General Authority. President Hinckley ultimately worked at Church headquarters for nearly seventy-five years!

"Someday I'm Going to Run This Place"

President Hinckley was searching for a job during the brief interval between his return home from his mission and his employment with the committee chaired by President McKay. Because of his love of literature and his boyhood aspirations to become a writer, he decided to try to get a job with the *Deseret News*. He made an appointment to visit with Samuel O. Bennion, general manager of the *News*, and asked him for a job. Brother Bennion was also serving at the time as a member of the First Council of the Seventy. President Hinckley told me that Brother Bennion, who was then a member of the First Council of Seventy, was quite brusque with him and turned him down cold. Moreover, he told President Hinckley that even if there were an opening, which there was not, there were others far better qualified than young Gordon B. Hinckley who would be given preference.

President Hinckley told me that as he left the interview with Samuel O. Bennion, he said to himself, "That's alright. Some day I'm going to run this place."

Years down the road, President Hinckley became the chairman of the board of the Deseret News. He did, indeed, run the *Deseret News*. This experience with Elder Bennion is very revealing of President Hinckley's character. Most young men would have been overawed by this man who was both the head of the *Deseret News* and also a General Authority of the Church. Moreover, to be turned down in this brusque way and to be told there were others better qualified than he would have been deflating and calculated to cause feelings of inferiority. But instead of leaving low and downhearted, this young man was positive and upbeat and not only confident of his future, but confident he one day would head the company which had just so summarily turned him away.

This experience reveals the supreme self-assurance that characterized President Hinckley's entire life and ministry.

"HE WAS THE WORKHORSE"

From the time of his return home from his mission in 1935 until his call as a General Authority in 1959, President Gordon B. Hinckley was employed. in various capacities at Church headquarters. His work on the staff was in three areas—Radio and Publicity, Temples, and Missionary Work.

President Hinckley's first assignment at Church headquarters was to become the secretary to the newly formed Radio and Publicity Committee, comprised of six members of the Twelve and chaired by Elder Stephen L. Richards. According to President Hinckley this committee had responsibility for all the radio and other public communications for the Church.

President Hinckley was paid a salary of $65.00 per month and supplemented that with $35.00 he received for teaching Seminary. He was the workhorse for the Committee—preparing scripts, editing, preparing and supervising their budget, etc. Later, after he had proven himself, he was asked by President J. Reuben Clark, President Stephen L. Richards, and others to edit their radio, conference, and other talks.

Interestingly, I first met Gordon B. Hinckley in 1942 while he was still serving as the Secretary of the Church Radio and Publicity Committee. At the time, I was in the mission home in Salt Lake City, preparing to go to the Southern States Mission. At that time the missionaries were housed in several old two-story homes north of the Beehive House on the west side of State Street. Brother Hinckley was among those who came to instruct the missionaries. He was then only thirty-one years old. The impression that has stayed with me over the years was that of an able younger man who gave us good tips about how to obtain free airtime at radio stations to present our message. He seemed to be very self-confident and to know his subject. But I did not detect in this young Gordon B. Hinckley the surpassing eloquence he showed later. It could be I was not then tuned in to eloquence.

"President Lee saw what was ahead"

It was obvious to me from the time I became associated with the First Presidency that a strong bond existed between President Harold B. Lee and President Gordon B. Hinckley. It extended back to the days when they were both staff employees of the Church. President Hinckley began his work with the Radio and Publicity Committee in 1935, which was only a year before President Harold B. Lee was employed by the Church as the general manager of the newly formed Welfare Department of the Church. In that period, President Hinckley and President Lee had offices side by side on the second floor of the Administration building, and from that association formed the friendship which persisted for nearly forty years, until President Lee's death in 1973.

Also, it was President Lee who called President Hinckley as a stake president. President Lee later told President Hinckley that when he set him apart as a stake president, President Lee "saw what was ahead for him."

"THE LAND OF MIRACLES"

In the early 1980s, I had a lengthy conversation with President Hinckley about his special relationship with President Harold B. Lee. Shortly after President Lee was sustained as the President of the Church in July of 1972, he and President Hinckley and their wives went on a trip together that took them to Italy, Greece, and the Holy Land. At Jerusalem, President Lee, who had been having respiratory problems, took ill with heavy congestion in his lungs. Concerned about him, Sister Lee asked President Hinckley to administer to him. He in turn invited Ted Cannon (who was then serving as the mission president in Switzerland with jurisdiction over Jerusalem) to assist him. Brother Cannon anointed and President Hinckley sealed.

Later that night, President Hinckley said he heard loud coughing from President Lee's adjoining room, which continued for some time and then stopped. The next morning at breakfast when the Cannons were present, President Lee said nothing. But the following day, after the Cannons had left, President Lee said at breakfast, "I guess we have had to come to the land of miracles to see miracles in our own lives." He then explained that some time after President Hinckley's priesthood administration, the Prophet was taken ill and so seriously that he felt he was going to die. Finally, he said, he coughed up a large clot of blood and that the coughing then stopped. (It apparently was a similar attack that took President Lee's life only about sixteen months later).

President Hinckley told me that he later prepared a narrative of this unusual trip with the Prophet, based upon his journal, which he titled "A Trip to Remember" and had it bound in leather as a gift for President and Sister Lee.

There was one final journey that President Hinckley took with the Prophet before his death. In 1973, following the Munich Conference, Presidents Lee and Hinckley and their wives took a trip to Florence, Vienna, and through Northern Europe. On this trip, as well as the earlier one to the Holy Land, President Hinckley made all the travel arrangements for the four of them, there being no security personnel, doctors etc. nor travel agents, as is now the case when the President of the Church travels abroad. It was like a senior companion travelling with a junior companion with their wives along. Judging from his comments and tone, I inferred President Hinckley still felt that way toward President Lee—that he was like a senior companion—a feeling I also share.

"Conciliation and negotiation"

Another assignment that President Hinckley performed during these early years at Church headquarters was to work with President Stephen L. Richards in supervising the missionary work. One particularly thorny assignment involved the negotiation of draft deferments for LDS missionaries. President Hinckley told me that the policy followed by President Richards in this sensitive issue was always one of conciliation and negotiation. At the outset, Elder Hinckley told President Richards that the Brethren really needed a lawyer in the position they wanted Elder Hinckley to fill. President Richards' response to Gordon B. Hinckley was, "I'm a lawyer, and I don't want another one involved in this delicate matter. Another lawyer would want to fight and litigate this issue, and it is one that cannot be resolved that way."

President Richards' philosophy of conciliation and negotiation prevailed despite one instance when it appeared that President David O. McKay was determined to follow another course. A missionary who had been out for 19 months had been ordered by his local draft board to report for duty immediately. The anguished parents came to President McKay for help, and he invited President Richards and Elder Hinckley to join them. President Hinckley told me that during the emotional conversation with this family, President McKay said, bringing his fists down on the desk, "They shall not have him! We shall fight this to the very last, even if it consumes all the resources of the Church!" When the Prophet asked President Richards to comment, he asked: "But what if we should lose the case, President? Then our whole missionary effort would be frustrated."

President McKay ultimately yielded and the policy of conciliation continued.

"WE WANT TO COMPOSE THIS MATTER"

Based upon many private conversations I had with President Hinckley over the years, I believe that President Stephen L. Richards was one of the giants in his life. As a young Church employee, President Hinckley quickly became a protégé of President Richards and he was obviously partial to him.

I remember that President Hinckley once characterized President Richards as the "best head" he had ever known. He was intelligent, wise, and careful. When faced with a difficulty, such as the problem with the draft deferments for missionaries, President Richards would often tell President Hinckley, "What we want to do is to compose the matter." According to President Hinckley, he was able to do this. He said one of the finest compliments President Richards ever received was a letter from U.S. General Lewis Blaine Hershey, which said, in effect, that if everyone dealing with his department had been as cooperative and reasonable as had the LDS Church, that his life would have been much simpler.

The philosophy of "composing" difficulties rather than fighting a bitter fight became almost a motto with President Hinckley. Over the years I often saw him transfer this principle into action. In this, President Hinckley was simply applying the remedy he had learned from President Richards of trying to "compose" differences and avoiding litigation.

"I WANT TO SEE HOW YOU DO IT"

Another exemplar in President Hinckley's life was President Henry D. Moyle of the First Presidency. President Moyle was in charge of missionary work while President Hinckley served as an Assistant to the Twelve. Once President Moyle asked Elder Hinckley how he gave instructions to missionaries and mission leaders. He explained that he taught how to find, to teach, to convert, to baptize, and to fellowship investigators. President Moyle said, "I want to see how you do it." So the two of them toured a mission together in California. Thereafter, they went out together to most of the missions in the United States, each discussing portions of these subjects. From this developed a very close relationship.

So close was President Hinckley to President Moyle, that he wrote a biography. of James H. Moyle, President Moyle's father, who had personally interviewed David Whitmer and recorded the personal testimony which David Whitmer bore to him of the visitation of the Angel Moroni.

"INFLUENCE IN THE HIGHEST COUNCILS"

I had no personal contact with Gordon B. Hinckley between 1942, when I met him in the mission home in Salt Lake City, and April 9, 1970, when I met him again in the Upper Room of the Salt Lake Temple at the weekly Thursday meeting of the Council of the First Presidency and the Quorum of the Twelve. That was the day I received the unexpected call by the First Presidency to serve as the secretary to the First Presidency. On that occasion, I was introduced to Elder Hinckley—and all the members of the Council—by President Harold B. Lee.

I have no recollection about anything special that happened that day when I shook hands with him. It was not long afterward, however, that I became acutely aware of him and of the strong influence he exerted in the highest councils of the Church. I found that his voice was heard there more often and more persuasively than any other member of the Twelve. I infer the self-confidence that emboldened a junior member of the Twelve to do this traces from these main sources: First, President Hinckley seemed to have been endowed inherently with a supreme self-confidence. He never seemed to have been at a loss as to the course of action he or the Church ought to take in any given situation. Nor was he ever at a loss for well-chosen and apt words to express his thoughts, which always was done in good temper and spirits. And second, he was unusually well trained scholastically and in Church doctrine and procedure. As a young missionary, he literally sat at the feet of two Apostles, and observed their work and ministry day by day. Then, after his mission, he was asked by the First Presidency to fill a key role at Church headquarters, ultimately spending three quarters of a century in the inner circles of influence of the Church.

"He Used the Talmage Room as his Office"

In the early 1980s, two solemn assemblies were held on the fifth floor assembly room of the Salt Lake Temple for local priesthood leaders in the Salt Lake City area. As we prepared for those special events, President Hinckley asked me to accompany him to the temple to inspect the great fifth floor assembly room, where the special meetings were to be held. As the two of us walked through the upper floors of the temple, President Hinckley shared with me some very interesting experiences from his personal history.

He told me that it was on the fifth floor of the temple that the first film presentation of the temple endowment was prepared in the 1950s. President Hinckley was the one who oversaw the day-to-day work on this special project. He took great pleasure in showing me the places (on the north side of the assembly room) where the screen was set up as the backdrop for the filming, and where the cameras were placed (which were hoisted by cranes to the fifth floor, where they were brought into the building through one of the great round windows). He then showed me the rooms east of the assembly room where files and other documents were kept during the filming.

President Hinckley told me that he used the "Talmage Room" (the small chamber in the temple where Elder James E. Talmage wrote his *magnum opus, Jesus the Christ*) as his office. President Hinckley then showed me two other rooms beneath the Talmage Room, on two different levels. These two rooms are of approximately the same size as the Talmage Room. One of these two rooms had been sealed up for many decades until it was "discovered" by workmen in the temple in the 1950s.

As President Hinckley showed me around, I was amazed by the beauty and dignity that characterize these rooms, which have no present use and which stand bare and unoccupied. The décor is marked by the same beauty and careful workmanship that are seen in the other rooms of the temple that are regularly occupied and used. The master builders who constructed it obviously felt that "The House of the Lord" should be perfect from basement to attic, and the builders spared no effort or expense in making it so.

It was a source of great interest to me to observe the sense of excitement and pride in President Hinckley as he led me on a tour of these seldom-seen rooms. And he was anxious to explain to me the arrangement of the furnishings and equipment used in the planning and execution stages of producing the first temple ordinance film.

As this project unfolded, President Hinckley was brought into intimate contact with President McKay, and that exposure likely was influential in his call as an Assistant to the Twelve in 1958.

President Hinckley pointed out to me the location of one work desk he used, located behind the screen on the north side of the Assembly Room, where President McKay would often confer with him when he came to the temple to inspect the progress of the work.

President Hinckley told me that he continued to work directly with President McKay in preparing the first film presentation of the temple endowment. When the film was completed, President Hinckley personally carried it to Switzerland for use in the Bern Temple, which was dedicated in September 1955. He was not a General Authority at the time. This was the first temple built in

Europe and the first temple to use the film presentation. Significantly, as a counselor in the First Presidency, he rededicated this temple in October 1992.

"HIS ARTICULATE SUPREMACY"

Among President Gordon B. Hinckley's many talents, his persuasive eloquence stands above all others. During my career, I have heard many eloquent men and women, but none to excel Gordon B. Hinckley. It has always been my personal belief that he was the most eloquent and effective speaker among all the General Authorities of his generation. His conference talks prepared in advance were always models of eloquence. But to me, the true test of his articulate supremacy was seen in the extemporaneous talks I heard him give in in a multitude of other settings, including area and stake conferences, administrative meetings, and in conversations in small groups. These impromptu sermons were on a variety of subjects that arose out of the discussions of the moment, so they were wholly unplanned on his part. On these occasions, the words came out as if played from an internal tape. They came out in complete sentences, each word seeming to have been carefully chosen to fit in its proper place. And the words were not ornate and abstruse, but were simple, plain words anyone could understand. But it was not the words alone and the carefully crafted sentences that made his speech so effective and memorable. His manner of delivery added to the impact. It was measured and reasonable, never strident or impassioned, and spoken with a sense of supreme self-confidence. Nor did he ever have to pause in search of a word. The precise word needed for the moment always seemed to be there ready to be spoken. I believe this was not an entirely learned skill but that much of it was an inheritance from father, Bryant S. Hinckley, who was also a most eloquent speaker.

"Impelled by President Hinckley's talk"

During the administration of President Spencer W. Kimball, I witnessed the fruits of President Hinckley's powerful and persuasive eloquence. President Kimball came to my office one afternoon, bearing thirty-one one hundred dollar bills, which the Prophet had received from an anonymous donor in the mail. There was a letter of explanation with the cash. It had come from a conscience-smitten member who had committed some act of dishonesty and was impelled by a talk which President Hinckley had given in general conference about honesty, and who wanted to atone for some real or fancied sin of omission or commission.

"A GRUELING DEPOSITION"

One of my first impressions of President Hinckley was his kindness. He was one man I would choose, were I given the choice, to sit in judgment upon my blackest sins. He was forgiving, merciful, charitable, and kind. He was also prayerful in the face of adversity. I often heard him pray that our hearts and the hearts of our enemies would be softened.

I observed these qualities in President Hinckley early in my association with him in the early 1970s. At the time, President Hinckley was involved in a lawsuit being litigated in Federal District Court involving the question whether the military deferment of our young men to serve missions was unlawful. In connection with this lawsuit, President Hinckley underwent a grueling deposition. Before attending the deposition, President Hinckley requested that the Brethren engage in a special fast and prayer, to the end that his mind would be enlightened and that the hearts of his adversaries would be softened toward him. After this event he expressed thanks to the Brethren and expressed the conviction that their faith and prayers were felt and had great effect.

"A RECURRING PHENOMENON"

President Hinckley exerted great influence upon all the Presidents of the Church with whom he worked. Each of the Prophets that President Hinckley served under and with whom I also worked with personally—Joseph Fielding Smith, Harold B. Lee, Spencer W. Kimball, Ezra Taft Benson, and Howard W. Hunter—had great confidence in him. An example of this confidence was demonstrated shortly before the Church's sesquicentennial in 1980. While final plans were being laid for the various celebrations that were to take place, I was sitting one day with President Spencer W. Kimball while he had a discussion with President Hinckley and President Boyd K. Packer about Church history. The comment was made that, at various times, great persecutions had arisen and almost overwhelming pressures exerted against the Church. President Hinckley then said that this was a recurring phenomenon in Church history and always would be. President Packer then made the comment that "the bells of hell" always ring when the saints set about to build temples.

Not long after this conversation, President Kimball asked me to write down for him my recollection of the conversation, as he wanted to use some of President Hinckley's thoughts in preparing his own talk and the dedicatory prayer to be delivered April 6 at the dedication of the new chapel at Fayette, New York.

"A HIGHLY DEVELOPED SENSE OF HUMOR"

President Gordon B. Hinckley had a highly developed sense of humor. President Hinckley once told me this story about a certain local leader of the Church. This man and his wife were very hospitable to leaders of the Church who visited the saints in their community and provided lodging for the General Authorities, but both were also noted for their unorthodoxy. President Hinckley told me that when he had stayed overnight in their home, the wife had pointed to the closet in the bedroom and said, "You can hang your clothes in there." Later, in the evening, when President Hinckley opened the closet door he found there were no hangers.

On another occasion, President Hinckley received a particularly aggravating letter, which he read to me. In the letter, the writer pulled out all the stops in criticizing President Hinckley for his service in the First Presidency and offered a list of suggestions on how he could improve. After reading me this letter, President Hinckley told me this story: He said that U.S. President Theodore Roosevelt once received a letter from a woman who asked, "President Roosevelt, is it true that as you charged up San Juan Hill you shouted at the top of your voice, "Damn it, damn it!" In answering the woman, Teddy Roosevelt said, "Madam. I don't remember what I said as I charged up San Juan Hill, but I do remember what I said when I read your letter."

"The Decision to Sell Their Home"

President Hinckley lived for many years in East Millcreek, where he had a large property with many trees. It was from one of these trees, planted decades before by the Prophet, that the new pulpit in the great Conference Center was constructed. There in East Millcreek, President Hinckley learned his first lessons of administrative leadership in the Church, ultimately serving as the stake president. The Hinckleys remained in the old family home up until the time President Hinckley was called as a counselor in the First Presidency.

As his duties in the first Presidency weighed down on President Hinckley, he sought living arrangements, which would ease his burdens and provide the peace and privacy that he and Sister Hinckley needed. He often spoke to me about his thoughts on finding a new home, commenting particularly about the unrelenting need for doing yard work at the old place.

One morning President Hinckley came to visit me in my office and told me that he and Sister Hinckley had reached the decision to sell their home and to move into a condominium. He was growing very weary of the problems of yard work, snow removal, and security at his home. With my help, he began to look at condominiums in downtown Salt Lake City, including one on the penthouse floor of the Canyon Road Towers, where Helen and I lived, which contained over 3,000 square feet comprised of two units that had been consolidated into one.

Ultimately, however, President Hinckley decided to move into the then-recently-constructed Governor's Plaza Condominiums on South Temple Street. The Hinckleys remained there until he became President of the Church several years later. Not only was he greatly relieved to be done with snow shoveling and lawn mowing, but it was convenient for him to be only a few minutes away from President Kimball—and later Presidents Benson and Hunter—and from his office at Church headquarters.

"A place unique in Church history"

In 1981 President Hinckley was called as an additional counselor in the First Presidency. Within a fairly short time following his call, the other three members of the First Presidency, Presidents Spencer W. Kimball, N. Eldon Tanner, and Marion G. Romney, were beset with a multitude of physical problems as the result of their advanced age. Following President Tanner's death in 1982, President Romney became the first counselor and President Hinckley the second counselor in the First Presidency. From that point forward until the death of President Kimball, President Hinckley was the only member of the First Presidency who carried out the day-to-day work of the First Presidency. Presidents Kimball and Romney were largely confined to their homes and unable to come to the office, except on rare occasions. That is not to say that they were not aware of and directly involved in leading out in the work. President Kimball still held the keys and was consulted on every major decision. But President Hinckley really carried the lonely burden of leading out in the work on a day-to-day basis.

A few months after President Tanner's death, at a time when he was the sole healthy and active member of the First Presidency, President Gordon B. Hinckley shared with me a special spiritual experience he had received. He told me that he had been feeling the burden placed upon him, and indeed that he felt oppressed by the weight of his responsibilities. In this circumstance, he implored God for help and in answer received a powerful witness of the Spirit and the whispered assurance, "Be still and know that I am God."

President Hinckley then occupied a place unique in the history of the Church. He was, for all purposes, directing the Church. He had good help from the Twelve and other General Authorities. And, because of the long time he had been at Church headquarters (since 1935, with two years away during the war), he had a clear understanding about all aspects of headquarters administration. And it was my privilege and blessing to be at President Hinckley's elbow, as it were, during these lonely years when he alone stood at the helm of the ship.

"You Brethren Go Forward"

In the late 1970s and early 1980s there were several significant events that pointed toward the eventual calling of President Gordon B. Hinckley as an additional counselor in the First Presidency.

The first hint of the need for such a call came in about 1979, when after a long day of meetings, President Spencer W. Kimball expressed a deep weariness. I remember that he turned to President Tanner and President Romney and said, in essence, "I am done. I am finished. I can't talk. I can't write. I can't think. It seems that everything is arrayed against me. You brethren go forward with the work. I will try not to get in your way."

As he talked, tears came to the Prophet's eyes. His personal secretary, D. Arthur Haycock, who was with us, told me later he had never seen the Prophet cry before. He seemed so forlorn, so vulnerable, so disconsolate.

A day or two later, President Marion G. Romney came to speak with me. He said that he had received what he called "spiritual stirrings" of late that some new crisis was about to break upon us. He also expressed great concern about "three old men leading the Church."

President Kimball rallied again from this low point he experienced, but the ominous forebodings expressed by President Romney continued to unfold into reality.

"I'M JUST ABOUT AT THE END OF THE ROAD"

At the end of the 1970s and into the early 1980s, the three members of the First Presidency, Presidents Spencer W. Kimball, N. Eldon Tanner, and Marion G. Romney, continued to gradually decline in physical health. Old age was simply catching up with them, and they were becoming unhinged physically.

I remember one especially sweet and private conversation I had with the Prophet, not long before President Hinckley's fortuitous call to the First Presidency. One morning following a slate of meetings, President Kimball lingered behind, seeming to want to talk with me alone. After giving me a fatherly kiss, he said rather disconsolately: "Frank, I'm just about at the end of the road. I know the counselors don't like to hear me say that, but it is so."

As the months passed, more ominous signs of physical decline emerged. In early 1980 President Tanner's health took a serious turn for the worse. His eyesight was failing rapidly, and his doctors told him that there was little hope that he would ever be able to see well again. He had peripheral vision, but could not identify someone sitting directly across the table from him. Nor could he read, which was a significant handicap that greatly impaired his ability to direct the work. Acutely aware of this, President Tanner raised the question whether he should be released from the presidency and given emeritus status. This led him to mention in private conversation, or rather to imply, the possibility of calling a new counselor to the First Presidency. However, having spoken this thought out loud, he rejected this idea almost the moment he advanced it.

Within a few weeks, President Tanner was practically blind. He told me one morning that his eye doctor had told him that he had "reached the end of the road" as far as any hope of recovery was concerned. He confided in me that he felt incapable of assuming more responsibility than he already had, and that he did not feel "on top" of his work. He then again mentioned the possibility of suggesting to the Prophet that an additional counselor or counselors in the First Presidency be called, or even of beginning to use the members of the Twelve in that role, though unofficially.

About the same time as President Tanner was dealing with his advancing blindness, I one day walked with President Kimball to his office, giving him an arm to lean upon. As I left the Prophet at his door, he turned to me, saying, "You see the difficult situation we are in."

"THE TWO OCTOGENARIANS WENT RUNNING"

In 1980 and 1981 the Church began gradually to face administrative problems arising from the fragile condition of the health of all three members of the First Presidency. Up until that point, the three brethren, Presidents Spencer W. Kimball, N. Eldon Tanner, and Marion G. Romney, were strong in mind and body. For example, I recall walking to the temple one day in about 1979 with President Tanner. As we walked, President Romney suddenly drew alongside.

"Why don't you lead the way?" President Tanner said to President Romney. At that, President Romney accelerated his speed into what was almost a run—and President Tanner picked up his pace to stay even with him. These two octogenarians then went running down the tunnel toward the south entrance to the temple, as frisky as young colts. It was one of the most charming sights I carry in my memory, especially because of President Tanner's crouching, skimming walk. God bless the memory of these three giants—Spencer W. Kimball, N. Eldon Tanner, and Marion G. Romney, who carried heavy administrative burdens of the Kingdom into their high old age.

"POISE AND ADROITNESS"

It was evident to me that President Spencer W. Kimball had perfect trust and confidence in President Hinckley even before his call to the First Presidency in July of 1981. In the months preceding his call, President Gordon B. Hinckley was repeatedly called upon to assist President Kimball and his counselors. Thus, during the Rochester Area Conference in April of 1980, Elder Hinckley accompanied the Prophet. Because President Hinckley could not see well, Elder Hinckley sat behind the President on the stand with a copy of his script in hand. Several times during the course of the meeting, Elder Hinckley prompted the President when he seemed to be having difficulty reading the teleprompter, thus saving him great public embarrassment. Then, at the October 1980 general conference, when three or four women in the balcony shouted, "No!" during the sustaining voice, Elder Bruce R. McConkie stood up and said that their vote had been noted, and that they should see Elder Gordon B. Hinckley. And, in March of 1981, Elder Hinckley joined President Kimball in paying a courtesy call on President Ronald Reagan in the White House in Washington, D.C. These and other sensitive and crucial assignments he handled with poise and adroitness, making him invaluable to the ailing Presidency.

President Gordon B. Hinckley's call as a member of the First Presidency in July of 1981 was not a surprise to his Brethren in the leading councils of the Church. They were aware of his distinguished family background, of his wide experience in Church affairs, and of his unusual verbal and diplomatic skills. When the call had been extended, there was general recognition of the appropriateness of the call.

He came to his new position well prepared in every sense. He had been intimately acquainted with the operation of the Church at headquarters for over forty years. For almost half that period he had been a member of the Twelve. His work as the Chairman of the Boards of the *Deseret News* and Bonneville International and as the Chairman of the Special Affairs Committee had given him special insights that would be invaluable to the Prophet. He had good judgment and was, in my estimation, by far the most eloquent of all the Brethren. The Lord had surely raised him up for this work.

At the meeting on July 23, 1981, when President Hinckley was set apart as a counselor to President Kimball, Elder Neal A. Maxwell was also ordained an Apostle and was set apart as a member of the Quorum of the Twelve Apostles, thus filling the vacancy in the Twelve created by Elder Hinckley's call.

"The Dominant Administrator"

President Gordon B. Hinckley served as a counselor in the First Presidency under President Spencer W. Kimball from the time of his setting apart on July 23, 1981, until President Kimball's death on November 5, 1985. During the intervening four years and four months he served as the dominant administrator in the Church.

His service under President Kimball can be divided into three general periods. First, the forty-one day period from the time of his setting apart on July 23, 1981, until President Kimball's major head surgery on September 3, 1981. During this time period, President Kimball was quite active and strong, and though Presidents Tanner and Romney were beset with a myriad of physical problems, the First Presidency operated with four members. Second, the period from September 3, 1981, until the death of N. Eldon Tanner on November 27, 1982. During this period, President Kimball's condition was extremely weak, and he seldom took any active role in Church administration. President Tanner was in a serious decline, but was about to rouse himself to active leadership. President Romney's condition was poor during this period. Third, the period from President Tanner's death on November 27, 1982, until the death of President Kimball more than three years later on November 5, 1985. During this final period, President Hinckley was essentially the lone man at the wheel, and except for a handful of major decisions and actions that President Kimball was able to participate in, President Hinckley essentially directed the Church under broad delegations of authority from President Kimball.

Never before nor since, in the long history of the Church, has there been a time when such a heavy burden rested upon the shoulders of one man. The only comparable period of time might have been from the fall of 1838 until the spring of 1839, when the Prophet Joseph was incarcerated in the Liberty Jail. Surely the Lord raised up Gordon B. Hinckley to serve in this significant role, which, in turn, prepared him for his own service as the sixteenth President of the Church.

"A COUNSELOR *IN* THE FIRST PRESIDENCY"

Not long after President Hinckley was called as President Spencer W. Kimball's counselor, I received a phone call from Roy Doxey, one of the editors of the *Church News*. He was calling to tell me that an article would be appearing in the next issue of the *Church News* about the new change in the First Presidency. He said that the reporters and editors at the *News* had been discussing the proper nomenclature to refer to President Hinckley's new position, and that the consensus was that President Hinckley would be serving as a counselor *to* the First Presidency rather than as a counselor *in* the First Presidency.

I raised the question with President Kimball, and he told me to look into the history and brief him on what had been done under previous Presidents of the Church in the unusual circumstance of calling more than two counselors. I knew that additional counselors had been called during the administrations of Presidents Brigham Young and David O. McKay. In the days of President Young, the extra counselor was set apart as a counselor *to* the First Presidency, but later, during the administration of President McKay, his extra counselors were sustained as counselors *in* the First Presidency. I gathered all the evidence available on the issue for the consideration of President Kimball. He then decided that President Hinckley would be sustained as a counselor *in* the First Presidency.

When I advised Roy Doxey at the *Church News*, he was surprised—and I think a little disappointed. His view—a view shared by many—was that the revelation provides that the First Presidency consists of only three high priests and that if others are called to counsel with them, they really counsel that body which is already filled to capacity.

For all practical purposes, the different terminology was without significant distinction. Whether he served as a counselor *in* or *to* the First Presidency, President Hinckley still filled the same role.

"Providential Timing"

Only six weeks after President Hinckley's call to the First Presidency, President Kimball faced one of the most significant medical crises of his life. A brain scan revealed an accumulation of scar tissue and blood beneath the membrane covering his brain. He was admitted to the hospital for major surgery. The surgeons removed a four-inch square section of his skull in the right front portion of his head near the eye. The offending matter was then removed through the membrane and the section of the skull cut out to allow the operation was wired back in place.

It was a major medical procedure, and the prognosis for President Kimball was very uncertain. The Prophet remained in intensive care for two or three days and then stayed in the hospital for another two or three weeks.

President Gordon B. Hinckley faced a daunting task. Though he lived for more than four years, President Kimball was never really the same following his September 1981 surgery. Nor were Presidents Tanner and Romney up to shouldering the heavy load of the Presidency. With general conference and the dedication of the Jordan River Temple looming, as well as a list of other meetings, conferences, and councils, and the usual crush of administrative business, President Hinckley certainly had his work cut out for him in the coming months and years. And he was surely up to the task.

Each day I became more and more impressed with the providential call of President Hinckley to the First Presidency, coming as it did at such a crucial time. President Kimball was almost completely incapacitated following his September 1981 surgery, attending meetings only sporadically. President Tanner was almost blind and heavily dependent on his secretaries, Dee Anderson and Larue Sneff. And President Romney struggled with poor eyesight, forgetfulness, and an increasing lack of self confidence caused by his physical disabilities and loneliness from the loss of his beloved wife, Ida.

The introduction into this group of three great, aged Prophets of a vigorous, able, and experienced younger man of only seventy-two had a remarkable effect on the administration of the Church. President Hinckley's hand was greatly strengthened by the uniform respect and confidence he received from the other members of the First Presidency and from the Twelve. It was indeed the hour and the day of President Gordon B. Hinckley.

"I WISHED THAT MORONI HAD A HOWITZER"

One of the most pressing tasks facing President Kimball's counselors as the Prophet lay in the hospital following his September 4, 1981 surgery was the dedication of the Jordan River Temple. President Kimball had broken ground on the structure on June 9, 1979, and by September of 1981 the temple was ready for the open house and dedication. Because President Hinckley was the only physically active member of the First Presidency, the brunt of the preparations and carrying out of the open house and temple dedication fell on his shoulders.

At the cornerstone laying ceremony, a news helicopter from Salt Lake City's Channel 2 flew over the audience several times in order to get good pictures for the evening telecast. The noise practically drowned out the remarks of President Hinckley who was speaking at the time.

Later, we received a telephone call from the director of news at Channel 2. He apologized profusely for the noise of the helicopter and said that the news staff was very embarrassed. In apologizing, the news director said, "At the time, I wished that Moroni had a howitzer instead of a horn."

"A MIRACLE OF THE FIRST MAGNITUDE"

Within days of President Kimball's September head surgery in early September of 1981, there was great pessimism expressed by his doctors and others about his chances of survival. Indeed, as general conference approached, the consensus of nearly everyone was that President Kimball would not survive until conference, and that he surely would never again be able to lead out in guiding the Church.

There were others, however, who believed that President Kimball would survive. Chief among them was President Gordon B. Hinckley. He had great faith that not only would President Kimball survive, but that he would "stand again before the people."

I recall being with Presidents Tanner and Hinckley shortly before the start of general conference in 1981. President Tanner raised the question of what the counselors should do were President Kimball to pass away before or during the coming general conference. President Hinckley was uncharacteristically quiet during this discussion. Then he spoke up and said, "I just have the feeling that President Kimball is going to get well."

President Kimball was unable to attend that conference, but President Hinckley continued to express confidence in the Prophet's recovery. He would often pray during meetings, with apparent conviction and faith that President Kimball would again be allowed to "stand before the people."

By March of 1982, President Kimball's physical condition was, if anything, worse than ever before. His eyesight and hearing continued to deteriorate; he was using a brace intermittently for his weakened back; his voice continued to weaken and to become more whispery; and his equilibrium became more shaky, and he occasionally fell as he tried to walk around his apartment. However, the Prophet seemed determined to attend the coming general conference, and, if he had his way, to speak at it.

On the Sunday of general conference in April of 1982, we all beheld a miracle of the first magnitude in fulfillment of President Hinckley's repeated prayers. President Kimball stood at the pulpit of the Tabernacle at the end of the afternoon session and bore his testimony and blessed the people. I never thought it would happen.

I will admit that I was among those who doubted that the Prophet would ever again stand and speak before the saints in a general conference. Shortly after his head surgery, President Hinckley began to pray in the meetings of the First Presidency that the Prophet would be allowed "to stand before the people again as Thy Prophet." On several occasions when he uttered these words, the thought came to me that he was asking the impossible. Moreover, I had the feeling that it was unfair to pray in such a way because of the great travail through which the President would have to pass in order to achieve it. But now that it was an accomplished fact, one had to acknowledge the rightness of it as demonstrating the power of faith and prayer in a most dramatic and convincing way.

"The Checked Everything but my I.Q."

President Gordon B. Hinckley was briefly hospitalized in May of 1982, which was a source of great concern to those at Church headquarters, since the Church could ill-afford to lose its only truly active member of the First Presidency. Given the weakened condition of the other members of the First Presidency, President Hinckley's illness could not have come at a worse time. And this fact was obviously weighing very heavily on the patient. His positive injunction to his doctor was, "Get me out of here as soon as possible."

He had been suffering from a lingering high fever due to an infection, and his doctor felt that he should be hospitalized in order to get the problem under control. He apparently had a similar attack several years previously during the dedication of the Washington Temple. Arthur Haycock told me that we almost lost him at that time.

President Romney and I went to the LDS Hospital to visit President Hinckley. He told us that it was the first time in his life he had ever been in a hospital as a patient. That was quite a record considering the fact that he was then in his early seventies. When we asked President Hinckley how he was doing, he told us about the multitude of tests the doctors were running on him, and then said, "They checked everything but my I.Q."

Gratefully, President Hinckley was soon healed and back on the job. Such a heavy burden rested upon him.

"Not Afraid to Move Forward"

There was almost no aspect of the work President Hinckley did not carry forward in the months and years following his call to the First Presidency in July of 1981. He installed new temple presidents, he trained new mission presidents, he traveled to Nauvoo to dedicate a number of newly restored homes, he traveled to the Far East to break ground for temples in the Philippines and in Taiwan, and he greeted political officials and foreign dignitaries to Church headquarters.

President Hinckley was not afraid to move forward with administrative changes. For example, he approved the completion of the placing of hundreds of satellite dishes outside stake centers in North America, which allowed special broadcasts to be viewed by members and Church leaders.

"No Shrinking Violet"

Following his surprising and providential call, President Gordon B. Hinckley lost no time in magnifying his new calling as a counselor *in* the First Presidency under President Spencer W. Kimball. Immediately after his call, I briefed President Hinckley about procedures in the Office of the First Presidency, and then I suggested that President Hinckley move into the office I had been occupying on the southeast corner of the first floor of the Church Administration Building. President Hinckley readily agreed, and I, in turn moved upstairs to the second floor.

Within a very few days after his calling, it was evident that President Hinckley's voice in the Presidency would be the dominant one. President Kimball appeared to have complete confidence in him. The fact that President Hinckley had been at Church headquarters for nearly a half a century, from 1935 until his calling in 1980, that he was blessed with great intelligence and judgment, that he had two decades of tenure in the Twelve, and that he was no shrinking violet in taking necessary action—all of this gave his comments powerful weight and influence. And the fact that he just came from the Twelve gave President Hinckley great status and rapport with that body, even beyond that of the other two counselors in the First Presidency.

"WITHIN THE BOUNDS OF HIS AUTHORITY"

Although he was alone at the helm for much of the time in the succeeding years, I observed that President Hinckley was very careful to never overstep the bounds of his authority. He always conferred with President Kimball on key initiatives and always deferred to the Prophet. And even though President Kimball's other two counselors, Presidents N. Eldon Tanner and Marion G. Romney, were suffering from the weaknesses of old age, President Hinckley always deferred to them, as well. President Hinckley, of course, began at that time to exert a dominant influence in the carrying out of the work of the First Presidency. Indeed, as a practical matter it could be said that Gordon B. Hinckley directed the Church for several years before the death of President Kimball. But, he always stayed within the bounds of his delegated authority. He never took action that plowed new ground unless he had the express authority of the Prophet.

"A MARK OF HIS GREATNESS"

President Hinckley's influence was quickly felt at every level of Church administration after his call. His voice was heard most often and most persuasively in the meetings of the First Presidency and with the Twelve. Almost overnight he became the member of the First Presidency to whom everyone turned for counsel and direction in practically all things pertaining to Church governance. Only a few days before the surprising call in July of 1981, President N. Eldon Tanner filled that role. But because of President Tanner's weakened condition, his blindness and the ravages of old age, he seemed willing and pleased to yield that role to Gordon B. Hinckley. This was another mark of President Tanner's greatness—that he willingly took a more senior, advisory role and relinquished the role of chief leadership to the younger and more vigorous man.

"He was walking a very tight rope"

President Hinckley's task in serving as a third counselor in the First Presidency required a great measure of discretion and balance. He was walking a very tight rope. During this time period, I asked him how he was holding up, and he told me, "I live from day to day." The difficulty lay in the need for President Hinckley to keep the ship afloat, yet to do it in such a sensitive, skillful way as not to infringe on the authority and prerogatives of the aged men who outranked him in the First Presidency. I would rate him a grade of "A plus" for the way in which he performed under these difficult circumstances.

"THE SITUATION HAD NEVER EXISTED BEFORE"

Not long before the death of President N. Eldon Tanner, President Gordon B. Hinckley came to my office to discuss a couple of matters. While he was there he seemed to be in the mood to talk and discussed a variety of subjects about his responsibilities in the First Presidency. It was apparent to me that he felt the full weight of the responsibility that rested on him. He mentioned how difficult it was to avoid overstepping his bounds when the senior members of the First Presidency were ailing. When I likened his situation to President Lee's while President Joseph Fielding Smith was alive, he observed, "Yes, but he was the first counselor." President Hinckley then commented that it was providential that President Kimball made broad delegations of authority to his counselors before he had his major surgery in September of 1981. He then commented that the organization of the Church was set up in such a way that almost any difficulty could be surmounted. President Hinckley pointed to Doctrine and Covenants 90:6:

> And again, verily I say unto thy brethren [the counselors in the First Presidency], . . . they are accounted as equal with thee in holding the keys of this last kingdom.

By virtue of the keys they hold, the counselors in the First Presidency have full authority to move forward with the work, despite the illness or even the disability of a President.

Shortly after I had this long conversation with President Hinckley, all of the older members of the First Presidency were afflicted with medical problems, which kept them from attending the regular meetings. President Tanner suffered a severe hemorrhaging of the nose, and President Kimball was also unwell and absent, as was President Romney. This was the first of many occasions over the next four years when President Hinckley was the only member of the First Presidency present at a presidency meeting. On this first occasion, however, it was a novelty, and I'm sure President Hinckley felt very alone.

Before the meeting began, President Hinckley visited with me and mentioned that the pattern of having an aged President in office likely will be perpetuated into the foreseeable future. I commented that the situation had never existed before which then existed, with the President and his first and second counselors being very infirm—and that this situation would not likely occur again. President Hinckley responded by saying that the answer would appear to lie in the President of the Church reaching down to call younger men to serve as his counselors and to release them promptly when it is seen that their effectiveness was impaired.

"The Office of Archbishop"

From an early period during his service as a counselor to President Spencer W. Kimball, President Hinckley had been impressed with the need to decentralize the administration of the Church. I recall that a few months after he joined the First Presidency, I had a long conversation with him about the great challenges facing the Church, brought about in large part because of the unprecedented and explosive growth of the Church that had occurred in the previous decade or two. President Hinckley then made this interesting observation—he said, in essence, "I now begin to see why the Catholic Church created the office of Archbishop." As we discussed this further, it became apparent that President Hinckley had in mind the idea that members of the Twelve, say five at a time, would be placed in charge of large areas of the world, under broad delegations of authority and responsibility from the First Presidency, to direct the affairs of the Church in these areas. Under this concept, two members of the Seventy would be assigned to act as counselors to each member of the Twelve. These reflections were prompted by the special insights President Hinckley had received during the early months of his service in First Presidency, as he witnessed the bureaucratic structure that had been created at Church headquarters and the complications that existed at home and out in the world.

As he discussed these ideas with President Kimball and members of the Twelve in the succeeding months and they were prayed about and pondered, the Brethren were inspired to divide the international world into areas and to domicile three General Authorities in each area with authority to direct the Church there, subject to the overall direction of the apostolic leaders in Salt Lake City. However, it was decided that these area presidencies would be comprised of members of the Seventy, not members of the Twelve, who would remain in Salt Lake City and have worldwide jurisdiction over the Area Presidencies.

President Hinckley was the chief architect for two key organizational changes implemented at this time. The first was the creation of three executive councils chaired by members of the Twelve, and the second the creation of Area Presidencies with three General Authorities in each presidency, living the year around in the area served.

An integral part of this change was to give the Area Presidencies jurisdiction over all ecclesiastical and temporal affairs in that area. Until that time there was a split jurisdiction between what was called executive administrators and the directors of temporal affairs who were answerable to the presiding Bishopric.

This organizational set-up positioned the Church to expand globally in an efficient, concerted way, dividing the areas as the work requires it. It provided for decentralization by giving the Area Presidencies wide discretion, while giving adequate overall control by the hierarchy through other administrative mechanisms, which President Hinckley was chiefly responsible for implementing.

Under this control mechanism, three headquarters executive Councils were created—Priesthood, Missionary, and Family History and Temples. Each Council was comprised of three members of the Twelve, two presidents of the Seventy, and a member of the Presiding Bishopric. The senior member of the Twelve on a council was the chairman. In addition to having authority over the headquarters departments falling under it, each executive council had authority and responsibility for a third of the areas around the world. Thus, President Hinckley envisioned that each Area Presidency would go to the executive council under which it fell for direction and advice. Actually, the headquarters contact man for an Area Presidency was the chairman of the executive council. Should the executive council be unable to respond, the matter could be taken to the Twelve for handling and ultimately to the First Presidency, if necessary. Because members of the Executive Councils would be in regular sometimes daily contact with their area presidencies and because Area Presidencies would be in regular contact with stake and mission presidents through stake and district conferences and mission tours, as well as through correspondence and telephone communications, President Hinckley believed the Church would be able to move forward as an integrated whole on a worldwide basis. The fact that members of the Seventy have apostolic authority, which enables them to set in order the affairs of the Church in their respective areas, provides the necessary flexibility and discretion so that local problems can be solved in a special, tailored way. And the Area Presidencies receive regular instruction from members of the Twelve during area, regional, and general conferences to insure that governing, apostolic standards are met. As already indicated, such an organization will make it possible to continue the accelerated growth of the Church worldwide through the increase of seventies and new areas as the work requires.

These proposals resulted in the establishment of areas in the Church, presided over by Area Presidencies, a major dismantling of the huge bureaucracy at Church headquarters and a major reassignment of duties to the Presiding Bishopric of the Church.

In retrospect, the contribution of President Hinckley in the implementation of these changes is Providential. These changes essentially equipped the Church to deal with almost unlimited growth in the future.

"Broad Delegations of Authority"

With the death of President Tanner and with the new and heavy responsibilities given to him, President Hinckley entered into a new important phase of his training as a future President of the Church. President Hinckley's duties increased dramatically after President Tanner's death. Shortly after his death, President Kimball called President Romney as his first counselor and President Hinckley as his second counselor.

President Romney, aware of his own advanced age and exhibiting great humility and unselfishness, suggested several times to President Kimball that Gordon B. Hinckley be called as the first counselor. President Kimball resisted this noble suggestion, but it is a mark of the greatness of Marion G. Romney.

President Kimball set apart President Romney as his first counselor, and President Romney set apart President Hinckley as the second counselor. Shortly thereafter, broad delegations of authority to President Hinckley were given by both President Kimball and President Romney. They essentially authorized him to act on behalf of the First Presidency in all matters pertaining to Church governance. This really made Gordon B. Hinckley the de facto President of the Church. Notwithstanding his authority to act, President Hinckley, however, was extremely deferential to President Kimball and always consulted with him before breaking any new ground or moving forward on significant callings or initiatives. In many respects, the following three years were the finest hour, not only for President Hinckley, but for Presidents Kimball and Romney as well. All three were great men and true stalwarts of the restored gospel.

In the early days after President Tanner's death, President Hinckley was not alone in the council meetings. President Kimball and President Romney frequently attended, most often in wheelchairs. President Kimball contributed to the discussion and made all the ultimate decisions. This was truly inspiring to see, as it was clear that notwithstanding his physical limitations, President Kimball was still at the helm.

"President Hinckley bore a heavy burden"

In the early months after President Tanner's death, President Hinckley made the wise decision to enlist the more active assistance of the Twelve, and President Ezra Taft Benson in particular, in handling the heavy load of the work. For example, President Hinckley decided that he would ask President Benson to conduct the opening and closing sessions of the general conference and to speak at the general priesthood meeting and the Sunday morning general session. It was decided that President Hinckley would make a brief statement at the beginning of the Saturday morning session, turning the conducting over to President Benson. Even with President Benson's able assistance, President Hinckley still bore a heavy burden at this and succeeding conferences.

"One of our Greatest Presidents"

My regular interaction with President Gordon B. Hinckley ceased following my release from the Seventy in 1991, and thus I have little personal knowledge of the events surrounding his service after that date. However, having spent much of two decades in close proximity to him, including a period of nearly five years of almost daily interaction, I think I am qualified to offer some insights about his character, his contributions, and his legacy for the Church.

It is difficult to assess the relative strength and greatness of the Presidents of the Church—in fact it is impossible to do so. The Lord raises up His servants to serve during specific times. Each brings his own unique qualities, which are perfect for his generation. However, in examining the broad sweep of Latter-day Saint history, it is possible to see some giants standing in the long shadow of history. President Gordon B. Hinckley is surely one of these. He is undoubtedly one of our greatest Presidents. Born into one of the great families of the Church, he was chosen almost in his youth for conspicuous service at Church headquarters. For a period of nearly seventy-five years, he worked closely with the highest leaders of the Church, first as a staff employee, then as a General Authority, then as a member of the Twelve, and finally for a period of several decades as a member of the First Presidency.

As with every leader, he faced unique challenges. One of the greatest tests of his character and leadership occurred during the final five years of President Spencer W. Kimball's administration, when President Hinckley was the only physically active member of the First Presidency. This was a circumstance that never before nor since has occurred in Church history. During those years, most of the meetings of the First Presidency included President Hinckley alone, with me taking minutes. I can testify that he was magnified greatly during that period and was under the constant guidance of heaven. It was during that difficult time that President Hinckley began to envision administrative solutions to problems that had dogged the Church for many years. Those problems arose primarily from the explosive growth of the Church. President Hinckley had the vision to see long-term solutions to those problems, which outfitted the Church for almost unlimited growth in the future. He harnessed the revealed structure of the priesthood in a way that set the Church on a firm and certain course. In all of this, President Hinckley was the architect, acting under the delegated authority of President Kimball.

On a personal level, we have rarely seen a more eloquent President of the Church. President Hinckley at the pulpit was inspiring, enlightening, almost poetic. He spoke best, it seemed, when he spoke extemporaneously. In private settings he was, if possible, even more eloquent, moving people to tears, inspiring change in individuals and organizations.

As one who spent many years literally at President Hinckley's elbow, I can testify that he was truly a Prophet of God.

THOMAS S. MONSON

Sixteenth President of The Church of Jesus Christ of Latter-day Saints

January 2008 to present

Thomas S. Monson Chronology

August 21, 1927
Thomas Spencer Monson is born in Salt Lake City, Utah, to G. Spencer and Gladys Condie Monson.

March 15, 1944
President Thomas S. Monson receives his patriarchal blessing.

Fall 1944
President Thomas S. Monson enrolls at the University of Utah and meets Frances Beverly Johnson.

1945-1946
President Thomas S. Monson completes his naval training.

1948
President Thomas S. Monson graduates from the University of Utah and begins working at the Deseret News as a classified advertising manager.

October 7, 1944
President Thomas S. Monson marries Frances Beverly Johnson in the Salt Lake Temple.

March 12, 1950
President Thomas S. Monson is sustained as the second counselor to Bishop John R. Burt in the Sixth-Seventh Ward of the Temple View Stake.

May 1950
President Thomas S. Monson is called and ordained as bishop of the Sixth-Seventh Ward at age twenty-two, after serving in the bishopric for only two months. He serves for five years, until **July of 1950**. At the time, President Monson is the youngest bishop in the Church.

June 1955
President Thomas S. Monson is called as second counselor to Percy K. Fetzer in the presidency of the Temple View Stake. He serves until **June of 1957**.

April 1959
President Thomas S. Monson serves as president of the Canadian Mission. He serves until **January of 1962**.

1962
President Thomas S. Monson is named General Manager of the Deseret News Press.

October 4, 1963
President Thomas S. Monson is sustained as a member of the Quorum of the Twelve Apostles. He is ordained on **October 10, 1963**.

1968 to 1985
President Thomas S. Monson supervises the work in Europe.

14 June 1969
President Thomas S. Monson organizes the Dresden Mission with Henry Burkhardt as president.

1976 to 1982

President Thomas S. Monson serves as chairman of the Missionary Committee.

June 29, 1985

President Thomas S. Monson participates in the dedication of the Freiberg Germany Temple.

November 10, 1985

President Thomas S. Monson is sustained and set apart as second counselor to President Ezra Taft Benson.

June 5, 1994

President Thomas S. Monson is sustained and set apart as second counselor to President Howard W. Hunter.

March 12, 1995

President Thomas S. Monson is sustained and set apart as first counselor to President Gordon B. Hinckley.

February 3, 2008

President Thomas S. Monson is ordained and set apart as the sixteenth President of the Church.

"I HAVE A NEW BISHOP FOR *YOU!*"

It is well known that President Thomas S. Monson was called as a bishop in the Church at age twenty-two. What is less well known is that his mother, Gladys Monson, predicted his call on the date of President Monson's birth. As she lay in St. Mark's hospital with her newborn son on a Sunday morning in 1927, her husband, G. Spencer Monson, reported to her that a new bishop had been installed in Church that day. The mother's response was, "I have a new bishop for *you!*"

"Long on Caring and Short on Statistics"

President Thomas S. Monson was the youngest bishop in the Church when called as a bishop at age twenty-two. His ward was on the west side of Salt Lake City where there were many unemployed members and eighty-five widows. I understand that President Monson's ward had the largest welfare responsibility in the Church at the time. There, in that humble little ward, President Monson learned the principles of welfare and caring in a very practical way. He was a bishop long on caring and short on statistics.

Bishop Monson laid into his new duties as a bishop with great vigor. He began to visit each member of his flock, one by one, and to instill a sense of love and community in the neighborhood. He gave particular care to the fatherless and the widows in the ward. I believe that his care of his widows stands as the most enduring accomplishment of his service. Each Christmastime, he would call personally at the home of each widow, leaving them a gift and a bishop's blessings. After his release, this practice continued down through the years. I can attest that even when he was a member of the Twelve and in the First Presidency, he continued, year by year, to visit the former members of his flock. He would usually take a week of his vacation in order to visit all of the widows each Christmas season.

"Have Courage, My Boy, to Say Yes"

After serving as a bishop, President Monson was called as a counselor in the stake presidency of the Temple View Stake in June of 1955, when he was twenty-eight years old. The first notice he had of the call was when his name was read from the stand in the Assembly Hall. The presiding authority was President Joseph Fielding Smith, then a member of the Twelve, who announced the new stake president, Percy K. Fetzer. Then, presenting the counselors, President Smith announced Thomas S. Monson as the new second counselor, saying, "Bishop Monson knows nothing of this appointment, but if he will accept it, we will be pleased to hear from him now!" President Monson, caught totally unaware of his new calling, had to improvise. Walking to the pulpit, he paused and then referred to the song which had just been sung in the conference, whose lyrics admonished adherence to the Word of Wisdom: "Have courage, my boy, to say no." This became President Monson's text for his impromptu sermon, which he developed into the theme, "Have courage, my boy, to say yes!"

This early sermon of the Prophet can be seen as a theme for his entire ministry. Have the courage to say yes. It beautifully illustrates the positive, energetic, happy, and courageous aspects of President Monson's personality and service.

"HE SAW TOM MONSON SITTING ON THE END SEAT"

In 1973 I attended the funeral services for Elder Thomas S. Monson's mother, Gladys Monson, which were held in the Rosecrest Ward chapel. While there, I learned these additional inspirational details regarding his 1955 call to the Temple View Stake Presidency.

One of the speakers, Brother John R. Burt, who served in the Temple View Stake presidency with President Monson, told this unusual story about his call: Brother Burt had preceded President Monson as bishop of the Sixth-Seventh Ward, and in fact President Monson had served briefly as Brother Burt's counselor, so the two men were well acquainted. At the reorganization of the stake presidency, President Joseph Fielding Smith, who effected the change, asked the new stake president, Percy K. Fetzer, to nominate counselors. He immediately chose John R. Burt, a former bishop, but was uncertain about the second counselor. Finally, pressed for time, President Fetzer said that the only other man who came to his mind was Bishop Thomas S. Monson. President Smith then asked Brother Burt if he could work side by side with President Monson. Brother Burt smiled, because he had already served in a bishopric with Thomas S. Monson, and then enthusiastically endorsed President Fetzer's nomination.

Later that day, as Brother Burt looked at a picture of the interior of the Salt Lake Tabernacle, which hung on the wall of the stake center, he said that he clearly saw, as if in vision, the seats where the Twelve Apostles sit, and he testified that he clearly saw Tom Monson sitting on the end seat.

THOMAS S. MONSON

On the morning before Elder Monson was sustained as a member of the Quorum of the Twelve in October of 1963, Brother Burt called his wife, who asked if he knew who the new member of the Twelve would be. Without any prior knowledge other than that received through the Spirit in 1955, he said, "Tom Monson."

"A SPECIAL YOUNG MAN"

Very early in his life, President Thomas S. Monson caught the caught the eye of the leading Brethren of the Church. While he was still in his early thirties, he was called as the president of the mission whose headquarters were in Toronto, Canada. In those days, released mission presidents reported directly to the First Presidency, so President Monson met personally with President David O. McKay and his counselors when he returned home from Toronto.

While I was writing the biography of President McKay, I was given access to all of his private diaries. President McKay made one entry in which he mentioned young Thomas S. Monson, and he made the comment that he was "a special young man," and that the Brethren should "keep their eye on him."

"Love and admiration for President Clark"

Shortly after his mission to Canada, President Monson was called to serve on two of the general Church councils (missionary and home teaching), for which he regularly attended stake conferences with General Authorities, who had the opportunity to watch him in action. At the same time, he was the manager of the Deseret News Press, which brought him in contact with General Authorities whose books were being prepared for publication.

President Monson often spoke of his shepherding one of President J. Reuben Clark's books, *Our Lord of the Gospels*, through the process of publication. From that experience and perhaps others, he acquired a great love and admiration for President Clark. His youngest son is Clark Monson, named after President Clark. So in the months and years after his mission, President Monson's daily work and his weekend work brought him into regular contact with the highest leaders of the Church. Given President Monson's great talents and spirituality and the deep impression he had made on President McKay, it is not surprising that he would be called to the Twelve. But I would go further to say that Thomas S. Monson was one of the great and noble ones selected by God in the preexistence to come to the earth and to lead out in building the Kingdom of God on earth.

"A CONSUMMATE TEAM PLAYER"

President Thomas S. Monson was a reserve basketball player on the University of Utah team that won the 1947 National Invitational Tournament. In those days the NIT was far more prestigious than that of the National Collegiate Athletic Association, or NCAA.

President Monson has always been a consummate team player. He is as enthusiastic sitting on the bench as he is on the court, so to speak. I have often pondered his role as a reserve basketball player and thought it mirrored his history in Church leadership over the course of his ministry. For more than two decades he was a "bench player," so to speak, laboring as a member of the Twelve, following his team leaders. Then, in November of 1985, he was suddenly placed "in the game" as a counselor to President Ezra Taft Benson. It was inspiring to observe him at this juncture in his service. Like a good "reserve player" coming off the bench, he was ready in every way to take a leading role.

"CALLED TO THE ATTENTION OF PRESIDENT McKAY"

President Monson once told me that in his opinion he was called to the attention of President McKay by two unusual events: First, he was called upon to report his mission to Canada before the First Presidency almost a year after his release, but just a few months before his call to the Twelve. Second, he said by chance he was able to conduct President McKay on a tour of the new plant at the Deseret News Press, where he worked, not too long before he was called.

"HE DID SAY 'THE TWELVE,' DIDN'T HE?"

President Monson was called as a member of the Quorum of the Twelve in October of 1963, when he was just 36 years old. President Monson once shared with me this insight about his call:

When President David O. McKay extended the calling, he told Thomas S. Monson that because he, too, had been called to the apostleship as a very young man, he could understand the trauma through which Elder Monson would pass. Afterwards, as President Monson left the Prophet's office, the first person he saw was Henry Smith of the *Deseret News*, who had been confidentially notified of President Monson's call and who was there to get information to fill in the gaps for an article about the new appointment to the Quorum of the Twelve. President Monson told me that when he saw Henry, who was an old friend, he wanted to be sure it was a call to the Twelve and not as an Assistant to the Twelve! President Monson said to Henry, "He did say Quorum of the Twelve, didn't he?"

"TO TELL HER ABOUT THE CALLING"

Shortly before his call to the First Presidency, President Monson shared with me this additional detail about his call to the Twelve in 1963. After receiving his call from President David O. McKay, he debated about how to share this earth-shaking news with his wife, Frances Monson. He decided to take her for a drive to the This is the Place Monument at the mouth of Emigration Canyon on the foothills overlooking the Salt Lake Valley. There, they got out of the car and walked around the monument, looking at the statuary and the bronze inscriptions. Finally, after President and Sister Monson had been there for some time in silence, she finally said, "What's wrong?" President Monson then told her about his new calling.

President Monson told me, "I just felt that I wanted to tell her about the calling in that special place."

"Some far-reaching event"

I once asked President Monson if he had any premonition or hint that he was to be called as a member of the Twelve. He said that he had not, although he had felt rather unsettled for several weeks before the call. He told me that the Sunday before he met with President McKay, he went to his church meetings, as usual, but during the meetings he had the subconscious feeling that he would prefer to be elsewhere, doing something other than church work. It was almost as if he was being tempted away from his path of duty. But praying within himself, the negative feeling passed, and he told me that at that moment, he was filled with a feeling of deep peace and satisfaction that he was in his place doing his duty in the Church, even though he might have preferred to be elsewhere. With these feelings, he said, came an impression that some far-reaching event would soon occur in his life.

"THE YOUNGEST APOSTLE"

After his call to the Quorum of the Twelve in 1963, President Monson brought an unusual youth to the Quorum of the Twelve. Only thirty-six years old at his ordination, he was the youngest Apostle for twenty-one years, from 1963 until the call of Elder Dallin H. Oaks in April of 1984.

When Elder Oaks was called, it was the first time in a generation that a person younger than President Monson sat in the circle. Still, President Monson is only about five years older than Elder Oaks.

"A HAPPY WARRIOR"

President Monson has a very happy, positive, enthusiastic personality. He always radiates an unusual cheerfulness from his countenance. His attitude is always upbeat, always optimistic. In my decades of personal interaction with him, I never once saw him depressed or disappointed. He has the personality of a "happy warrior." No obstacle seems too difficult for him to surmount. He is whole souled, able, sincere, and a great catalyst among the Brethren and all the membership of the Church.

This radiant, cheerful personality in President Monson is contagious. Just being around him causes people to become hopeful and enthusiastic. I suppose this quality in President Monson might be called "charisma," but it is really more than that. He is a truly converted soul, with a love the Lord and His Gospel.

"A STRIKING PROFILE"

For sixteen years, while serving as secretary to the First Presidency, I sat on the stand in the Salt Lake Tabernacle facing the speakers' stand from the side. From that vantage point, I saw all of the speakers in profile. Over and over through the years, the features of Thomas S. Monson reminded me of the Prophet Joseph Smith. From the various portraits we have of the Prophet Joseph, and especially from the profile paintings done in Nauvoo, he had a striking profile with a towering physique, a regal bearing, prominent features of nose and chin, and an aura of confidence and cheerfulness. The countenance of President Monson, seen in profile, had the same qualities.

But, the similarities between the Prophet Joseph and President Monson do not end there. His friendliness, interest in people, his common touch, his energy, and compassion are of a kind that matches the qualities of the Prophet Joseph. These qualities naturally attracted followers both to the Prophet Joseph and to President Monson.

"CORDIALITY AND FRIENDLINESS"

I first met President Thomas S. Monson in the Upper Room of the Salt Lake Temple on April 9, 1970, the date I began my service as the secretary to the First Presidency. On that morning, I was taken around the circle by President Harold B. Lee and introduced to each member of the Quorum of the Twelve before the beginning of the Council Meeting. I was impressed by the cordiality and friendliness of President Monson. He was very open and warm. A bond of friendship and mutual admiration grew up between us. I soon developed a very close relationship with him. He often called me or visited me in my office to counsel about the work. As the frequency of these and other contacts increased, the nature of our relationship became one of a more confidential kind. Such was the trust between us that we shared matters of the most sensitive kind pertaining to the work that I never felt free to record nor discuss. I believe that I became his confidant and sounding board on many subjects.

One of the things I enjoyed most about my work with the Brethren was my association with President Monson. From the beginning we had a special understanding and camaraderie. I treasured my relationship with President Monson and never want to betray it. I admire and respect him and fully sustain him in his prophetic office.

"My mentor"

Beginning in the early 1970s, I began, in the early mornings, to write a biography of the Prophet Joseph Smith. I had never written a full-length biography before, and this project was undertaken on my own time to fulfill a long-held ambition to write about the Prophet.

Over time, I shared this private endeavor with President Monson, and he began to play a key role in this aspect of my life. During the years I labored over this project, President Monson would often inquire about it and offer me encouragement. Then, in the mid 1970s when my manuscript was completed, he offered to read it to give me his honest appraisal. Thus began a long literary mentorship with President Monson. He offered several suggestions to me, which I welcomed. This first biography of the Prophet Joseph Smith was ultimately published in 1977, and in the succeeding years I wrote and saw published biographies of fourteen of Joseph Smith's successors.

President Monson became my mentor and kindly offered to review my manuscripts. For my part I gladly accepted because of his experience as the manager of the Deseret News Press, as a member of the board of the Deseret Book Company, and as an aide in shepherding many books through to press for President J. Reuben Clark and others. President Monson reviewed all of my manuscripts about Presidents of the Church up until the time he became a member of the First Presidency in late 1985. He probably would have reviewed the later manuscripts, had I asked him, but I was reluctant to do so, for fear of burdening him or causing him embarrassment.

It will be found that most of my biographies express indebtedness to the "Mentor," who was President Thomas S. Monson. Only my wife, Helen, knew the identity of the "Mentor" for certain. Others may have guessed at it. Only two people had the nerve to ask me who my "Mentor" was, and I declined to reveal to them that it was President Thomas S. Monson.

I am grateful for President Monson's support and for all he has done to help me in my endeavors to write the lives of the Presidents of the Church.

"A VERY SKILLED ADMINISTRATOR"

President Thomas S. Monson is a very skilled administrator. He has always had the ability to inspire confidence, and to create and maintain unity in a group. He also has one of the most positive and enthusiastic personalities I have ever encountered. In all my years of close association with him, I never saw him depressed or disappointed. He is also a man of great integrity. There is no pretense in his makeup. What the membership of the Church sees of him in public is the same in private.

I would say that President Monson has the skill of a good chess player—he is able to envision future moves. He is very adept at long-range planning. And, like a good chess player, he sometimes achieves his goals through indirection or adroit maneuvering. President Monson is a very tough man, a very strong personality. Once he knows what he wants to achieve and how to do it, he is relentless.

"HE RECOGNIZES, ENCOURAGES AND BUILDS UP"

In his relationships with people, President Thomas S. Monson always remembers and lifts.

President Monson has a phenomenal memory for names. I have seen him instantly recall the names of people he met briefly decades before. To hear a Prophet of God recall and speak your name is a powerful motivation. It is one of his natural gifts.

President Monson not only remembers names, he also lifts people up. He is a builder of men and women. He recognizes, encourages, and builds up his followers in very personal ways. I have seen him go out of his way countless times to lift people up and to recognize them. He is especially apt to recognize and uplift those who are laboring in obscure roles. In this respect, President Monson reminds me of the story of the Savior, who saw the man "of little stature" called Zacchaeus, who climbed a sycamore tree by the side of the road in order to catch a glimpse of the Lord over the heads of the taller people who were pressing close to the Lord. The Lord "looked up" and saw the little man in the tree, publicly recognized him, and invited him to dine with him. (See Luke 19:1-10).

I was often the recipient of President Monson's out-of-the-way kindnesses as I worked in a relatively obscure role at Church headquarters. For example, on one rare occasion I was asked to share my testimony in a Council Meeting with the Brethren. Afterwards, President Monson went out of his way to share with me a special poetic couplet he had composed:

Vision without work is daydreaming.

Work without vision is drudgery.

Vision coupled with work brings success.

After sharing this little saying with me, President Monson told me that it exemplified my service to the Brethren. This moved me deeply, and I later had this couplet engraved on special plaques, which I gave to all of my children. This was a great motivation to me. It exemplified one of the most salient leadership qualities of his ministry. How many people would take the time to seek out a relatively obscure person, laboring in the Kingdom, and then pay them a compliment, such as I received from President Monson? I have no doubt that the experience I had with President Monson has been repeated thousands of times through the years with others in similar contexts. The effect of this action of President Monson is to create a strong bond of love and loyalty and to provide an incentive to do better.

"They Often Showed Deference"

This feeling that President Monson was "a special young man" was shared by many of the Brethren during the early years of his service in the Quorum of the Twelve. I noted that the senior members of the First Presidency and the Twelve often showed deference to young Thomas S. Monson, although he was still in his thirties and forties. The respect they gave him belied his relatively junior status.

An example of this deference could be detected in President N. Eldon Tanner. Though he had served as a counselor to four Presidents of the Church and was a man of honorable age and significant accomplishment and ability, I noted that President Tanner never criticized President Monson in my presence. This was unusual for President Tanner, as he was a very straight-shooting, frank, and outspoken man, and his leadership style was to freely correct those with whom he worked, including members of the Twelve. But not so with President Monson—President Tanner treated him with the highest respect and deference. This was also true with President Marion G. Romney, who always spoke with equal praise about President Monson.

"The Most Aggressive Member of the Twelve"

After beginning my service with the Brethren in April of 1970, I soon learned that the most assertive member of the Quorum was Thomas S. Monson. Over time I became more and more impressed with his great leadership abilities. He was very aggressive and a driver, but he also had the great ability to draw people together and to make them feel a part of what was going on. Sometimes his aggressiveness and energy had the effect of exhausting those who worked with him, but he seemed to be sensitive of this feeling; and when he became aware of even a hint of a negative reaction setting in, he withdrew and then went out of his way to bridge any gap that may have opened up. In this way, he never made any enemies, but only friends and supporters.

"A SWEEPING CHANGE"

In the early 1980s, when President Gordon B. Hinckley was the only physically active member of the First Presidency, President Monson stepped up to take a strong leadership role in the Quorum of the Twelve. This was a period of significant challenge and opportunity in the Church, brought about in large part by the unprecedented growth in the membership of the Church, which had begun in the administration of President David O. McKay and greatly accelerated during the administrations of Presidents Joseph Fielding Smith, Harold B. Lee, and especially Spencer W. Kimball. The explosive growth of the Church was straining the then-existing administrative structure of the Church at the headquarters level, and it was also spreading thin the time and energy of the General Authorities.

In about 1983, President Monson chaired a committee that prepared a very significant report for the First Presidency. This report proposed significant administrative changes in the work. These changes included the establishment of Area Presidencies in the international areas of the Church and the elimination of artificial distinctions between ecclesiastical and temporal affairs. These proposals from President Monson's committee, which were ultimately implemented in substance, brought about a sweeping change in the way the Church operated at the highest level.

"Making the gospel clear to the masses"

President Thomas S. Monson is extremely articulate and expresses himself freely and convincingly. His General Conference talks are masterpieces of clarity and inspiration. They strike a near perfect tone between the colloquial and the sublime. In many ways, his sermons are reminiscent of the powerful sermons of the greatest orators of Church history, in days before microphones or recording devices.

President Monson once shared with me that his patriarchal blessing promised that he would have a special gift of "making the gospel clear to the masses." In fulfillment of this patriarchal promise, President Monson does have a very clear, simple means of exposition, which could hardly be misunderstood. His talks are also delivered with great enthusiasm and fervor and are never read. He may memorize them, or at least have them so well in mind that he delivers them flawlessly without benefit of notes.

"He Prayed During the Entire Journey"

During his years in the Twelve, President Thomas S. Monson was one of the most physically active and widely traveled of all members of the Twelve, with special assignments in Europe. In this assignment he often traveled to Europe to create stakes or dedicate new areas for the preaching of the gospel. For example, he once traveled to Portugal to offer a dedicatory prayer in that land. But there was no nation closer to his heart than East Germany, where he had a multitude of special spiritual experiences.

Elder Joseph B. Wirthlin, who as an Assistant to the Twelve assisted President Monson in the work in East Germany, told me about this special experience he had with the future Prophet in 1978: At that time it was very difficult for the Church to arrange for President Monson and Elder Wirthlin to travel to the Communist-held East Germany, and after one trip it appeared it might not be legally possible for the Brethren to return. However, during their trip, Brother Walter Krause, the sole Patriarch in East Germany, came to President Monson and Elder Wirthlin before they left and promised them in the name of the Lord that they would both be back together in East Germany.

Elder Wirthlin told me that he had the same impression, that the way would be opened for them both to go back. He also told me that President Monson literally prayed during the entire journey that they would be permitted to return. This prayer, and the prophecies of Brother Krause and Elder Wirthlin were fulfilled within a few months.

"A FUTURE TEMPLE IN EAST GERMANY"

Through more than a decade, President Monson became a strong advocate for the humble saints of East Germany in the leading councils of the Church. This is nowhere more evident than in President Monson's advocacy for a future temple in East Germany.

The saints in East Germany at the time were under the leadership of Henry Burkhardt, the longtime president of the East German Mission. During one of President Monson's trips there, President Burkhardt expressed the strong desire that the worthy members in that country be permitted to receive their endowments and sealings, even though they did not have access to a Temple. At the time it was virtually impossible for citizens of East Germany to obtain exit visas to leave the country for any reason. I was present on several occasions when President Monson spoke privately with President Kimball about the desires of the faithful East German saints.

After his discussion with President Monson, President Kimball really took hold of the idea of helping the East German saints receive temple ordinances. The Prophet gave a great deal of thought to how the Brethren might administer the ordinances and blessings of the endowment and marriage sealings upon worthy members behind the Iron Curtain, despite the lack of a temple there.

Within a year President Monson was able to put into President Burkhardt's hands architectural plans for a small temple to be submitted to the East German officials. This resulted in the miraculous construction and dedication of the Freiberg Temple in 1985.

None of this would have occurred but for the passionate advocacy of President Thomas S. Monson.

"HE HAD A VIVID DREAM"

For many years President Monson had a special role as a member of the Quorum of the Twelve with responsibility for the welfare program of the Church. In this role, he worked very closely with President J. Reuben Clark and President Harold B. Lee, two of the earliest visionaries and architects of the program. My sense is that both President Clark and President Lee saw President Monson as the next generation of leadership in welfare matters. Because of this, both of these senior Brethren took President Monson under their wings, and he received special tutelage from both of them. They also expected a great deal from President Monson and even pushed him in sometimes-uncomfortable ways, but he responded with great obedience and humility and quickly developed great leadership skills.

Several years after the death of President Harold B. Lee, President Monson told me that he had a vivid dream, to which he attached great spiritual significance. He said that in his dream, President Harold B. Lee appeared to him. President Lee did not speak, but merely smiled benignly at President Monson, in a way that imparted to him that he was pleased with the way in which the welfare program was developing. President Monson was very moved when he related the circumstances of this dream.

About the Author

Daniel Bay Gibbons is a writer living in Holladay, Utah. The youngest son of Francis M. Gibbons and Helen Bay Gibbons, he is a former trial attorney and judge and is the author of several previous books. He has served as a full-time missionary, twice as a bishop, and as president of the Russia Novosibirsk Mission.

INDEX

Acropolis, 180
Albion State Normal
  School, 105, 115
Allen, James, 365
American Institute of
  Cooperation, 303
Anderson, Dee, 448
Anderson, Elder Joseph,
  5, 371
  and Francis M.
    Gibbons, 8
  and Yalecrest Ward, 27
  call as an Assistant to
    the Twelve, 8
  service on high council,
    27
  statement about Francis
    M. Gibbons, 30
Anderson, Jack
  and Francis M.
    Gibbons, 21
Anderson, Norma, 9
Angel Moroni, 420
Apache County, Arizona,
  14
Arapahoe, 185
Archbishop
  GBH on office of, 460
Area Conferences, 205
  Buenos Aires, 205

Manchester, 41, 98,
  109, 203
Manila, 205
Mexico City, 110, 204
Munich, 110, 204
Sao Paulo, 205
Scandinavia, 205
Seoul, 205
Taipei, 205
Tokyo, 205
Area Presidencies
  creation of, 460
Argentina, 40, 202
Arizona, 211, 218
Arizona School of
  Commerce, 15
Arizona Superior Court,
  14
As a Man Thinketh, 365
Ashman, Brother
  patriarch, 403
Ashton, Elder Marvin J.,
  177, 387
Assembly Hall, 23, 478
Assembly Room, 424
Assistants to the Twelve,
  213
Atlanta, Georgia, 21
Australia, 40, 202
Austria, 199

Bamboo Curtain, 285
Beehive House, 61
Belgium, 199
Ben Gurion, David, 328
Bennion, Elder Samuel
   O., 139, 160, 410
Benson, Flora Amussen,
   300, 314, 316, 319
   death of, 304, 341
   missionary service, 318
Benson, George T., Jr.,
   299
Benson, President Ezra
   Taft, 42, 397, 475, 483
   and Francis M.
     Gibbons, 343
   and GBH, 337, 466
   and HBL, 310
   and New York Governor
     Thomas E. Dewey,
     303
   and President Dwight D.
     Eisenhower, 303
   boyhood friendship with
     HBL, 114
   death, 355
   life
     Apostolic service, 302,
       303
     birth, 299, 308
     Boy Scouts, 321
     call to Twelve, 302,
       322
     childhood, 309, 311
     Church service, 301,
       320
     courtship, 315
     death of, 304
     education, 299, 300,
       301, 314, 318, 320
     employment, 300,
       301, 320
     family, 340
     health problems, 312
     in Europe after WWII,
       302
     marriage, 300, 319
     military, 299
     military service, 312
     mission, 299
     mission to England,
       315, 316
     patriarchal blessing,
       318
     political career, 303,
       324, 325, 326, 327,
       330
     President of the
       Church, 304, 339
     President of the
       Twelve, 303
     Secretary of
       Agriculture, 303
     World War II, 324
   motto, 342
   personal qualities, 305

eloquence, 331
faith, 344
genuineness, 306
humility, 307
integrity, 344
kindness, 306
patriotism, 344
poise and self-control, 344
sense of humor, 332
spirituality, 312, 334
unpretentious, 307
scripture carried in wallet, 345
service in the Twelve, 133
SWK mistaken for, 214
Benson, Sarah Dunkley, 299, 308
Bern Temple, 425
Bern, Switzerland, 179
Bible
Smith family, 46
Boise Stake, 301
Boise, Idaho, 300, 320, 349, 357, 359, 373, 374
Bolivia, 202
Bonneville International, 442
Bonneville Stake, 27, 174, 334, 362, 372, 376
Bountiful, Utah, 356
Bowen, Albert R., 28

Bowen, Elder Albert E. and Francis M. Gibbons, 23
Boy Scouts of America and ETB, 321
Brazil, 40, 202, 277
Brazil Area Presidency, 278
Brazil Fortaleza Mission, 278
Brewster, Hoyt, 78
Brigham Young University, 4, 153, 318, 373
Brittain, Commodore, 16
Broadhead, Daken K., 363
Brown, President Hugh B.
as a lawyer, 361
Buenos Aires, Argentina, 202
Bulgaria, 179
Burkhardt, Henry, 474, 503
Burt, John R., 473
vision of TSM in Tabernacle, 479
Burton, Elder Theodore M., 129
Burton, Suzanne Gibbons, 149, 158
Burton, Timothy A., 149, 158

Cache Valley, 112, 115, 119
Caleb, 231
Callis, Elder Charles A., 108
  death of, 108, 141
  vision of the Savior, 139
Camp Pendleton, 245
Canadian Mission, 473
Cannon family, 322
Cannon, Ted, 182
Canyon Road Towers, 432
Carthage Jail, 47
Cederlof, Bjork, 24
Central America, 201, 275
  Church growth in, 273
Central States Mission, 198
Cheyenne, 185
Chicago, 54
Chicago Law School, 153
Chile, 40, 202
Christmas, 213
Christopherson, Elder D. Todd
  as a lawyer, 361
Church Administration Building, 10, 49, 80, 83, 124, 158, 232, 289, 371, 454
Church Auditors, 266
Church Board of Education, 230
Church Finance Committee, 267
Church Historian, 353, 373
Church Historian's Office, 45, 59, 61
Church News, 445
Church Office Building, 232
City Creek Canyon, 130
Clark
  President J. Reuben and HBL, 135
Clark, Donna Murray, 264
Clark, Max B., 264
Clark, President J. Reuben, 107, 137, 138, 216, 412, 492, 505
  and HBL, 133, 144
  as a lawyer, 361
  fear of flying, 81
  prophecy of, 107, 144
Clark, President Stephen L., 412
Clawson, President Rudger, 124
Clayton, William, 5
Clifton Ward, 115
Clifton, Idaho, 112, 113, 309
Coffee, 256
Coke, 256

Copenhagen, Denmark, 38, 77
Council Room in Salt Lake Temple, 305
Cove Fort, 374, 402
Cowley, Elder Matthew, 133
Curtis, Marvin, 376
Death Valley, 145
Denver, Colorado, 116
Derby, England, 57
Deseret Book Company, 492
Deseret News, 410, 442, 472, 485
Deseret News Press, 474, 482, 484, 492
Deseret Stake, 402
Dew, Sheri L., 343
Dewey, Governor Thomas E., 303
Dixon, Kitty, 15
Douglas Street, 37, 46, 67
Douglas Ward, 376
Doxey, Roy, 445
Dresden Mission, 474
Duncan, Arizona
  SWK prophecy uttered at, 274
Dunkley, Ann, 314
Dupaix, Ray, 26
Durham, Elder G. Homer, 406

Eagle Gate, 46
East Germany, 501
East High School, 70
East Millcreek, 395
East Millcreek Stake, 395
Ecuador, 40
Edling, Wilford, 267
Edmunds-Tucker Act, 50
Egypt, 352
  ETB opens doors in, 329
Eisenhower, U.S. President Dwight D., 303, 324, 325, 327
Ellsworth, Homer, 254
Emigration Canyon, 302, 322, 486
England, 35, 39, 56, 179, 199
Ensign Stake, 106
Essentials in Church History, 37, 59
Europe, 201, 251
European Mission, 303, 408
Evans, David W., 74
Evans, Elder Richard L., 98, 372
  and GBH, 407
Executive Councils
  creation of, 461
Eyring, Dr. Henry J., 262, 263
  death of, 262

Far East, 246
Faust, President James
 E., 279, 285
 and Helvecio Martins,
  279, 280
 as a lawyer, 361
 call to the Twelve, 280
Fayette, New York, 430
Federal District Court,
 429
Federal Heights, 174
Fetzer, Percy K., 245, 473,
 478, 479
Fiji, 203
Fillmore, Utah, 402
First Council of the
 Seventy, 139, 213
First Presidency, 40, 107,
 222
First Quorum of Seventy,
 205
Flight Attendant
 and SWK, 256
Florence, Italy, 37
Fortaleza, Brazil, 278
Fotheringham, William,
 273
France, 199
Freiberg Germany Temple,
 474
Freiberg Temple, 503
Fyans, Elder J. Thomas,
 369

Garden Park Ward, 74
Genealogical Society, 352
General Authorities, 273
 from many nations, 277
General Conference, 8, 63,
 230, 233
 JFS leaves to watch son
  play football, 71
Germany, 38, 199
Gibbons, Adeline
 Christensen, 14
 vision of, 21
Gibbons, Daniel Bay, 90
 testimony of, 5
Gibbons, Francis M., 3
 and Elder Albert E.
  Bowen, 23
 and ETB, 343
 and HBL, 17
 and HWH, 380
 and TSM, 492
 biographer, 4
 buys home in Yalecrest
  Ward, 26
 dream of DOM, 28
 dream of HBL, 20
 first acquaintance with
  HBL, 146
 impression to see Bjork
  Cederlof, 24
 last conversation with
  HBL, 193
 law practice, 24

meets ETB, 305
mission, 16
naval service, 16
preparation, 7, 13
　shorthand, 13
secretary to the First
　Presidency, 4
SWK visit to home, 251
three year residence in
　South America, 278
Gibbons, Helen Bay, 8,
　161
　and Gregg shorthand,
　　16
　blessing from HBL, 147
　given blessing by HBL,
　　19
Gibbons, Judge Andrew
　S., 13
　death and appearance
　　of, 20
Gibbs, William F., 5
Gila Valley, 211
Governor's Plaza
　Condominiums, 432
Grand Canyon, 201
Granite Mountain Record
　Vaults, 353
Grant, President Heber J.,
　42, 106, 107, 119, 130,
　132, 322, 400, 408
　and Bryant S. Hinckley,
　　374

calls ETB to Twelve, 302
Grant, President Heber J.
　Grant, 200
Great Britain, 77, 201,
　203, 352
Great Depression, 127
Greece, 179, 202
Greenhalgh, Joseph, 199
Gregg, John Robert
　inventor or Gregg
　　shorthand, 15
Guatemala, 40
Haight, Elder David B.,
　228, 229
　and blessing of Helvecio
　　Martins, 282
　call to the Twelve, 261
　sees map of Africa in
　　vision, 282
Hammond, Elder F.
　Melvin, 273
Hanks, Elder Marion D.,
　236, 242
Harold, Bennett
　call as patriarch by
　　ETB, 334
Harrison, U.S. President
　Benjamin, 51
Hawaii, 51, 203
Hawaii Mission, 318
Haycock, Arthur, 194
Haycock, D. Arthur, 76,
　93, 249, 436

and ETB in Washington,
D.C., 326
Heap, Ward
court reporter, 14
Hill, Napoleon, 365
Hinckley, Ada Bitner, 394
death of, 394
Hinckley, Arza, 400
Hinckley, Bryant S., 374,
394, 400, 402
death, 396
Hinckley, Elder Alonzo A.,
400, 402
Hinckley, Ira, 374, 400
Hinckley, Marjorie Pay,
179, 395
Hinckley, President
Gordon B., 42, 47, 55,
98, 166, 195, 206, 259,
268, 372, 374, 475, 499
administrative changes,
453
and delegations of
authority, 464
and ETB, 337, 466
and HBL, 163, 179, 396
and President Henry D.
Moyle, 420
and Temples, 423
architect of Church
administration, 468
call as counselor to
SWK, 206

contribution, 467
greatness of, 467
life
Apostolic service, 396
Assistant to the
Twelve, 396
birth, 394
call as Assistant to
the Twelve, 424
call to the Twelve, 396
childhood, 400, 405
Church employment,
394
Church service, 395
counselor in First
Presidency, 396
counselor in the First
Presidency, 397,
429, 438
death, 398
education, 394
ehealth, 452
employment, 395,
410, 412
health, 397
home, 395
marriage, 395
mission, 394, 406,
407
President of the
Church, 397
writing, 405, 420
office, 454

on authority of counselors, 458
on creation of Area Presidencies, 460
patriarchal blessing, 406
personal qualities
  adroitness, 441
  boldness, 453, 454
  discretion, 457
  eloquence, 426, 468
  loyalty, 455
  persuasion, 428
  persuasiveness, 421
  self-confidence, 421
  sense of humor, 452
  vision, 460
prepares draft statement of Revelation on Priesthood, 293
prophecy regarding SWK, 450
providential call to First Presidency, 447
spiritual experience, 434
travels with HBL, 110
with HBL in Israel, 181
Holy Land, 202, 352, 355
Hotel Utah, 259
Hungary, 199

Hunter, Clara May Jeffs, 350, 354, 360, 368
  death, 354, 368
Hunter, Howard William Jr., 350
Hunter, Inis Stanton, 355
Hunter, John William, 349
Hunter, Nellie Rasmussen, 349
Hunter, President Howard W., 42, 81, 98, 112, 397, 475
  and accident in Egypt, 389
  and Elder LeGrand Richards, 378
  and Francis M. Gibbons, 380
  and HBL, 167
  and SWK, 352
  focus upon Temple, 385
  gives blessing to childless woman, 387
  leadership style, 380
  life
    Apostolic service, 352, 353, 355, 383, 387, 389
    Apostolic service, 373
    birth, 349
    call to the Twelve, 352, 362

childhood, 349, 357, 359, 374
Church service, 351, 362
courtship, 350
death, 356
death threat, 355
education, 349, 350, 375
family, 350, 354
health problems, 354, 356, 367
home, 384
legal career, 351, 361
marriage to Clara May Jeffs, 350, 360
marriage to Inis Stanton, 355
musical career, 349, 350, 359, 360, 374
President of the Church, 356
President of the Twelve, 354, 355
life preserved, 389
love of music, 357
motto, 365
office of, 365
on Islam, 386
personal qualities
  cordiality, 380
  endurance, 367
  faith, 370
  faithfulness, 368
  genuineness, 372
  hopefulness, 367
  humor, 367
  independence, 357
  kindness, 370, 385
  love of books, 365
  love of children, 382
  musical talent, 358
  quiet strength, 391
  sense of humor, 382
  spirituality, 387, 391
  studious nature, 357
  vision, 369
prophecy regarding LeGrand Richards, 390
Hunter's Croonaders, 359, 374
Hyde, Elder Orson, 190, 328
Illegal Aliens, 276
Iowa State University, 300, 320
Iraq, 352
Iron Curtain, 285
Israel
  ETB opens door in, 329
Italy, 179, 202
Jacksonville, Florida, 108, 141
Jensen, Harriet
  prophecy of, 116

Jenson, Andrew, 59
Jerusalem, 182, 415
Jerusalem Center, 355
Jesus the Christ, 423
Job, 225
Jordan River, 231
Jordan River Temple, 449
Joshua, 231
Kimball, Andrew, 198, 209, 211
Kimball, Camilla Eyring, 198, 199, 201, 202, 257, 262, 263
Kimball, Elder J. Golden, 213
Kimball, Elder J. Golden Kimball, 213
Kimball, Olive Woolley, 198, 209, 210
Kimball, President Spencer W., 98, 144, 195, 362, 386, 396
   1981 medical crisis, 447
   and GBH, 441
   and Helvecio Martins, 278, 279, 282
   and HWH, 352
   and legacy of HBL, 189
   death of, 304
   delegations of authority, 464
   final years, 337
   life
   advocate for oppressed, 209
   and missionary work, 205
   and missionary work, 240
   Apostle to the Lamanites, 200, 273, 275
   Apostolic service, 201, 202, 203, 218, 274
   birth, 198, 209
   business, 199
   call to the Twelve, 199, 214
   car accident, 201
   church service, 199
   death, 206
   final years, 259, 443
   health problems, 200, 201, 203, 204, 206, 218, 221, 222, 225, 228, 229, 230, 245
   humility, 214
   marriage, 198
   mission to Central States, 198
   naming of, 209
   open heart surgery, 222, 224, 225
   President of the Church, 204, 205, 206, 212, 233, 260

President of the
   Twelve, 203, 204,
   232
sense of humor, 213,
   214
sermons, 270, 272
service in Army, 198
spiritual experiences,
   228
travels, 201, 202, 203
travels, 242
vacations, 245, 250
voice, 219, 226
milestones of his
   administration, 243
   Revelation on
   Priesthood, 278
motto, 365
office of, 262
on his rest theory, 250
on hunting, 255
on hymn Come Let Us
   Anew, 250
on illegal aliens, 276
on old age, 251
on plowing new ground,
   268
on raising up leaders
   from foreign nations,
   277
on salvation and
   exaltation, 249
on the day of the
   Lamanite, 274
on the great feast, 272
personal qualities
   advocate for the
      oppressed, 275,
      276, 277
   boldness, 208, 234,
      240, 243, 268
   compassion, 232
   confidence, 240
   delegation, 244
   detail focused, 238,
      293
   discipleship, 208, 266
   dreams and visions,
      269
   energy, 208, 227, 234,
      238, 251
   humility, 226, 233,
      236, 240, 253, 260,
      262, 294
   integrity, 233, 262
   kindness, 232
   leadership style, 236,
      238, 244, 261, 266
   love, 212, 261
   mottos, 246, 251
   perpetual motion,
      243, 246, 250
   perseverence, 208,
      226, 229, 244
   privacy, 225, 226

prophecy of, 274
resolution, 216
sense of humor, 216, 221, 242, 253, 254, 255, 256, 257, 261, 264, 267
sense of urgency, 238, 277
spirituality, 243, 266, 269, 272, 274, 294
stubbornness, 216, 229
vision, 208, 234, 238, 240, 247, 266, 277
work, 228, 230, 239, 242, 243, 247, 248, 249, 261
writing, 248
physical decline, 438
service in the Twelve, 133
travels, 199
Kimball, Sister Camilla Eyring
health problems, 225
Kimgall, Camilla Eyring, 202
Kings Hall in Manchester, 99
Kirtland, 46, 48
Kirtland Temple
SWK dreams about, 269
Knight, John M., 117, 119

Krause, Walter, 501
Laguna Beach, 245
Lamanite Committee, 200
Lamanites, 273
Latin America, 151, 275
Lava Hot Springs, 314
LDS High School, 394
LDS Hospital, 178
LDS servicemen, 245
Lee, Fern Tanner, 106, 119, 121
  death of, 109, 173
Lee, Joan Jensen, 109, 119, 179
  courtship of with HBL, 174
Lee, Louisa, 112
Lee, Louisa Bingham, 105
Lee, President Harold B, 218
Lee, President Harold B., 11, 42, 84, 98, 224, 233, 234, 236, 240, 305, 371, 491
  ancestry, 112
  and dream of Native American leader, 186
  and GBH, 181, 396, 415
  and picture of the Savior, 139
  and the Temple, 160

and the Welfare
   Program, 122, 127,
   129, 130
and TSM, 505
and Welfare Program,
   135
blessing to Helen Bay
   Gibbons, 147
boyhood friendship with
   ETB, 114, 309
conducts funeral for
   Charles A. Callis, 142
courtship with Joan
   Jensen, 174
death of, 204, 303
dreams of, 125, 145,
   161
experience in Los
   Angeles Temple, 160
extemporaneous
   Conference sermons,
   171
gift of tongues, 170
home of, 174
legacy, 189
life
   and the Welfare
      Program, 107
   Apostolic service, 107,
      133, 138
   birth, 105
   call to the Twelve,
      132, 135, 141, 144
   childhood, 112
   Church service, 106,
      115, 122
   counselor to JFS, 109
   death, 110
   death of, 193
   death threats, 190,
      192
   education, 105, 114
   employment, 121
   funeral of, 195
   health problems, 177,
      182
   marriage to Fern
      Tanner, 106, 121
   marriage to Joan
      Jensen Lee, 109
   miraculous healing in
      Jerusalem, 110
   mission, 105, 116,
      117
   political career, 106,
      122, 130
   President of the
      Church, 110, 155,
      184, 185
   travels, 107, 108, 110,
      179, 181
   work, 105
   writing, 108
musical talent, 112
office of, 160

on call of Francis M.
    Gibbons, 11
personal qualities, 112
  administration, 156,
    187
  eloquence, 164
  faith, 183
  mentor, 151
  optimism, 168
  organizational genius,
    163
  pesuasion, 166
  sense of humor, 167
  spirituality, 113, 116,
    121, 124, 130, 158,
    162, 169, 170, 172,
    188
  spirituality, 108
  vision, 128
prophecy of regarding
  SWK, 222
receives blessing
  Jerusalem from GBH,
  182
SWK mistaken for, 214
Lee, President Spencer W.,
  42
Lee, Samuel Marion, Jr.,
  105
Lehi, Utah, 254
Liberty Jail, 444
Liberty Stake, 400, 402
Lion House, 232, 260

Little Cottonwood Canyon,
  49
Liverpool, 56
Logan, Utah, 299, 312
London Temple, 39
London, England, 324
Lord Thompson of Fleet,
  179
Los Angeles Temple
  dedication of, 160
Los Angeles, California,
  349
Lund, President Anthon
  H., 59
Lyman, Elder Richard R.
  SWK mistaken for, 214
Malad, Idaho, 188
Manchester, England, 41,
  99, 109, 203
Marriott, Ally, 173
Marriott, Bill, 173
Mars Hill
  HBL preaches on, 180
Martins, Elder Helvecio,
  278, 292
  and Elder David B.
    Haight, 282
  and SWK, 278
    1977 conversation,
      280
  attends November 1977
    conference, 280

receives personal message from SWK, 280
Maxwell, Elder Neal A., 442
McConkie, Amelia Smith, 41
McConkie, Elder Bruce R.
  as a lawyer, 361
McConkie, Elder Bruce R..
  prepares draft statement of Revelation on Priesthood, 293
McConkie, Oscar W., Jr.,, 145
McConkie, Oscar W., Sr.
  dream of, 145
McKay, President David O., 40, 55, 107, 218, 234, 353, 363, 481, 484, 499
  1954 trip to Santiago, Chile, 273
  and ETB's appointment to U.S. Cabinet, 325
  and GBH, 408
  and TSM, 485
  death, 8, 28, 40
  death of, 109, 203
  mission president to ETB, 317
Meeks, Heber, 141

prophecy of, 21
Meg
  Smith family horse, 52
Mercy Fielding, 44
Merrill, Elder Joseph F., 380, 407
Merrill, Elder Marriner W., 188
Metcalf, Derek, 158
Mexico, 107, 275, 277
Mexico City, 110, 353, 356
Miami, Florida, 141
Middlemiss, Claire, 363
Millard County, 402
Millard Stake, 374
Millennial Star, 407, 408
Mission Home, 164
Missionary Training Center, 164
Missouri, 40, 44
Mobile, Alabama, 78
Monson, Clark, 482
Monson, Frances Beverly Johnson, 472, 473, 486
Monson, G. Spencer, 472, 476
Monson, Gladys Condie, 472, 476, 479
Monson, President Thomas S., 43, 98, 372
  and East Germany, 501, 503

and Francis M.
  Gibbons, 492
and HBL, 156
and President J. Reuben
  Clark, 482
Apostolic service, 499
appearance, 490
dream of HBL, 505
life
  Apostolic service, 474
  birth, 472, 476
  call to the Twelve, 474
  call to the Twelve,
    485, 487
  call to Twelve, 480
  Church service, 472,
    473, 476, 477, 478,
    479, 481
  counselor in the First
    Presidency, 475
  education, 472
  education, 483
  employment, 474
  marriage, 473
  naval service, 472
  President of the
    Church, 475
patriarchal blessing,
  472
personal qualities
  assertivness, 498
  cheerfulness, 489
  eloquence, 500
  enthusiasm, 489
  friendliness, 491
  inspiring, 495
  leadership, 494
  memory for names,
    495
  positive attitude, 478
  positive attitude, 489
  prayerfulness, 501
  team player, 483
sermons, 478, 500
youngest Apostle for a
  generation, 488
Montevideo, Uruguay, 202
Monument Park First
  Ward, 376
Monument Park Second
  Ward, 376
Monument Park Stake,
  376
Mormon Tabernacle
  Choir, 74
Morrill Anti-Bigamy Act,
  50
Morrill Anti-Bigamy Act of
  1862, 35
Mount Graham Stake,
  199
Moyle, James H., 420
Moyle, President Henry
  D., 133
  and GBH, 420
  as a lawyer, 361

Munich, Germany, 110
Mussolini, 77
National Collegiate Athletic Association, 483
National Council of Farm Cooperatives, 301, 320
National Invitational Tournament, 483
Native Americans, 185, 273, 276
Nauvoo, 44, 46
Nauvoo Legion, 47
Nauvoo, Illinois, 356
Navajo-Zuni Mission, 200
Nelson, President Russell M., 98, 229, 334
  and Francis M. Gibbons, 27
  and SWK's open heart surgery, 204, 222, 224
  calls Francis M. Gibbons as bishop, 28
Nelson, William O., 390
Netherlands, 199
New York, 218
New York City, 109, 201
New Zealand, 202
Nigeria, 78
North Thirty Third Ward, 376
Nottingham, England, 56

Oaks, Elder Dallin H., 488
  and HBL, 153
  as a lawyer, 361
  as BYU president, 373
Official Declaration 2, 287
  drafting of, 293
Ogden, Utah, 56, 315
Oliver Cowdery test, 286
Oneida Stake, 321
Oneida Stake Academy, 114, 309, 312
Orlando, Florida, 356
Oswald, Coach Mickey, 70
Our Lord of the Gospels, 482
Oxford, Idaho, 105, 115
Pacific, 246
Pacific Islands, 203
Packer, President Boyd K., 84, 98, 173, 178, 234, 242, 255, 290, 372
  and HBL, 137
  call to the Twelve, 8
  ordination of, 12
  prepares draft statement of Revelation on Priesthood, 293
Palo Alto, California, 18, 147
Paraguay, 202
Parkinson, George B., 313
Parthenon, 180

Pasadena Stake, 380
Pasadena, California, 362
Patriarch to the Church, 138
Peru, 40, 202
Petersen, Elder Mark E., 133
Peterson, Elder Mark E. accident in Egypt, 389
Peterson, Lamonte, 376
Piccadilly Hotel in Manchester, 98
Pioneer Stake, 106, 107, 121, 122, 124, 127, 129, 130, 151, 216
Plutarch, 4
Polynesian Cultural Center, 353
Poplar Grove Ward, 121
Portugal, 202, 501
President, Spencer W., 499
Presiding Bishopric redefined role, 463
Preston, Idaho, 114, 300, 309
Promised Land, 231
Provo, Utah, 214
Quito, Ecuador, 401
Quorum of the Twelve, 71, 132, 200, 228, 238, 287, 293, 302, 363, 390, 474
Quorum of the Twelve Apostles, 36
Radio and Publicity Committee, 181
Reagan, U.S. President Ronald, 441
Regional Representatives Seminar in 1974, 205, 240
Relief Society Building, 232
Relief Society General Board, 73
Republican Party, 303
Revelation on Priesthood, 206, 278, 391
  background
    appearance of President Wilford Woodruff, 287, 289, 290
    Elder David B. Haight's vision of a map of Africa, 282
    SWK begins counseling with Twelve, 286
    SWK's 1977 message to Helvecio Martins, 280
    SWK's 1977 promise to Helvecio Martins, 278

SWK's invites Brazilian missionaries to temple dedication, 285
SWK's March 22 decision, 284
SWK's mention of Exodus 20 2 as a point of departure, 283
SWK's prayerful struggle, 283, 284, 286, 289
SWK's preoccupation with question in early March, 283
SWK's tentative statement of May 30, 1978, 290
SWK's time spent alone in Upper Room, 289
unanimity of the Twelve, 290
drafting of statement announcing, 293
events preceding 4. SWK seeks unanimity among General Authorities, 292

formal decision made by First Presidency and Twelve, 293
Reynolds v. United States, 35, 50, 62
Reynolds, Elder George, 61
Reynolds, Ethel, 36
Richards, Dr. Thomas, 188
Richards, Elder George F., 39
Richards, Elder LeGrand, 238, 287, 290
  and HWH, 378
  illness, 390
  vision in Salt Lake Temple, 278, 287
Richards, Hilda Merrill blessed by HBL, 188
Richards, President Stephen L., 143, 417
  and GBH, 409
  as a lawyer, 361
  on, 419
  SWK mistaken for, 214
Rio de Janeiro, 280
Roberts, B.H., 209
Roberts, Elder B. H., 59
Romney, President Marion G., 71, 98, 133, 177, 195, 205, 206, 234, 266, 279, 362, 436, 497

racing President Tanner, 440
reaction to change in Priesthood restrictions, 284
Romney, President, Marion G. physical decline, 438
Roosevelt Junior High School, 69
Roosevelt, U.S. President Teddy, 431
Rosecrest Ward, 479
Rotary International, 199
Russia Novosibirsk Mission, 3
Sabbath, 270
Safford, Arizona, 107, 144, 200, 201, 218
Salt Lake Central Stake, 376
Salt Lake City, 46, 198, 200, 202, 209, 211, 242, 254, 257
Salt Lake City Commission, 106, 122
Salt Lake Stake, 61
Salt Lake Tabernacle, 186, 212, 218, 480
Salt Lake Temple, 35, 36, 37, 39, 49, 62, 94, 106, 109, 139, 149, 158, 160, 198, 232, 305, 360, 378, 473
missionary training in, 164
Samoa, 203
San Juan Hill, 431
Santiago Temple, 273
Santiago, Chile, 273
Sao Paulo Brazil Temple, 283
construction of, 279
Sao Paulo Temple, 285
Sao Paulo, Brazil, 202, 279
Scandinavia, 77
Secretary of Agriculture, 325, 330
Secretary to the First Presidency, 305
Senior and Senior, 26
Seventy, 152, 236, 242, 279
Shurtliff, Louie, 35
Shurtliff, Louie Shurtliff, 36
Sixth-Seventh Ward, 473, 479
Smith, Bishop Alfred B., 228
Smith, Douglas, 47, 67, 70
Smith, Elder Nicholas G., 138

Smith, Emma Hale, 44
Smith, Ethel Reynolds, 61, 97
　death, 37, 73
Smith, Henry, 485
Smith, Hyrum, 44
　trunk belonging to, 46
Smith, Jessie Evans, 37
　background, 74
　courtship, 74
　death, 41, 97
Smith, Jessie Evans:, 76
Smith, Joseph Fielding Jr., 55, 67
Smith, Joseph Fielding, Jr.
　son of JFS, 47
Smith, Joseph Richards, 35, 56
Smith, Julina Lambson, 35, 45, 48, 56
Smith, Lewis, 38, 67
　death in World War II, 38
　death of in World War II, 78
Smith, Louie Shurtliff, 56, 97
　death, 61
Smith, Mary Fielding, 47, 48
Smith, Milton, 67
Smith, Milton, 71

Smith, Patriarch John
　son of Hyrum Smith, 55
Smith, President David O., 42
Smith, President George Albert, 39, 42, 124, 200
Smith, President Joseph, 42, 44, 190, 490
Smith, President Joseph F., 5, 35, 36, 42, 48, 49
　death of, 36
　safe belonging to, 46
　vision of the redemption of the dead, 65
Smith, President Joseph Fielding, 11, 109, 135, 157, 185, 234, 236, 305, 371, 478, 479
　and Francis M. Gibbons, 90
　and Francis M. Gibbons, 100
　death of, 109, 204
　life
　　additional counselor in First Presidency, 40
　　ancestry, 42
　　Apostolic service, 36, 37, 38, 39, 59, 63, 77
　　athletics, 92

attends dedication of
    SL Temple, 49
birth, 35, 44
boyhood, 49, 52
call to Twelve, 36, 63
children, 38, 61, 67,
    69, 70
church service, 61
courtship of Louie
    Shurtliff, 56
death, 41, 101
death of first wife, 36
education, 53
employment, 52, 59
flying, 81
home, 37, 61, 80
    Douglas Street, 67
humor, 81, 88, 89, 91
love for temple, 94
marriage to Ethel
    Reynolds, 36
marriage to Jessie
    Evans, 37
marriage to Louie
    Shurtliff, 35
mission to England,
    35, 56
old age, 83
patriarchal blessing,
    55
personal qualities, 83,
    85, 86, 100
preaching, 64

President of the
    Church, 8, 41
President of the
    Twelve, 39, 40, 80
private secretary to
    his father, 65
vegetarian, 93
vigor, 96
writing, 37, 59
Smith, Reynolds, 67
    and Word of Wisdom, 69
Sneff, Larue, 448
Snow, President Lorenzo,
    42, 44
Solemn Assemblies, 373
Solemn Assembly, 212
Solomon, Angie Hinckley,
    403
South Africa, 255
South Africa Mission, 108
South America, 40, 108,
    202, 275
    Church growth in, 273
South Pacific, 39, 202,
    229, 387
Southeast Asia, 202
Southern States Mission,
    16, 21, 412
Southwestern University,
    350
Soviet Union, 77
Spain, 202

Special Affairs Committee, 442
St. George Temple, 373, 402
St. George, Utah, 373
St. Joseph Stake, 211
St. Mark's Hospital, 476
Stanford University, 16, 146
Stanley, Elder F. David
   and HBL, 152
Stapley, Elder Delbert L., 133, 372
Stevenson, Robert Louis, 405
Sunday School General Board, 395
Swiss Temple, 39, 246
Switzerland, 182, 199
Tabernacle, 71
Tabernacle Choir, 54
Talmage Room, 423
Talmage, Elder James E., 119, 423
   corrects young HBL, 117
Tanner, Ida, 448
Tanner, President N. Eldon, 11, 84, 177, 195, 205, 225, 234, 251, 266, 305, 371, 497
   administrative strengths, 266, 267
   death, 397
   death of, 206
   greatness of, 456
   health crisis, 448
   on call of Francis M. Gibbons, 11
   physical decline, 438
   racing President Romney, 440
   reaction to change in Priesthood restrictions, 284
Tate, Lucile, 287
Taylor, President John, 42, 44
Tea, 256
Ted, Cannon, 415
Temple Square, 49, 372
Temple View Stake, 216, 473, 478, 479
Temple Work
   SWK dreams about, 269
Temples, 356
Temples, plans for a small temple, 246
The Salt Lake Tribune, 63
Think and Grow Rich, 365
Thirty-Third Ward, 376
This is the Place Monument, 486
Tonga, 203
Toronto, Canada, 481

Trapped by the Mormons (Anti-Mormon silent film), 316
Twelve, 213, 242
U.S. Army, 198
U.S. Supreme Court, 35, 50
University of California at Berkeley, 301, 320
University of Idaho, 300
University of Utah, 16, 71, 394, 472, 483
Upper Room of the Salt Lake Temple, 16, 279, 287, 289, 294, 371, 378, 391, 421
  described, 371
Ursenbach, Brother, 359
Uruguay, 40, 202
Utah Air National Guard, 81
Utah Constitutional Convention, 209
Utah County, 254
Utah Highway Patrol Trooper
  and SWK, 257
Utah State Agricultural College, 314
Utah State University, 312
Utah Territory, 209
Ute Stadium, 71
Van Valkenburg, Mac, 148

Washington D.C. Stake, 301
Washington, D.C., 301, 327, 441
Welfare Program, 107, 122, 135
Western States Mission, 105, 121
Weston, Idaho, 105, 115
White House, 441
Whitmer, David, 420
Whitney, Elder Orson F., 59, 300, 309
  and ETB, 316
  vision of the Savior, 139, 316
Whitney, Idaho, 299, 300, 309, 314
Whittier Elementary School, 122
Widtsoe, Elder John A., 407
Wilkins, Ernie, 18, 147
Wilkins, Maurine Lee, 18, 147
  appearance in Temple, 158
Wilkinson, Dr. Ernest L., 222, 229
Wilkinson, Ernest, 153
Wirthlin, Elder Joseph B., 501

and Francis M.
Gibbons, 27
Women's Suffrage, 209
Wood, Edward J.
  gives prophetic blessing
  to Joan Lee, 175
Woodruff, President
Wilford, 5, 42, 44, 49,
288
  appearance in Salt Lake
  Temple in 1978, 279,
  391
  JFS travels with as a
  boy, 54
Woolley Family, 216, 217
Word of Wisdom, 69, 270
World Conference on
  Records, 353

World War II, 38, 78, 302,
  324
World's Fair, 54
Wright Brothers, 81
Yalecrest Ward, 8, 27,
  372, 403
Young Men's General
  Board, 61
Young, President
  Brigham, 42, 155
  on lawyers, 361
Youth and the Church
  book by HBL, 108
Yugoslavia, 199
Zacchaeus, 495
ZCMI, 52

www.ingramcontent.com/pod-product-compliance
Lightning Source LLC
Chambersburg PA
CBHW071552080526
44588CB00010B/881